John Dickson Carr

John Dickson Carr: A Critical Study

S. T. Joshi

Bowling Green State University Popular Press
Bowling Green, Ohio 43403

To
Will Murray

Contents

Preface

I have been reading John Dickson Carr sporadically for more than half my life; but only recently, while writing articles for the forthcoming *Penguin Encyclopedia of Mystery and Suspense,* did I sense that a full-length study of Carr might be profitable. The time seems right for such a study: many of his novels are being reissued; his miscellaneous stories, radio plays, and articles are being collected (although much more still needs to be done in this regard); and, most importantly, Douglas G. Greene, the leading Carr authority, is working on a full-scale biography. Such a work is long overdue, and should resolve many questions which I do not have the resources to answer. As a result, my own study will be almost purely critical, with only intermittent reliance on the facts of biography and conjectures on the possible biographical significance of certain passages in Carr's writing.

The critic of detective fiction—especially of the sort of detective fiction Carr wrote—faces a very ticklish dilemma encountered in no other field: to what extent should one reveal the solution to a work? Carr himself, in his column in *Ellery Queen's Mystery Magazine* (October 1970), writes that "while a critic must say what he likes about the merits of any book, it's not quite the clean potato carefully to give away secrets on whose effect its author so much depends". Although I agree wholeheartedly with this utterance, I have in a few instances found it impossible to discuss a work intelligibly without mentioning the culprit or some other vital but concealed point in the case. My only comfort is, firstly, that few who have not already read Carr's works are likely to read this book, and secondly, that it is often as enjoyable to read Carr's work when one knows the outcome as when one does not. In any event, I have tried to spill the beans in as few instances as possible, even by occasionally supplying an intentionally erroneous or misleading summary of the plot so as not to give the ending away.

My study is divided into two parts: in Part I, I discuss Carr's work by detective, in a roughly chronological sequence within each chapter; in Part II, I consider the entirety of Carr's work from a broader thematic standpoint, discussing his political and social philosophy, the very complex issue of his theories and practise of mystery writing, his use of the supernatural, and points of style and characterisation. I am not interested in providing a book-by-book analysis of each work: some novels I study in considerable detail, others I mention only to cite some interesting trends or patterns they exemplify. I can also discuss the same novel in several different

i

chapters, on each occasion emphasising some different feature or aspect of it as it suits my purpose. In my chapters on individual detectives, I have probably not recorded absolutely everything known about them: this sort of fanatical fact-gathering is very popular in certain schools of detective criticism, but unless all these little tidbits can be shown to have some wider significance, it is all so much useless and irrelevant information.

My method of citing Carr's work is a little unconventional. Since I myself have had access to relatively few first editions of Carr's novels and story collections, and since it is likely that many readers similarly do not have such access, I have felt it more convenient to cite Carr's novels by chapter. Most of Carr's stories are short enough that citation of the volume in which they appear is probably sufficient. (It may be worth noting that the majority of the paperback editions of Carr's work are notoriously misprinted; the recent editions are not necessarily superior to the earlier ones in textual accuracy. Even some of the hardcover editions are error-riddled; I wonder, for example, whether anyone—including the author—ever proofread the Harper & Row edition of *The Hungry Goblin.*)

My bibliography of primary and secondary sources is a composite of several previous bibliographies (although in nearly every case I have verified data listed by my predecessors) with much new information, especially as regards foreign translations of Carr's work. Probably much more work needs to be done for a definitive Carr bibliography, but I trust I have supplied a starting-point.

I now need only acknowledge those individuals who have supported me in my first major venture into the criticism of detective fiction: Will Murray, who gave me a chance to write on Carr and many other writers for the *Penguin Encyclopedia;* Neil Barron; Virginia Boucher of the University of Colorado Library; Marie Claire Cebrián; Leslie D'Acri; Martin Davis of the Alderman Library, University of Virginia; Richard Fumosa; Jerry Aliotta; Marc A. Michaud; and Steven J. Mariconda. I wish to make particular note of the help of James E. Keirans and Douglas G. Greene, who both read the entire manuscript and saved me from many errors. I alone am responsible for those mistakes and misinterpretations which, in my stubbornness, I may have refused to correct or alter.

Introduction

John Dickson Carr was born on November 30, 1906 (the date of 1905 is found with peculiar frequency—in reference works, card catalogues, even in blurbs in Carr's own books), in Uniontown, Pennsylvania. His father was a lawyer, and in 1912 was elected to the House of Representatives as a Democrat. Interestingly enough, Carr's own mature political philosophy was conservative and even reactionary; but in his youth Carr must have enjoyed the four years (1913-16) spent in Washington, D.C., although it would require nearly fifty years for him to express his sentiments on the Washington of this period in *The Ghosts' High Noon* (1969).

As the family returned to Uniontown, Carr joined the legal interests derived from his father with the journalistic interests of his grandfather, a part owner of a newspaper in Uniontown: at the age of eleven he began writing articles on court proceedings and murder cases. By fifteen Carr had his own column, largely concerned, curiously, with boxing. Although an undistinguished student at The Hill School, which he attended from 1921 to 1925, Carr absorbed an enormous fund of knowledge from independent reading, and in later years could boast impressive autodidactic expertise on true crime, English and European history, fencing, and other, more esoteric subjects: curious bits of this learning find their engaging way into his novels at odd moments.

At Hill Carr wrote for the literary magazine, although no trace of the future detective writer has been found in its pages. Far different is his work for the literary magazine of Haverford College, which he entered in 1925. *The Haverfordian,* of which Carr was an editor, is filled with his stories and even a few poems; but what is interesting is that a good proportion of them are tales of historical adventure. Carr was absorbing history avidly at Haverford, and it ought not to be a surprise that history and detection dominated his early literary interests in roughly equal proportions. But detection was clearly on the rise in Carr's horizon; Robert Lewis Taylor, in his celebrated *New Yorker* article on Carr, relates an amusing anecdote about one of Carr's earliest tales:

Murder, only dormant at best in his thinking, reappeared in the form of a mystery story minus the ending; he wrote it and put it in the journal, together with the princely offer of twenty-five dollars to the first person who could come forward with the solution. It was, he felt, a foolproof puzzle, and he sat back with enjoyment to witness the discomfiture of his fellows. To his stunned dismay, a bored youngster came in about an hour after the magazine was distributed, presented a detailed and accurate solution, and, not unnaturally, asked for his cash. Carr, penniless, was obliged to call on his father to make up the deficit. His father, in a letter forwarding a

1

check, inserted a gratuitous essay on the follies of mystery writing.[1]

The story in question is one of the early Henri Bencolin tales, "The Shadow of the Goat", published in *The Haverfordian* for November and December 1926.[2] It was perhaps the last time anyone ever guessed the solution to a Carr story so easily.

In 1928 Carr's parents sent him to the Sorbonne in Paris for further study; but Carr spent all his time writing, and here produced the short novel *Grand Guignol,* an early version of his first novel, *It Walks by Night* (1930); it was published in *The Haverfordian* in the issues for March and April 1929. In 1929 he expanded *Grand Guignol* into *It Walks by Night,* and it was promptly bought by Harper & Brothers, largely through the efforts of Carr's friend H. M. Tomlinson, Jr., a salesman at Harper. When the novel was published, Harper unprecedentedly advertised it in a full-page ad in the *New York Times,* and it ultimately sold 15,000 copies. Carr's career as mystery novelist was launched.

Robert Lewis Taylor writes charmingly of Carr's life at this time:

He moved into a duplex flat on Columbia Heights, in Brooklyn, with Tomlinson and Edward Delafield, also a Harper's salesman and a friend of Carr's from his college days. It was an offhand, prankish household, given to mild roistering. Both Delafield and Tomlinson regarded themselves as singularly blessed, for they were able to sit back and watch a top mystery writer at work, an exhibit available to only the privileged few. Ideas came to Carr at odd moments. He was apt to come sprinting out of the shower, crying, "I've got it!" He would pick up a newspaper and, seeking out the crime notes, as was his habit, seize cheerfully on a brief, routine suicide. "He would begin to twist it and turn it around," says Delafield, "and before long it would emerge as a full-fledged book plot. And the next thing we knew, he'd have it written and published." Tomlinson once asked Carr if he had undue trouble with plots. Fixing him with a Holmesian glare, Carr replied, "I've had exactly a hundred and twenty complete plots outlined, for emergencies, since I was eleven years old."[3]

Whether Carr had used all 120 plots by the end of his career is not certain; I suspect he had, for we shall see that several short stories and radio plays provided the nucleus for later novels, and plots of other novels and stories are mere variations upon one another. And yet, Carr's originality and fecundity cannot be praised too highly, especially in light of the fact that his plots were almost always restricted—even in many of his "historical mysteries"—to the locked-room murder or, more generally, the "impossible crime". Given such an extreme self-imposed limitation, it is remarkable how many changes Carr rung on this basic formula, and how fresh and vigorous the whole corpus of his work remains.

During his New York period (1930-33) Carr would make frequent trips to England and the Continent, and still more exotic places like Africa and Madagascar; but he met his future wife, Clarice Cleaves, aboard ship as she came to the United States to visit relatives. In 1932 Carr married Clarice, abandoned his native country, and settled in England; he became so devoted an Anglophile that he was frequently mistaken for a British author. His life revolved entirely around writing. Between 1930 and 1941 he published thirty-nine books—thirty-six novels, one short novel (*The Third Bullet*), one short-story collection (*The Department of Queer Complaints*), and a nonfiction study (*The Murder of Sir Edmund Godfrey*). What is remarkable is not merely the staggering productivity of Carr's writing but its consistently high quality; it is what led Anthony Boucher to write nostalgically:

You can argue as you will about which was the most enjoyable period for a reader of detective stories: My allegiance remains irrevocably fixed to the 1930s, when you could count on four new novels a year by John Dickson Carr.

Carr was young ... and fertile and inventive and tossed off plots and devices and gimmicks the way Schubert tossed off melodies—and with the same canny craftsmanship to lend substance to his fertility. He was publishing about a third of a million words a year, but each book was as painstakingly shaped (and often as detailedly researched) as if he'd spent a year or two on it alone.[4]

The pattern of Carr's early writing is of some significance. Henri Bencolin, the hero of Carr's college short stories, is featured in his first four novels (excluding *Grand Guignol*); but after a year or two focusing on Bencolin and drawing upon his Paris experiences, Carr faced the first of what I see are two major turning-points or crises in his career. Let us examine the next several novels he wrote: *Posion in Jest* (1932) is set in his native region of Pennsylvania and features Patrick Rossiter; *Hag's Nook* (1933) and *The Mad Hatter Mystery* (1933) are the first and second Dr. Fell novels; *The Bowstring Murders* (1933), published under the not very clever pseudonym Carr Dickson (a publisher's decision; Carr wished to use the pseudonym Nicholas Wood, derived from his father's first two names), features John Gaunt; *The Eight of Swords* (1934) is a Dr. Fell novel; *The Plague Court Murders* (1934) is the first Sir Henry Merrivale novel; it was followed by *The Blind Barber* (1934; Fell) and *The White Priory Murders* (1934; Merrivale); then came *Devil Kinsmere* (1934), published under the pseudonym Roger Fairbairn, an historical mystery; after several more Fell and Merrivale novels we find *The Murder of Sir Edmund Godfrey* (1936), a nonfictional work conceptually very close to an historical mystery, and a little later we have *The Burning Court* (1937), a supernatural mystery, and *The Four False Weapons* (1937), where Bencolin unexpectedly reappears. The point to be made here is that it was not at all obvious to Carr, as it is to us in hindsight, that he would focus upon Fell and Merrivale as his two principal detectives; during the early and middle thirties he was experimenting in a wide variety of themes, genres, and settings, and in some ways it is curious that he would settle down to alternate between Dr. Fell novels and Sir Henry Merrivale novels for a large part of his career.

It is worth pausing over *Devil Kinsmere* and *The Murder of Sir Edmund Godfrey* here, although they and other historical mysteries shall be studied in greater detail in a later chapter. The former is perhaps the least-read Carr work, for the simple reason that it has not been reissued since its original American and British editions of 1934. True, Carr rewrote this novel thirty years later as *Most Secret* (1964), changing little but the language; but in some ways *Devil Kinsmere* has a freshness and vitality, if at times a stylistic clumsiness, lacking in its more polished revision. The most significant thing about it is the odd pseudonym used for it, one never again employed by Carr: I can only imagine that at this time he did not feel that his already loyal following of mystery readers were ready for an historical novel from his pen, one where there is a murder, to be sure, but where that simple event is overshadowed by the more significant political machinations of Charles II. Carr may have been worried about its critical reception, and rightly so: it was not widely reviewed (understandably for what appeared to be a first novel from an unknown author), and was not a popular success. Very different is *The Murder of Sir Edmund Godfrey*, which Carr published under his own name. As a purportedly nonfictional work (although it is really an historical novel which adheres with extreme fidelity to known historical fact, with a conclusion giving a detective writer's conjectures on the solution of this still-unresolved murder in the later Stuart era), it was reviewed more exhaustively than most of Carr's novels (the same would be true for the later *Life of Sir Arthur Conan Doyle*), including a lengthy and favourable review in the *Times Literary Supplement* and a highly favourable review in the *New York Herald Tribune* by the young Alfred Kazin, later to become one of the most distinguished American critics. Some have maintained that it is Carr's single best work.[5] Given Carr's early historical stories and these two historical works, it is actually surprising that Carr would wait another decade and a half before writing his next historical novel, *The Bride of Newgate* (1950).

In some ways it is significant that the novels featuring Sir Henry Merrivale were written under the Carter Dickson pseudonym. Carr in his early years was simply writing more than any publisher could reasonably handle; and Harper presumably decided that it could take no more than two novels by Carr a year, and so Carter Dickson was born. I have always felt that Dr. Gideon Fell was closer to Carr's heart than Sir Henry Merrivale; the Fell canon endures longer—the first Fell novel appeared in 1933, the last in 1967, whereas Merrivale makes his debut in 1934 and bows out in 1955 with the novelette "All in a Maze"—and the Fell works are more consistently meritorious. The later Merrivale novels are thin and uninspired, and several commit the aesthetic blunder of not even having an actual murder committed.

Carr's first English sojourn (1933-48) must surely have been the most enjoyable period of his life; he had a new wife, he was a successful and prolific author, and he gradually began associating in English social and literary circles. He was elected to the Savage and Garrick clubs and, in 1936, to the exclusive Detection Club (the first American to be so elected); to his disappointment, however, G. K. Chesterton, then president of the Club and a writer who strongly influenced Carr, died just prior to Carr's attendance of his first meeting.

Part of the reason for Carr's relative decline in productivity in the forties (only fourteen books published from 1942 to 1949) was his extensive work for the BBC during World War II. His radio plays and talks for American and British radio from 1940 to 1945 (with a few more in 1948 and 1955) are only now coming to light; and although Carr wrote relatively few short stories in his career, the radio plays range from original stories of detection, adaptations of tales by Poe, Bierce, Chesterton, and others, war propaganda, and even some literary criticism ("New Judgement: John Dickson Carr on Edgar Allan Poe"[6]). There is a wealth of interesting and worthy material here both for the Carr follower and the general mystery enthusiast, and it is to be hoped that more of these scripts shall one day be published.

Another reason for Carr's diminishing fecundity in the forties is the fact that he spent two years researching his *Life of Sir Arthur Conan Doyle* (1949). This "authorised" biography, written with the cooperation of Doyle's heirs, signalled the second significant turning-point in Carr's career. For a while in the late thirties and forties it seemed as if Carr would produce a Fell and a Merrivale novel alternately until time immemorium (what a shame that it never occurred to Carr, as it did to Michael Innes in *Appleby and Honeybath*, to join these two detectives in a single work!). But Carr's own work was slowly metamorphosing: perhaps incited by criticism that his works were too much mere logical puzzles without emotional involvement (a fundamentally true assessment for the work of the late thirties, although as "mere logical puzzles" they are among the finest of their kind), Carr began consciously augmenting the melodrama and dramatic tensity of his writing. Successful in this vein are *The Emperor's Snuff-Box* (1942), the only non-series detective novel of this period, and *Till Death Do Us Part* (1944); much less successful is the bathetic and pulpish *Curse of the Bronze Lamp* (1945). But Carr may have been sensitive to another and still more telling charge—that his novels, while technically and structurally brilliant, really broke no new ground in the field. When Carr started to work on the Doyle biography and read (or reread) such of Doyle's historical romances (they have little or no detection in them) as *Micah Clarke* or *The Refugees*, set in the late seventeenth century, or *The Exploits of Brigadier Gerard*, set in Napoleonic France, Carr may well have come to the conclusion that he could combine the detective tale and the historical novel as he had done tentatively in *Devil Kinsmere;* the results are *The Bride of Newgate* (1950), *The Devil in Velvet* (1951), *Captain Cut-Throat* (1955), and other historical mysteries of the fifties and sixties. It is no accident that nearly all the early historical novels are set in late Stuart or Napoleonic times.

The Doyle biography provided the impetus for some other, rather slight works—the collaborations with Adrian Conan Doyle, *The Exploits of Sherlock Holmes* (1954), introductions to several reissues of Doyle's detective and science fiction novels, and Carr's edition of Doyle's *Great Stories* (1959). Meanwhile Carr was continuing to experiment: a new detective, Patrick Butler, is featured in *Below Suspicion* (1949) and *Patrick Butler for the Defence* (1956), the first with Fell. *The Nine Wrong Answers* (1952) is described by

Carr in the dedication as "a novel of character combined with one of very fast action...without police investigation"; it is a radical expansion and elaboration of a radio play. The Merrivale canon's last novel was *The Cavalier's Cup* (1953), and after *Below Suspicion* Fell would not return for nearly a decade.

In 1948 Carr, now entrenched in his conservative politics, found the Labour government of England so offensive that he left his adopted homeland and the setting for so many of his novels and returned to the United States, purchasing a house in Mamaroneck, in Westchester County. Much later, in *Panic in Box C* (1966), he would draw upon his memories of this region. Upon his return he was elected president of the Mystery Writers of America, serving a year term. By 1953 the Labour party had been ousted and Carr promptly returned to England, remaining until 1965. The bulk of his writing was historical mysteries, although Fell was revived in *The Dead Man's Knock* (1958) and would be dragged through four more novels in the next decade.

In 1965 Carr returned to the United States, and not surprisingly settled in the South—Greenville, South Carolina—no doubt because its social and political conservatism suited him better than the liberalism now dominant in the Northeast and throughout much of the country. Carr could not have felt comfortable during Lyndon Johnson's Great Society, and one can picture his relief at the election of Richard Nixon in 1968. But by this time Carr's career was petering out. Always a heavy and unrepentant smoker (all the characters in his novels smoke like chimneys), he became afflicted with cancer and his productivity waned. His fiction-writing career came to an end in 1972 with *The Hungry Goblin;* but he had commenced a book review column in *Ellery Queen's Mystery Magazine* in 1969, and continued it with wit and enthusiasm until 1976. Carr died of cancer on February 27, 1977.

It was a distinguished career: seventy-one novels, three or four novelettes or short novels, seven collections of short stories and radio plays (two posthumously compiled by Douglas G. Greene), two fine works of nonfiction, articles, introductions, and miscellany. I would not be surprised to see a volume of his letters if someone has the resources and tenacity to compile it. Not having access to much biographical information, I can only conjecture from his published work what sort of man Carr was; but he will strike any reader as one who lived life amply, had very pronounced opinions (subject—perhaps unfortunately—to very little change over the course of his life), and one who was naturally inclined to writing. The key word to describe John Dickson Carr is *ingenuity;* it might well be said that he had more of it than any writer in literary history, but we may find at the end of our analysis that this quality, if it is not tempered with any others, may force us to limit or qualify Carr's achievement and his place in literature. In large part he adhered doggedly to an extraordinarily narrow branch (the "impossible crime") of the already narrow field of detective fiction; he was the undisputed master of this tiny subgenre, but we are at times inclined to regret wistfully that he so restricted his talents.

PART I

Henri Bencolin

Henri Bencolin, prefect of police and later *juge d'instruction* in Paris, is strikingly different from Carr's two other principal detectives. Firstly, he is officially connected with the police department; Dr. Gideon Fell, on the other hand, is a pure amateur, while Sir Henry Merrivale is, in his early career, chief of Military Intelligence but with no direct ties to the police—indeed, his intrusion into certain purely criminal cases creates considerable annoyance on the part of such hardworking policemen as Chief Inspector Humphrey Masters. Secondly, Bencolin has very clear principles of detection, and these stand in stark contrast to the intuitional methods of Fell and Merrivale. Thirdly, and perhaps most importantly, Bencolin is not—and is not meant to be—a likeable character. Let us examine these last two points more closely.

Bencolin had appeared in four short stories and one short novel before making his grand entrance in Carr's first novel, *It Walks by Night* (1930); he was featured in three subsequent novels written in rapid succession— *The Lost Gallows* (1931), *Castle Skull* (1931), and *The Corpse in the Waxworks* (1932)—before retiring, only to be resurrected years later in *The Four False Weapons* (1937). The short stories (now collected in *The Door to Doom and Other Detections*) date to Carr's college years, the first written when he was twenty. They are impressive works, and Carr already reveals a surety of touch, vividness of prose style, and deftness in plot-weaving that would be the hallmarks of his entire career. And Bencolin's personality is already established in these stories, undergoing only elaboration in the novels. As early as "The Fourth Suspect" (1927) we hear that Bencolin "worked out his cases with an eye to the dramatic rather than to the truth";[1] in fact, this is a false dichotomy, for Bencolin strives for both drama and truth. But "unnecessary theatricality"[2] becomes a feature of all Carr's detectives, and Bencolin is no exception.

Carr, beginning his literary career in the late 1920s in the midst of the "Golden Age" of the formal detective story, could not do otherwise than create a succession of eccentric detectives; but the degree and nature of their eccentricity differ sharply, and Bencolin could never be mistaken for Fell or Merrivale, as those two can occasionally be mistaken for each other. To be sure, all Carr's detectives separate themselves from the crowd by their intelligence; but Carr wishes to endow Bencolin with a remoteness, cynicism, and even a certain misanthropy that make him a figure inspiring respect and occasionally a faint dread. He is not a man to be fooled with.

9

The most elaborate description of Bencolin appears early in *It Walks by Night:*

Your first impression...was one of liking and respect. You felt that you could tell him anything, however foolish it sounded, and he would be neither surprised nor inclined to laugh at you. Then you studied the face, turned partly sideways—the droop of the eyelids, at once quizzical and tolerant, under hooked eyebrows, and the dark veiled light of the eyes themselves. The nose was thin and aquiline, with deep lines running down past his mouth. A faint smile was lost in a small moustache and pointed black beard—the black hair, parted in the middle and twirled up like horns, had begun to turn grey. Over the white tie and white shirtfront, it was a head from the renaissance in the low light of the lamps. He rarely gestured when he spoke, except to shrug his shoulders, and he never raised his voice; but whenever you were in this man's company in public you felt uncomfortably conspicuous. (1)

To this largely physical description are added other traits of character: "You noticed not a little of the aristocrat in the back-thrown head, the slow, graceful speech, the faint and dominant contempt with which he faced Miss Mertz."[3] Well, few of us are aristocrats, and so Bencolin is automatically rendered remote and awe-inspiring. But the most common and most encapsulated description of Bencolin appears so early as *Grand Guignol* (1929), the short novel that served as an early version of *It Walks by Night:*

He rose and began to pace about, hands clasped behind his back, head bent forward. Mephistopheles smoking a cigar, several of him reflected in the mirrors around the walls as he passed up and down; a queer and absurd little figure in motion, but Paris's avenger of broken laws.[4]

"Mephistopheles smoking a cigar": there is more to this soubriquet, we are given to understand, than merely a description of Bencolin's moustache and goatee. The matter is spelled out explicitly in *Castle Skull,* where a frightened suspect (not, as it happens, the murderer), about to be questioned by Bencolin, remarks bitterly: "That Bencolin...could have crucified a certain Man we've heard about, and taken only an artistic pride in the way he drove in the nails" (10). This is really quite remarkable, even coming from someone who, like Carr, seems to have lacked any especial religious fibre. It is interesting that Carr chose to portray Bencolin in this manner: the thinking behind it being, evidently, that if he terrifies ordinary people, he will certainly terrify the guilty.

Bencolin's theories of detection are of considerable interest, but there seems to be a certain inconsistency or even paradox in their expression. The first elaborate statement on the subject appears in "The Murder in Number Four" (1928), where Bencolin first says, "We of the police cannot be content with knowing the identity of our guilty men. Unlike the detectives in fiction, we must have proof."[5] This is unobjectionable, and even the amateur Fell takes care to accumulate enough hard evidence to convict the criminal. But then Bencolin proceeds to deliver a long diatribe on the theory and practise of detection:

"The great chess player is the one who can visualize the board as it will be after his move. The great detective is the one who can visualize the board as it *has been* when he finds the pieces jumbled. He must have the imagination to see the opportunities that the criminal saw, and act as the criminal would act. It's a great, ugly, terrific play of opposite imaginations. Nobody is more apt than a detective to say a lot of windy, fancy things about reasoning, and deduction, and logic. He too frequently says 'reason' when he means 'imagination.' I object to having a cheap, strait-laced pedantry like reason confused with a far greater thing."[6]

Bencolin then ridicules the implausibility of the fictional detective:

"There is so much elaborate hocus-pocus around the whole matter of criminal detection that it makes a detective wonder why people think he acts that way. The fiction writers want to call it a science, and attach blood pressure instruments to people's arms, and give them Freud tests—they forget that your innocent man is always nervous, and acts more like a guilty one than the criminal himself, even his insides. They forget that these machines are operated by the most cantankerous one of all, the human machine."[7]

And yet, in *It Walks by Night* Bencolin says the following:

"One of the popular fallacies of the day...is that the detection of crime is *not* a science, and that its investigators do *not* achieve almost magical results. I do not know why this error should be so prevalent, unless it is because extraordinary analyses occur so often in fiction; therefore, the careful public reasons, they cannot possibly occur in life....Still, it is difficult to understand why the man on the street is prone to be so suspicious of what he is pleased to call 'book stuff' in this business. Tell him that a doctor—preferably a German with a sonorous name—has discovered a cure for cancer, and he will be very apt to believe you; but tell him the simple truth that by a single trace of mud-stain on a coat the identity of a murderer may be established, and he will probably sneer, 'Pah! you've been reading Gaston Leroux!' Yet we do not say, because the doctor's naked eye cannot see into a man's appendix, that the doctor cannot know this man has appendicitis. It is a field for specialized investigation, precisely like medicine." (11)

If we are not to accuse Bencolin (or Carr) of flagrant inconsistency here—is detection a science or isn't it?—I think the way out is to assume that the kind of science referred to in "The Murder in Number Four" is the science of psychology (" 'And your psychological detective wants to pick out the *kind* of man who committed a crime; after which he hunts around till he finds one and says, 'Behold the murderer,' whether the evidence supports him or not' "[8]), a science Carr always viewed with suspicion. The real science of detection, referred to and utilised in *It Walks by Night*, is forensic science—fingerprints, blood samples, and the like—although even this science must be under the control of a guiding intellect or "imagination" if its results are to be applied properly. This last caveat allows Carr elsewhere to ridicule "scientific" methods of detection without thereby ridiculing Bencolin. In *The Eight of Swords* (1934) a bishop using such methods is held up to scorn:

His information was enormous; he could recite to you the details of every atrocity in the last hundred years; he knew all the latest scientific devices for both the advancement and prevention of crime; he had investigated the police departments of Paris, Berlin, Madrid, Rome, Brussels, Vienna, and Leningrad, driving the officials thereof to the verge of insanity; and, finally, he had lectured all about it in the United States. (2)

Clearly the bishop has not the "imagination" to interpret what the scientists or technicians tell him. Still, the emphasis on science segregates Bencolin significantly from both Fell and Merrivale.

The Bencolin novels begin several patterns persisting through Carr's career—an elaborately convoluted structure that allows each chapter to end on a dramatic revelation or pseudo-climax; an assemblage of somewhat hyperbolic and theatrical characters; the narration of the case by an ingenuous and somewhat naive character who follows the detective about, even though he has no connexion with the police; and a rivalry, sometimes amiable and sometimes bitter, between the detective and other officers of the law. Some of these features will more profitably be studied in Part II, but the last two can be observed here.

The narrator of the first four Bencolin novels (not the short stories or *Grand Guignol* or *The Four False Weapons*) is the American Jeff Marle. We learn little of him—all four novels are narrated in the first person— but we assume that he is a vigorous young man, probably in his late twenties, eager to follow Bencolin even when he has no especial idea what Bencolin is about. In *Poison in Jest* (1932) we find that he is a novelist. He is not a Watson figure, for he has considerably greater intelligence and certainly more animation: in *The Corpse in the Waxworks*, when he is detected overhearing a conversation in a second-floor room of a sinister club, he leaps out the window, dodges the knives of the club's bouncers, knocks one of them unconscious, and finally contrives to escape by the aid of the club's manager, to whom he has imparted some vital information. This whole scene is good, rousing shoot-'em-up stuff, but Carr is unwilling to have this sort of thing dominate a work, and he restricts it here to a few chapters.[9]

Marle also finds himself attracted to the number of fetching young women who habitually fill Carr's novels. Indeed, in the first few novels it appears that Carr was attempting to establish a strain of continuity with several recurring characters; but he grew tired of the practise and let it subside. Marle develops a romance with the Englishwoman Sharon Grey, whom we first encounter—startlingly—lurking half naked in a dark room in *It Walks by Night*, awaiting a tryst from the man who has just been murdered. This romance—full of bickering and emotional fireworks—is admirably handled.

We do not learn how the affair turns out, but in *The Lost Gallows* we hear more of it:

...and when the Saligny case was over there had been an unforgettable, hectic week in a little village along the Seine before her father, who was wild, tracked us down and broke it up. She had been literally dragged away by that old son of a whatnot. I had received letters which indicated real captivity. Still, there had been that week! (2)

When Marle and Bencolin come to London and become entangled in the murder of El Moulk in *The Lost Gallows*, Marle rings her up by accident on the telephone:

I was picturing her as she would be now, with her lips close against the mouthpiece of the telephone, gesturing with a cigarette while she spoke. Sharon of the amber-coloured eyes, which wandered from perplexity to dreaminess, and then looked alive and questioning with devilment. Sharon of the long black eyelashes, the eager flushed face, and the dark-gold hair. Sharon the soft and clinging, who could drink like a sailor and swear like a newspaper man. I remembered her dreaming, her jealousy, her rages and tenderness, as I had known her in the old days at Paris.... (2)

And although Bencolin looks upon the whole romance with a certain cynicism ("Spare me the lover's point of view," he says in another context in *The Corpse in the Waxworks* [5]), Marle and Sharon resume their affair. But in the tumult of the case Sharon is forgotten in the latter half of the novel. In *Castle Skull* she makes no appearance at all. At the beginning of *The Corpse in the Waxworks* Marle tells another character that he is engaged (2), but does not mention Sharon's name, and she does not figure in this novel, either. Indeed, Marle now finds himself attracted to Marie Augustin, manager of the Club of the Silver Key. Why Carr did not develop the Marle-Grey romance—as Dorothy L. Sayers so carefully and sensitively portrayed the courtship of Harriet Vane by Lord Peter Wimsey over four novels, or as Margery Allingham depicted the courtship and marriage of Albert Campion and Amanda Fitton—can only be wondered at; it would have lent a richness and substance to his works that no amount of Bencolin's theatricality could have done.

The rivalry between Bencolin and other officials who are brought in to solve the case is an engaging feature of these novels: Bencolin, even more than Fell or Merrivale, seems to work best when he has a foil to oppose him. Three of the four short stories involve Bencolin and Sir John Landervorne, who engage in a cheerful contest to arrive at the truth. In *The Lost Gallows* Landervorne is resurrected, and we now learn that he has retired as assistant commissioner of the metropolitan police. The two have a somewhat heated dispute over methods of detection (Landervorne soberly asserts: "The qualities of a detective are practice, patience, and perseverance" [3]), in the course of which Bencolin makes the calm prediction: "I will bet you dinners for the three of us that I can name this man's murderer within forty-eight hours" (3). This is a little less hyperbolic than a similar boast he made in *It Walks by Night* ("I have never been baffled, and I have never been more than twenty-four hours in understanding the entire truth of any case on which I have been engaged" [11]); but if we have read the Bencolin saga up to this point (and it is to be admitted that few contemporary readers of *The Lost Gallows* would have read the early short stories), we are more than a little taken aback to learn that Landervorne himself is the culprit. Such a conclusion is almost underhanded: if it is not a case of the detective himself committing the crime, it comes very close to it.[10] Nevertheless, there may be some possible influences. In G. K. Chesterton's "The Secret Garden" (in *The Innocence of Father Brown*) Aristide Valentin, chief of the Paris Police, is the criminal; and Valentin himself had appeared in an earlier Father Brown story, "The Blue Cross". Perhaps even more direct an influence is Gaston Leroux's *The Mystery of the Yellow Room* (1907), pronounced by Dr. Fell in his locked-room lecture "the best detective tale ever written" (*The Three Coffins* [17]). Here the criminal is the detective Frédéric Larsan, who throughout the novel is involved in a heated rivalry with young Joseph Rouletabille to solve the case.

In any case, *The Lost Gallows* is one of several works where Carr comes close to breaking his own rules of fair play. Perhaps the one flaw in *The Corpse in the Waxworks* is that it presents a murderer whom we have seen in only one small scene prior to the revelation: here Carr is certainly skirting close to his rule not to impute the crime to a minor character whom the reader cannot be expected to remember.

Detective rivalry continues in *Castle Skull*, where Bencolin battles Baron Sigmund von Arnheim, Chief Inspector of the police at Berlin. This figure has been revived from Carr's first published short story, " 'As Drink the Dead...' " (1926), where von Arnheim is featured alone. Here von Arnheim is portrayed as a pompous buffoon, and yet Bencolin allows him to outline an entirely erroneous solution to the case because he wishes the actual murderer to go free; indeed—astoundingly for a police officer—Bencolin actually destroys evidence to protect the murderer. This sort of behaviour may be all right for Fell, but comes as a rude shock when attributed to Bencolin, even though here, as in *The Lost Gallows*, he is acting in an unofficial capacity outside his area of jurisdiction—a castle on the Rhine. We shall later consider the significance of such frankly criminal activity on the part of Carr's detectives.

Grand Guignol, the early version of *It Walks by Night*, allows us to examine carefully the early growth of Carr the detective writer. *Grand Guignol*, at 25,000 words, is a substantial novelette or short novel, and in its vivid Paris atmosphere, ingenious crime, and lively prose would be a credit to any detective writer; and it is only by comparison with *It Walks by Night* that we can both gauge Carr's advancement as a writer in less than two years' time and also recognise the greatness of the novel itself. *Grand Guignol*, probably written in 1928, is set in 1927, as is *It Walks*

by Night; the mechanics of the principal crime—a "locked room" murder—
do not differ appreciably, although events following this crime are elaborated
at considerable length in the novel. What is more, in *It Walks by Night*
all the characters are fleshed out much more substantially and vividly than
in *Grand Guignol:* not only do we have minor characters who do not appear
in the short novel (including Sharon Grey and also Dr. Hugo Grafenstein,
a clinical psychiatrist who acts as Bencolin's opponent in detection), but
all the figures—in particular the criminals, sketched very lightly in the short
novel—breathe with greater vigour. Whole passages of *Grand Guignol* have
found their way into *It Walks by Night,* but one would be hard pressed
to detect their presence in the 90,000-word novel.

There is also a depth of emotion in *It Walks by Night* not found in
its predecessor—and, indeed, not very often found in Carr's subsequent work.
The murder of Raoul, Duc de Saligny, provokes poignant reflexions from
Marle:

It was a curious way to die, not so much in its tragedy as in its lack of simple
dignity. Certainly the living Saligny must have cut a prouder figure than that, when
you fancied the lift of that powerful body smashing a tennis-ball white against a
glare of dust and sun. Was he, as I imagined, a sort of swashbuckling, back-slapping
chap, ingenuous and hearty with everybody?—a conscious D'Artagnan with a ready
jealousy and an equally ready sympathy? There was the head, with thick blond hair,
and the startled wide-set eyes of an oxlike and docile brown, lips open on magnificent
teeth. Now it was all smeared with a glaze. Yes, Raoul, you must have carried that
head to better purpose than being surrounded by jabbering and paunchy men, to
be accidentally kicked and set rolling by somebody's casual boot. . . . (6)

It is something we do not find very often in Carr, who too frequently succumbs
to the temptation of regarding the crime as an intellectual puzzle—the more
so because his crimes are the product of such fiendish ingenuity. Similarly,
we find few passages analogous to Sharon Grey's lament over Saligny, her
former lover:

"I mean, when a person dies, you don't have any sense of him any more; you
don't think of him as really living"—she gestured—"up there. It's as though he
had never lived, do you see? He isn't real any more. You wonder what he was like,
and you can't even visualize him, when you try, except as—as a kind of magic-
lantern picture on the wall. I wonder what's wrong with me? It doesn't mean anything
to me. . . ." (9)

The greatest formal difference between *It Walks by Night* and *Grand
Guignol* is its conclusion—specifically, the means by which Bencolin reveals
the criminal. In the short novel Bencolin stages an outlandishly theatrical
spectacle where the suspects are chained to chairs, gagged, and made to
see a film where actors reenact the crime according to Bencolin's
reconstruction. Clearly, when he wrote *It Walks by Night,* he considered
such shenanigans a little too outrageous even for Bencolin, and he here
adopts the usual lecture-room style common to nearly all early Carr novels,

as Bencolin merely recites—in an artful and dramatic fashion, to be sure—
the nature of the crimes. The most amusing thing about the hyperbolic
conclusion of *Grand Guignol* is the fun Carr pokes at it in *The Problem
of the Green Capsule,* where a character jeers: "Come now. Be fair. Is this . . . a
kind of French-police reconstruction of the crime, at which the guilty wretch
is supposed to scream out and confess?" (19). The writing and tempo of
It Walks by Night is wild and histrionic, but just short of absurdity. It
has nearly everything one could want in a detective story; although it is
his first true novel, it is one of Carr's great works.

The Lost Gallows* and *Castle Skull* are both entertaining, but hardly
prepare us for the brilliance of *The Corpse in the Waxworks.* Who but
Carr could have conceived of a murder victim resting in the arms of a waxen
satyr in a museum? This is what Dorothy L. Sayers in reference to another
Carr novel called "the crazy terror of the incongruous".[11] But Carr's horrific
tableaux are rarely designed merely for shock value; and here there is a
double symbolism involved. We are to think not merely of the juxtaposition
of the no-longer-alive with the never-alive; but, as we learn at the end, the
murderer placed his pretty young victim in the satyr's arms to signal his
(mistaken) impression that she was "a kind of procuress, a kind of brothel-
keeper" (18). The spuriously funereal atmosphere of the setting is handled
with great adeptness, as is the Paris setting in general:

Paris is unjustly blamed. Paris goes to bed early. The boulevards were grey and
shuttered, deserted under a few mournful lights. Bencolin's big Voisin swept down
into midtown, where the pale lamps of the Place de l'Opéra drowsed under electric
signs; buildings were washed with bluish-grey under the sharp stars, and muffled
auto horns called faintly. The trees of the Boulevard des Capucines looked ragged
and sinister. We were all crowded into the front seat, where Bencolin drove in his
usual detached manner, at his usual speed of fifty miles an hour, never seeming
to be aware that he was driving at all. The cry of our horn caught up echoes along
the rue Royale, and through an open wind-screen the chill breeze against our faces
smelt of wet pavements, of chestnut trees, and the turf of autumn. Threading that
forest of white lamps which is the Place de la Concorde, we turned right up to
the Champs Elysées. The brief, violent ride flung us out of the dinginess round
St.-Martin's Gate; we were in an atmosphere of sedate window-grills, of ordered trees
and the decorum of the Avenue Montaigne. (5)

Carr had the good sense to set his works only in places known to him
from experience; and passages like the above, as well as his many descriptions
of England in later novels, ring true because they are a part of Carr's own
background and fund of memories.

Such a claim could be made even more emphatically for *Poison in Jest*
(1932), a novel written directly after *The Corpse in the Waxworks.* It does
not feature Bencolin, but is narrated by Marle; and Bencolin figures as a
ghostly presence precisely because he is not there. Marle has now returned
to Pennsylvania—the place where he, like Carr, grew up. And as he becomes
enmeshed in a purely domestic crime focusing on the family of Judge Quayle,

Marle not merely yearns for Bencolin's presence ("I wished Bencolin were here" [8]) but ponders on the fact of murder so close to home:

In other lands we can take murder unquestioningly, as a deplorable part of the civilization, like the coffee of France or the cigarettes of Germany—inseparable from the weird minds of foreigners. But it does not occur in big dingy houses we have known since boyhood. It does not occur among our lifelong friends, whom we cannot conceive as having any emotions at all. (3)

Poison in Jest, with its atmosphere of brooding tragedy, very close character analysis, and absence of any "impossible" or sensational crimes (although two people are murdered and an attempt is made on a third), is a noble and successful experiment for Carr: in its way it anticipates by twenty years the psychological mysteries of Margaret Millar, where the only meaningful clues are those of a person's character. It is unfortunate that Carr did not attempt the experiment again, although he suggests it in *The Crooked Hinge* (1938), where Fell remarks that the mystery there is "what I've been half-dreading for a long time—an almost purely psychological puzzle" (7); but at least it is evidence to refute the claims of critics that Carr could not draw character. In the final revelation of the murderer Carr's portrayal of a demented personality becomes almost horrific.

I do not know why Carr abandoned Bencolin after *The Corpse in the Waxworks* nor why, five years later, he exhumed him in *The Four False Weapons*. By this time Carr seems to have become perfectly content altering between Fell and Merrivale in successive works, having written seven novels involving the former and five involving the latter. In *The Four False Weapons* we are once again in Paris, but Bencolin himself has changed considerably, at least outwardly: he has resigned from the police force "during those political rows a couple of years ago" (1), whatever that is supposed to mean, and the narrator (nor Jeff Marle but Richard Curtis, a London solicitor) finds Bencolin far from the immaculate and dignified presence he exhibited in prior days:

Curtis first noticed the smoke of the rankest and worst tobacco he had ever smelled; then the sleeves of the corduroy coat, worn at the elbows, of the man in the doorway. He was a tall, lean, stringy man, in the middle fifties, and his appearance was not improved by his hat. He was smoking a pipe. A genial eye was turned on them from under a wrinkled eyelid, and he needed a shave. Yet nothing could have exceeded the gravity with which he removed the pipe from his mouth and lifted his dilapidated hat. (5)

But his cynical character seems little altered, as Curtis observes: "If this were Henri Bencolin—and every intonation of the voice, every gesture told him that it was—certain things were missing, like the Mephistophelian eye. Or were they? He was not quite sure" (6).

Bencolin's unofficial status makes him ideal for the delicate business at hand—to ascertain facts about Rose Klonec, who has become involved with an Englishman represented by Curtis' firm—but when Klonec is murdered, Bencolin shifts back to homicide with startling alacrity. He even makes the incredible statement that "I should not be at all surprised if I were to direct matters for the present" (6); and, sure enough, the Paris police are more than happy to oblige. This whose business strains credulity somewhat, but less so than Bencolin's outrageous statement toward the end:

> "My dear young lady," said Bencolin very gently, "I can tamper with the law when, where, and how I like. I have tampered with the law when, where, and how I liked; and I will do it again." (16)

The Four False Weapons is a substantial work, but not quite up to the standard of Bencolin's best previous cases, *It Walks by Night* and *The Corpse in the Waxworks*. Both Bencolin and Carr seem to exude a certain exhaustion here, as if they cannot wait for the work to end.

The five Bencolin novels form a compact and satisfying series. Only the sheer paucity of works prevents the Bencolin casebook from rivalling the more impressive Fell and Merrivale files. Carr has everything going for him here: the vivid Paris atmosphere (the English and Rhine settings of *The Lost Gallows* and *Castle Skull,* respectively, are handled less ably); a dark, brooding atmosphere of grim cynicism occasionally livened by farcical humour; a depth and vividness of character portrayal not found quite as often in later works; and, of course, that lacing of the horrific and grotesque that became Carr's trademark. That Bencolin made his first major entrance in a work called *Grand Guignol* is only fitting; for all the Bencolin novels radiate an atmosphere of scarcely controlled hysteria and of horrors around the corner that distinguishes them in detective literature.

Works about Bencolin

A. Novels

Grand Guignol (1929).
It Walks by Night (1930).
The Lost Gallows (1931).
Castle Skull (1931).
The Corpse in the Waxworks (1932).
The Four False Weapons (1937).

B. Short Stories

"The Shadow of the Goat" (1926).
"The Fourth Suspect" (1927).
"The Ends of Justice" (1927).
"The Murder in Number Four" (1928).

Dr. Gideon Fell

Hag's Nook (1933) opens with a lyrical description of the English countryside:

There is something spectral about the deep and drowsy beauty of the English countryside; in the lush dark grass, the evergreens, the grey church-spire and the meandering white road. To an American, who remembers his own brisk concrete highways clogged with red filling-stations and the fumes of traffic, it is particularly pleasant. It suggests a place where people really can walk without seeming incongruous, even in the middle of the road. Tad Rampole watched the sun through the latticed windows, and the dull red berries glistening in the yew tree, with a feeling which can haunt the traveller only in the British Isles. A feeling that the earth is old and enchanted; a sense of reality in all the flashing images which are conjured up by that one word "merrie." For France changes, like a fashion, and seems no older than last season's hat. In Germany even the legends have a bustling clockwork freshness, like a walking toy from Nuremberg. But this English earth seems (incredibly) even older than its ivy-bearded towers. The bells at twilight seem to be bells across the centuries; there is a great stillness, through which ghosts step, and Robin Hood has not strayed from it even yet. (1)

Every American who has ever visited England has felt this way; and Carr, the American expatriate who fled to Paris during his college years to escape the narrowness of Calvin Coolidge's United States, felt himself drawn by inevitable racial and cultural ties to the British Isles. And if one is going to settle for twenty-seven years (1933-48 and 1953-65) in England, one had better come up with an English detective; Carr, of course, came up with two, Dr. Gideon Fell and Sir Henry Merrivale, but Fell proved to be the more enduring and, in the end, the more substantial.

The English turn in Carr's work is heralded, of course, by *The Lost Gallows* (1931), set in London; and even Bencolin, prototypical Frenchman that he is, at one point reveals an anomalous knowledge of a rather esoteric point of English history, as he explains the origin of Jack Ketch, the eighteenth-century term for hangman: "The hangman at Tyburn was nicknamed Jack Ketch from a man called Richard Jacquett, who owned Tyburn manor in 1678" (9). Bencolin explains away this erudition with the breezy "I'm up on that sort of literature", but it is really Carr who is speaking here. Both Fell and Merrivale may be, in their physical bulk, a gentle parody on the beef-eating Englishman.

19

Fell's physical proportions, indeed, are the first thing that strikes us; for, with Rex Stout's Nero Wolfe, he must be the largest detective in mystery fiction. He is frequently said to be more than three hundred pounds, and in the early novels he requires not one but two canes to move about; he must pass through a normal door sideways, and on the surprising number of occasions when physical exertion is necessary, he is found wheezing and puffing, well to the rear of his younger and nimbler colleagues. The prototypical description of Fell occurs in *The Mad Hatter Mystery* (1933), although very similar language is used in other novels:

There was the doctor, bigger and stouter than ever. He wheezed. His red face shone, and his small eyes twinkled over eyeglasses on a broad black ribbon. There was a grin under his bandit's moustache, and chuckling upheavals animated his several chins. On his head was the inevitable black shovel-hat; his paunch projected from a voluminous black cloak. Filling the stairs in grandeur, he leaned on an ash cane with one hand and flourished another cane with the other. It was like meeting Father Christmas or Old King Cole. (1)

Our first question is: Why? What does Carr intend by portraying this brilliant man as one whom, in some late novels, certain waggish characters take to calling "Gargantua"?

Carr never made a secret of the fact that G. K. Chesterton—the man G. K. Chesterton, himself a figure of some bulk—was the inspiration for Fell. In his *New Yorker* article, Robert Lewis Taylor reports Carr's testimony on the matter:

"Fell is G. K. Chesterton, of course," says Carr. "Chesterton and his Father Brown series were idols of my boyhood. When I got going good, I decided to create a detective in the great man's image."[1]

On the face of it, it is somewhat odd that a fictional detective would be endowed with the physical characteristics of a real author of detective stories: Fell does not resemble Father Brown (who is small and thin), save in his love of paradox (something common to all Carr's detectives and something which, as we shall see in a later chapter, may derive more directly from Sherlock Holmes than Father Brown), but resembles the creator of Father Brown. But the fact is that he does so only physically: although Fell is an author, he does not write either detective stories or the philosophical and literary works that make up the bulk of Chesterton's *oeuvre;* and in no other significant particular does Fell resemble Chesterton.

Even in physical details Fell may be more similar to another popular writer of the 1920s now largely forgotten: Arthur Machen (1863-1947), the man of letters now principally known for his tales of the supernatural. Machen was enjoying an unprecedented period of celebrity in the 1920s—especially in America—thanks to the many reprints of his novels and tales by Alfred A. Knopf in 1922-26 (a collected edition of Machen was published in 1923 by the London firm of Martin Secker); and Carr, who from youth was an avid reader of weird literature, could scarcely have been unaware of him. (Years later Carr reviewed Machen's *Tales of Horror and the Supernatural* in the 1 August 1948 issue of the *New York Times Book Review*.) Machen too was a large, rotund figure who frequently walked with a cane; but one further detail is telling. In *Hag's Nook* Fell is described as a lexicographer; the term inevitably brings Samuel Johnson to mind, and in a later novel— *He Who Whispers* (1946)—the link between Fell and Johnson is made explicit:

"Sir—" began Dr. Fell, rearing up with a powerful oratorical flourish like Dr. Johnson. (9)

The Machen connexion enters in the fact that Machen too made pretensions to being similar to Johnson—a photograph of Machen posing as Dr. Johnson received wide publicity in its day.[2] I have no idea whether Carr really was thinking of Machen in addition to Chesterton in creating Dr. Fell; but the point is worth considering.

More important is not the origin but the purpose of Fell's characteristics, physical or otherwise. It can scarcely be doubted that Fell—principally in his girth but also in nearly every other trait of his character—is meant to be the converse, even a parody, of Sherlock Holmes. If Holmes is gaunt or even skeletal, Fell must be grotesquely fat; if Holmes in his conversation adopts the stiff formality of a late Victorian, Fell speaks habitually with an orotund eighteenth-century diction that dynamites its own tongue-in-cheek pomposity with ludicrous wheezing (the celebrated "Harrumph") or slang ("WOW!"). The only link between Holmes and Fell is their detective genius.

Other aspects of Fell's personality and achievements can be seen as Holmesian parodies. Holmes is the author of a learned treatise on the various types of tobacco ash—such a work is to be expected from a detective, as it may be of direct relevance in the solving of a case. Fell, on the other hand, in *Hag's Nook* is found working on a subject no less esoteric—*The Drinking Customs of England from the Earliest Days*, "a monumental labour into which he has put six years of scholarly research" (3)—but one whose connexion to detective work is, to say the least, tenuous. It is as if Fell has chosen this subject precisely because it is useless and recondite. How typical of a man who takes the absurd seriously and finds the serious absurd![3]

In *The Mad Hatter Mystery* (1933) Fell is seen to have already published a work "on the history of the supernatural in English fiction" (2). This subject—tangentially pertinent, perhaps, in those many cases where the supernatural seems to have entered—may not sound especially odd nowadays, when much scholarship is being directed toward the weird tale; but in 1933 the subject was still sufficiently *outré* that Fell's authorship of the tract can be seen as another example of his penchant for storing up useless knowledge. Carr never gives the actual title of Fell's treatise, but his reference to it in *The Mad Hatter Mystery* makes one think immediately of the first modern treatment of the subject, Dorothy Scarborough's *The Supernatural in Modern English Fiction* (1917). H. P. Lovecraft published his "Supernatural Horror in Literature" in an obscure magazine in 1927, and it is unlikely that Carr knew of it.

The most startling way in which Fell differs from Sherlock Holmes is the fact that he is married. Mrs. Fell makes her only actual appearance in *Hag's Nook,* and it is a captivating one:

> And here was Dr. Fell, pottering about his domain in a broad-rimmed white hat, looking sleepily amiable and doing nothing with an engrossed thoroughness. Here was Mrs. Fell, a very small and bustling and cheerful woman who was always knocking things over. Twenty times in a morning you would hear a small crash, whereupon she would cry, "Bother!" and go whisking on with her cleaning until the ensuing mishap. She had, moreover, a habit of sticking her head out of windows all over the house, one after the other, to address some question to her husband. You would just place her at the front of the house when out she would pop at a rear window, like a cuckoo out of a clock, to wave cheerfully at Rampole and ask her husband where something was. He always looked mildly surprised, and never knew. So back she would go, previous to her reappearance at a side window with a pillow or a dustcloth in her hand. To Rampole, lounging in a deck-chair under a lime tree and smoking his pipe, it suggested one of those Swiss barometers where the revolving figures are for ever going in and coming out of a chalet to indicate the weather. (3)

It is regrettable that we never see Mrs. Fell in any subsequent works; in the majority of the other Dr. Fell novels she is not even mentioned, and when she is it is often in a passing note telling us that she is travelling or visiting in-laws. In *Death-Watch* (1935) the narrator goes with the Fells to the theatre (1); in *The Three Coffins* (1935) the wives of Dr. Fell, Superintendent David Hadley, and Rampole are mentioned as being in an upstairs room "conferring about something" (2). From this point on, however, Fell's wife ceases to appear even as a bit player or ornament to her husband. At the beginning of *The Problem of the Green Capsule* (1939) Fell is said to be taking the waters at Bath, but his wife is not mentioned. She is settling comfortably into new quarters with her husband at Hampstead in *The Problem of the Wire Cage* (1939 [18]). Eleven novels and twenty-seven years pass before Mrs. Fell is even referred to in passing, but in *Panic in Box C* (1966) Fell speaks of her in the present tense (9), so presumably she is still alive. It is unfortunate that Carr did not develop Mrs. Fell's character, for after *Hag's Nook* her presence is so insignificant that we begin to wonder what purpose she is meant to serve at all. It is, quite frankly, rather grotesque to imagine Fell engaging in marital relations with her— their marriage, unlike that of Sir Henry Merrivale, is childless—and Julian Symons is entirely to be excused when, in his survey of detective fiction, he forgets that Fell has a wife at all.[4] If the existence of Mrs. Fell is somehow meant to indicate that Fell, for all his eccentricities, is more "normal" and middle-class than Sherlock Holmes, it is something Carr never even suggests or intimates. In the end Fell's wife becomes merely an anomalous and inassimilable footnote.

Fell and Merrivale unite in being different from both Sherlock Holmes and Henri Bencolin by their air of harmless buffoonery. The later Fell novels are more explicit on this point than the earlier ones. In *In Spite of Thunder* (1960) a character remarks that Fell is "so absent-minded he doesn't even seem to know where he is" (6). In *The House at Satan's Elbow* (1965) it is said that "most of the time he looks absent-minded or even half-witted" (14). Fell's own constant references to his "woolgathering" show that he consciously wishes to convey this impression.

The very name Gideon Fell perhaps contributes to this deceptive image of foolishness. "Gideon" sounds superficially like a comically unusual name, but has ominous Biblical overtones ("The sword of God and Gideon"). "Fell" makes us think of the schoolmaster Dr. Fell (Gideon Fell is also an ex-schoolmaster), about whom Tom Brown (1663-1704) wrote the amusing epigram (quoted frequently—and erroneously—by several characters in the Dr. Fell novels), adapted from Martial:

> I do not love thee, Doctor Fell.
> The reason why I cannot tell;
> But this alone I know full well,
> I do not love thee, Doctor Fell.

But the adjective "fell" is always in the back of our minds, the more appropriately in that both it and the doctor convey an air of archaism and doom.

It need hardly be remarked, therefore, that Fell's buffoonery is a carefully crafted pose, largely designed to take in unwitting criminals who fail to see in him a formidable opponent. Rarely does Fell let the mask of clownishness slip off, but on those rare occasions when he does so he can be as ruthless and intimidating as any American private eye. Consider his interrogation of the gangster Spinelli in *The Eight of Swords* (1934):

> "Man," interposed Dr. Fell softly, "will you never let well-enough alone? There are a number of dangerous questions I could have insisted on your answering; and you evaded them. Very well. Since I don't believe you shot Depping, I am willing to let that pass. But, by God, my friend!—if you question me, or argue with me, or try to quibble about time limits, you will get no mercy at all." He struck the handle of his stick on the table. "Speak up! What's it to be? Freedom, or gaol?" (13)

Fell's clownish behaviour is also sloughed off when lives are on the line. In *Death-Watch* he becomes genuinely angry at his old friend Hadley when the latter tries to pin the murder on an innocent party. In other novels he often lets the guilty party escape; as he declares openly in *In Spite of Thunder,* he is "notorious for circumventing and flum-diddling the law when my personal feelings are involved" (19).

Fell's relationship with the law is, indeed, a curious one. Although he and Superintendent Hadley are not nearly as ill-tempered toward each other as are Sir Henry Merrivale and Chief Inspector Humphrey Masters, Fell works with Hadley and the police only when it suits him. Even more so than Merrivale, he is the consummate amateur, and takes pride in it. The problem of how Dr. Fell, as a non-police officer, becomes involved in case after case is not something that Carr spends much time worrying about; for the most part Fell is simply in the right place at the right time. His circle of acquaintances appears to be very wide, as in nearly every instance some character knows him and invites him to solve the case. Are we to infer that Fell is inspired by ties of friendship? Perhaps, although Carr does not make the point explicit. In *Hag's Nook* he lives near the site of the crime; in *The Problem of the Green Capsule* (1939) Hadley blithely tells the official in charge of the case, "Oh, and if you need any help, Fell is close at hand. He's at Bath, taking the cure" (2). Hadley had earlier justified his reliance on Fell by stating, in *The Mad Hatter Mystery*, "I am not one of those fools who distrust amateurs" (2). This is certainly handy for Fell, who would have been barred from several cases by a more rigid authority.

Sometimes it is the bizarre nature of a case that summons Fell; in *The Eight of Swords* Hadley tells Fell, "You are in your element with the sort of fantastic lunacy of a case which doesn't come our way once in a dozen years, ordinarily" (3), something Fell echoes in *Till Death Do Us Part* (1944): "I am merely your consultant on the *outré*" (15). In *The Blind Barber* and *The Arabian Nights Murder* (1936) Fell is consulted more conventionally at his home, and solves the case without leaving his study. This is armchair detection with a vengeance! But to the end Dr. Fell remains a free-lance:

"...I am under the impression, Dr. Fell, that you have no official connection with the police?"
    "Sir," replied Dr. Fell, "your impression is quite correct."
    (*The House at Satan's Elbow* [15])

This unofficial status allows Fell to perform antics unthinkable for an ordinary police officer—suppression of evidence, allowing the criminal either to escape or to commit suicide, and the like. Nothing, however, could surpass Fell's concluding act in *The Man Who Could Not Shudder*, where he sets fire to a Jacobean manor house to prevent one man from proving the guilt of another. Fell appears to express not so much regret as coy sheepishness at this act, and in later novels he talks of it in terms that scarcely conceal his pride.

In certain other novels, this unorthodoxy in upholding the law leads to less comical and much more disturbing results. In *Death Turns the Tables* (1941) Fell builds up an elaborate and seemingly sound case against one man in order to pressure the actual murderer, Judge Horace Ireton, into writing a confession of the crime. But then Fell cavalierly destroys the confession on the assumption that Ireton will merely step down from the bench. Fell's intention seems no more than to point a somewhat feeble moral: "So go your ways, and don't be so ruddy cocksure about your judgment in the future" (20). Whether the brutal and self-important Ireton will take this advice is far from certain. In *The Dead Man's Knock* (1958) a character is threatened and nearly killed to silence his tongue about the true facts of the crime; incredibly, the police also go along with Fell and drop the case.

Chief Inspector (later Superintendent) David Hadley figures in a number of the early Dr. Fell cases, and it is their joint participation in the investigation that makes several of these novels some of the finest in detective fiction. Hadley is the perfect foil to Fell: coldly rational, of military bearing and appearance, he exemplifies both the virtues and the limitations of conventional police work. His competition with Fell in solving the case is almost never acrimonious, and he is by no means a fool. The most elaborate description we receive of him is in *The Arabian Nights Murder*, as the third of the police officers assigned to the case:

> The third of the trio, Superintendent David Hadley, came originally from the north of the Tweed. He was Dr. Fell's best friend, and the doctor knew him as well as anybody; but, Dr. Fell often admitted, you never knew where you were with him. Cautious, even-tempered, and logical on the surface, he could be alternately slow and brilliant, alternately stolid and erratic. That calm stolidity of his—it is still told how he walked alone into the most odorous thieves' kitchen east of Poplar, arrested Myers and Bailey with a dummy gun, and calmly walked them out ahead of him with his back turned to every knuckle-duster in the place—that stolidity covered a streak of touchiness which was quick to take offense at any slight, even when none had been intended. He disliked scandal, was a great family man, and had possibly a too-great sense of dignity. Though he would have denied it angrily, he had perhaps a stronger imagination than either of the others. Finally, he was never known to turn down anybody in serious trouble, friend of his or not. ("Prologue")

Hadley appears in *The Mad Hatter Mystery, Death-Watch, The Three Coffins, The Arabian Nights Murder, To Wake the Dead* (1938), *The Problem of the Wire Cage* (1939), *Till Death Do Us Part, He Who Whispers, The Sleeping Sphinx* (1947), and *Below Suspicion* (1949) (which can boast an all-star cast of crime-fighters in Fell, Hadley, and Patrick Butler). This mere list of Fell-Hadley mysteries is sufficient both to indicate the vigour of Carr's early work and to suggest that the pairing of these two contrasting and complementary detectives somehow allowed Carr to rise to heights rarely reached by Bencolin or by the Merrivale-Masters tandem.

And yet, for a police officer who rigidly upholds the doctrine of proper police procedure, Hadley can be remarkably lax in dealing with Fell. We have seen how, in *The Eight of Swords*, he nonchalantly allows Fell to investigate a case on the grounds of its "fantastic lunacy", although the nominal police officer of rank is an Inspector Murch. In *Death-Watch* Fell, arriving at the scene of the crime ahead of Hadley, states, even more outrageously than the retired Bencolin of *The Four False Weapons:* "I'm afraid that until Hadley gets here I shall have to take charge" (3). Fell repeats this procedure in *The Sleeping Sphinx* ("Hadley thought it might be less embarrassing if I, the old duffer, looked into it first" [9]). The culmination of Hadley's irregularity occurs as early as *The Mad Hatter Mystery*, where Fell persuades Hadley to let the murderer go free. To his credit Hadley ponders the matter deeply before reaching his decision:

"I told you," he said, quietly, "I was getting old. I am sworn to uphold the law. But—I don't know. I don't know. The older I get, the more I don't know. Ten years ago I should have said, 'Too bad,' and...You know what I'm thinking, Fell. No jury would ever believe that boy's testimony. But I do." (21)

What is curious is that both Fell and Hadley seem to be approaching the end of their careers even in the very early novels. A long passage about Fell's career previous to *The Mad Hatter Mystery* must be quoted in full:

"I'm not sure what I am," he said. "Some people would say a Fossil. But in a manner of speaking you *have* come in contact with me, General. That would be some years ago. Do you remember Allerton, the naturalist?"
The general's hand stopped with the cigar halfway to his lips.
"He was a good man, Allerton was," Dr. Fell said, reflectively. "He'd been sending some beautiful and intricate drawings of butterflies to a friend of his in Switzerland. The patterns of the wings were perfect, in their way. They were plans of the British minefields in the Solent. But he got his Latin a trifle mixed in the notations....His real name was Sturmm, and I believe he was shot here in the Tower. I—er—accounted for him."
A rumbling sound apparently indicated a sigh.
"Then there was good old Professor Rogers, of the University of Chicago. If he'd known just a bit more about American history I don't think I should have been certain. I've forgotten his name, but he played a good game of chess and had a sound liking for drinking-bouts; I was sorry to see him go. He used to carry his information written infinitesimally small on the lenses of his spectacles....Or perhaps you recall little Ruth Wilisdale? I was her dear father-confessor. She would have a snapshot of herself taken at Portsmouth, with the newest thing in gun designs just in the background; but I hoped she wouldn't try to use it. If she hadn't shot that poor clerk, for no reason except that he was in love with her, I should have let her go."
Dr. Fell blinked at the steel crossbow bolt.
"But that was in the line of duty. I'm older now. Hadley insisted on that business of Cripps, the Notting Hill poisoner; and that chap Loganray, with the mirror inside his watch; and the Starberth affair was rather forced on me. But I don't like it. Heh. Hmf. No." (8)

Two things are interesting about this passage: first, the fact that several of the cases appear to involve espionage (presumably during World War I), even though none of the Fell cases actually written by Carr involve spies or political intrigue in the least; and second, the fact that only the last case mentioned—the Starberth affair, clearly referring to *Hag's Nook*—is one we have a record of. In other early novels we hear of similar unknown cases—"the case of the Two Hangmen" (*The Blind Barber* [7]), "the Weatherby Grange affair; or the six blue coins which hanged Paulton of Regent Street" (*The Arabian Nights Murder* [Prologue]). All this may be similar to Conan Doyle's penchant for referring to unwritten Sherlock Holmes stories, but there may be more to it than that. Neither Fell nor Hadley is a young man when we first meet them; it is not merely that they are veterans, hence worthy of respect, but that they both seem conscious holdovers from a prior day. They do not belong to the twentieth century. When Hadley, in *The Arabian Nights Murder*, declares that his favourite writer is Macaulay "because there is never a sentence which needs to be read a second time in order to make out the meaning" (18), he is not only expressing his desire for clarity, logic, and precision, but his adherence to the literary and perhaps the cultural standards of the nineteenth century (recall Hadley's "too-great sense of dignity"). Fell's own eighteenth-century predilections are evident not only in his speech but in the archaic title of his book on drinking customs; and his very occupation (although it is never described in any detail) of lexicographer unites him to the past: how can an individual be a lexicographer in the twentieth century, when all dictionaries nowadays are compiled by impersonal corporations?

Hadley is not quite so studiously archaic as Fell, but we are nevertheless somewhat startled to find that, so early as *Death-Watch*, he is about to retire as Chief Inspector. After the case, however, he does not retire but becomes Superintendent, and his career continues for nearly two more decades. By *The Problem of the Wire Cage* we learn that Fell has known Hadley for twenty-five years (10); Fell's hair is now streaked with grey (11). *The Dead Man's Knock*, although published in 1958, is set in 1948, yet Fell does not seem to have aged appreciably. Hadley has finally retired by *In Spite of Thunder* (12), but Fell carries on. *The House at Satan's Elbow* is manifestly set in 1964, and finds Fell now with hair "a dull grey-white" (11). He seems as well-preserved as his wife. Carr seems to have missed the opportunity of developing Fell's personality over this thirty-year span of novels, as Margery Allingham did with Albert Campion; in the later novels Fell seems a little more subdued, but this is more attributable to Carr's own loss of power than to any mellowing on Fell's part. Hadley does not seem to change much at all from one work to another.

If Hadley's most vivid role is *The Arabian Nights Murder*—where he himself narrates the latter third of the book in the first person, claiming with justifiable pride that "it was the best bit of work I ever did" (18)— his most affecting comes in *The Mad Hatter Mystery*, as he tries to coax information out of the childlike and easily flustered Sheila Bitton:

"Oh, please!" she said, "don't *you* preach! You sound like Daddy. He tells me what a fool I am, calling up every day, and I don't think he likes Bob, anyway, because Bob hasn't any money and likes poker, and Daddy says gambling's absurd, and I know he's looking for an excuse to break off our engagement and keep us from getting married, and..."

"My dear Miss Bitton," Hadley interposed, with a sort of desperate joviality, "I certainly am not preaching. I think it's a splendid idea. Splendid, ha! Ha, ha! But I only wanted to ask you..."

"You're a dear! You're a dear!" cooed Miss Bitton, as though she were saying, "You're another." "And they rag me so much about it, and even Phil used to phone me and pretend he was Bob and ask me to go to the police station because Bob had been arrested for flirting with women in Hyde Park, and was in gaol, and would I bail him out, and..."

"Ha, ha," said Hadley again. "Ha, ha, ha...I mean, er, how...er...bad. Shocking. Preposterous. Ha, ha." (13)

Those "ha-has" are probably more painful to him than admitting that Fell is right about the solution of a case. In *Death-Watch* Hadley finally and genuinely unwinds:

For the first time Melson heard Hadley laugh. He even told a mild anecdote from the many current concerning a certain celebrated film-actress whose broad charms were attracting attention, and showed all his teeth with unexpected mirth. (19)

It is moments like this that show us that Hadley is not—or, at least, is not always—the humourless and stone-faced policeman he affects to be.

Detective-Inspector Andrew MacAndrew Elliot fills in for Hadley in three novels, *The Crooked Hinge* (1938), *The Problem of the Green Capsule* (1939), and *The Man Who Could Not Shudder* (1940). He is not described with nearly the verve of Hadley, although it is arresting to see him fall in love with a suspect in *Green Capsule*, Marjorie Wills, whom—as we learn in *Death Turns the Tables* (7)—he later marries. Each of these three novels are among Carr's best, but it is Fell and other characters, not Elliot, who dominate the action and our attention.

Unlike Henri Bencolin, Gideon Fell does not appear to have very well-developed views on the nature and practise of detection. (Here I am not referring to Fell's celebrated "Locked-Room Lecture" in *The Three Coffins* [1935], self-consciously a discussion of how to write locked-room mysteries and not how to solve murder cases.) We have seen how Fell is held up in contrast to the bishop in *The Eight of Swords* who advocates "scientific" principles of detection; in a less self-parodic way Hadley is made to utter a similar sentiment in *The Arabian Nights Murder:* "Poetical values are all very well in their way, but I do not find them an efficient substitute for a tape-measure and good eyesight" (21). If Fell's methods are therefore "poetical", how is he so unerringly correct? The closest Fell comes to outlining his own methodology is a self-deprecating remark in *To Wake the Dead:* "Being afflicted with a real scatter-brain, I am full of a hideous curiosity about very small details, and tend to let the main picture go hang" (16). This is not especially helpful, but may mean that a reconstruction of a crime must take cognisance of *every* detail, however seemingly inconsequential or irrelevant, if it is to be correct: in several novels we have competing reconstructions, but all save one are shown to be erroneous because *all* the evidence has not been accounted for. (In a later chapter we shall see that this same principle leads to the supernatural conclusion of *The Burning Court.*) Fell's wry comment in *The Problem of the Green Capsule* (12) and elsewhere that his early life as a schoolmaster makes him more capable of catching liars than most other people is more an example of Carr's acerbic wit than it is a principle of detection. In *The Case of the Constant Suicides* Fell pontificates: "All evidence...points two ways, like the ends of a stick. That is the trouble with it" (10). But we do not learn how Fell or anyone else is supposed to be able to tell in which direction the evidence genuinely points. We can only conclude that Fell is either an intuitionist or, in fact, simply a more efficient fact-gatherer than Hadley himself: it is because he can keep all the "small details" in his mind, and somehow combine them into a unity, that he triumphs in ratiocination.

The course of the twenty-three Dr. Fell novels, written from the beginning to the end of Carr's career, reveals some interesting patterns and interrelationships. *Hag's Nook* and *The Mad Hatter Mystery* are narrated in the third person, but their virtual protagonist is Tad (later Ted) Rampole, a young American who has come to England to visit Fell. He is much like Jeff Marle, and like him falls for a character in the first novel, Dorothy Starberth; by the time of the second he has married her. Their romance in *Hag's Nook* is again handled with charm and poignancy, although rudely interrupted by the murder of Dorothy's brother Martin:

She had come out of the library, presently. Her red eyes showed that she had been crying desperately, in one of those horrible paroxysms; but she was steady and blank-faced then, squeezing a handkerchief. He hadn't said anything. What the devil was there to say? A word, a motion, anything would have seemed crude and clumsy; he didn't know why; it just would have seemed so. He had merely stood wretchedly by the door, in his soaked flannels and tennis shoes, and left as soon as he could. He remembered leaving: it had just stopped raining a moment before, and the grandfather clock was striking one. Through his wretchedness he remembered fastening foolishly on a small point: the rain had stopped at one o'clock. The rain had stopped at one o'clock. Got to remember that. Why? Well, anyway—

It wasn't as though he could feel any sorrow at the death of Martin Starberth. He hadn't even liked Martin Starberth. It was something he stood for; something lost and damned in the girl's face when she walked in to look at her dead; a squeeze of a flimsy handkerchief, a brief contortion of a face, as at pain too great to be borne. The immaculate Martin looked queer in death; he wore an ancient pair of grey flannels and a torn tweed coat...And how would Dorothy feel now? He saw the closed shutters and the crape on the door, and winced. (9)

But Carr tired of Rampole even more quickly than he tired of Marle—he is alluded to in passing in *Death-Watch* (12), reappears somewhat tepidly in *The Three Coffins,* and is never heard from again. Subsequent novels feature as protagonists many other young men who resemble Rampole and Marle considerably—Christopher Kent in *To Wake the Dead;* Dick Markham in *Till Death Do Us Part*—but aside from being the eyes through which the reader sees virtually all the action, they are not significant in themselves.

Although they blunder into the middle of murder cases, Carr carefully
contrives it that they not only never come under suspicion but could never
do so because they have manifestly sound alibis. This is why they can tag
along so insouciantly with Fell, Hadley, and others and learn all about
the progress of the investigation. Only in *Till Death Do Us Part* is there
a slight variation: Markham is not a suspect, but we feel keen anxiety as
we wonder whether his fiancée is a multiple poisoner. Bob Morrison in
The Man Who Could Not Shudder amusingly ridicules the narrator-as-
sidekick convention:

I have always been attracted but puzzled by those detective stories in which the narrator
is in on everything. He tags about everywhere without any real excuse, and yet the
police never seem to notice him. At least, they never object to his presence. They
never say, "Oi! What are you doing here, my lad? Get along home."
    This grouse is inspired by the fact that, just as Julian Enderby was going to
give some really important evidence, they tossed me out of the room. (12)

The Fell novels do not offer much variety of setting: of the twenty-
three, seventeen take place in England (many of these in London); one in
Scotland (*The Case of the Constant Suicides*); one in Switzerland (*In Spite
of Thunder*); three in America (*The Dead Man's Knock* [Virginia], *Panic
in Box C* [Connecticut], *Dark of the Moon* [South Carolina]); one is aboard
ship (*The Blind Barber*). One point to note in this regard is the number
of novels that take place, not in the conventional country manor house
(although there are several of these) but in public buildings: the Tower
of London (*The Mad Hatter Mystery*); a museum (*The Arabian Nights
Murder*); a hotel (*To Wake the Dead*); a theatre (*Panic in Box C*). This
is refreshing in that the topography of the site can put severe restrictions
upon what Carr can do—especially in the case of the Tower of London,
known to every tourist who has ever set foot in England—and compels Carr
to utilise still greater ingenuity in plotting and construction. Even when
the hoary, reputedly haunted castle is used—*Hag's Nook, The Case of the
Constant Suicides, The House at Satan's Elbow*—it is handled in a refreshing
way. *Constant Suicides* ends up being more a farcical comedy than a pseudo-
horror tale. Conversely, the first five chapters of *Hag's Nook* might have
served as the perfect introduction to a haunted house novel.

Hag's Nook is a notable success for its shuddersome setting, its
introduction of Fell, and its grim conclusion, where the murderer is offered
the chance to commit suicide but cannot, in his cowardice, bring himself
to do so. The concluding chapter, where Carr presents the murderer's self-
serving confession, could have been handled a little more subtly—the criminal
displays his own villainy too obviously and clumsily—but otherwise the
novel is a marked success. And yet, even *Hag's Nook* does not prepare us
for the spectacular brilliance of *The Mad Hatter Mystery*. The remarkable
thing about this novel is not merely its grotesque humour—the opening
paragraph is justly famous:

It began, like most of Dr. Fell's adventures, in a bar. It dealt with the reason why a man was found dead on the steps of Traitors' Gate, at the Tower of London, and with the odd headgear of this man in the golf suit. That was the worst part of it. The whole case threatened for a time to become a nightmare of hats. (1)

—but the fact that the whole nature of the case is more expansive, complex, and convoluted than any of Carr's previous works. It is not simply a matter of length: to be sure, the novel is considerably longer than any Carr had yet written, but the multifaceted character of the plot—involving such things as those omnipresent hats, a lost detective story by Poe predating "The Murders in the Rue Morgue", and a crossbow arrow as the murder weapon, all in the shadow of the Tower—engenders a structure more elaborate than any we have seen before and rarely to be equalled in later works. And although we spend much of the time following Fell, Hadley, and Rampole as they dash from place to place in search of clues and to interview suspects, all the characters in the novel come alive in a way Carr did not often achieve. *The Mad Hatter Mystery* is a classic of detection.

The Eight of Swords and *The Blind Barber* are both comic detective stories, the latter self-consciously so. They are different from *The Mad Hatter Mystery* in that the comic element is intended to dominate; and Carr is immediately faced with the ticklish situation that, as a character in *The Blind Barber* states clearly, "a murder isn't especially funny" (20). Fell attempts to defend the comic element as follows: "Don't be afraid of the nonsense. Don't apologise for the vast Christian joy of laughing when an admiral slips on a cake of soap and sits on his own cocked hat" (Interlude). But this is mere assertion, not justification. Carr does not so much address the issue of murder and humour as evade it: in *The Eight of Swords* the murdered man is someone not especially liked by anyone, hence we are evidently not to care about him or his murder; in *The Blind Barber* we do not have actual confirmation that a murder has been committed until the end, when the body is finally discovered. Carr attempts to provoke a certain sense of unease with such remarks as "behind this foolery there was moving something monstrous and deadly" (6); but such dire warnings seem contrived and half-hearted in the midst of so much hilarity.

The real flaw with *The Blind Barber* is not the conception—humour and murder can mix well, and Carr himself has done it better elsewhere— but the execution. Carr simply tries too hard to be funny; and he can seemingly do so only by crude slapstick, which he heaps up frenetically lest a single page go by without a chuckle or guffaw. The humour does not arise naturally from the circumstances, but is concocted artificially and self-consciously. And a passage like the following, describing Captain Sir Hector Whistler's reaction to being hit over the head with a whiskey bottle, will not place him in the company of P. G. Wodehouse:

"!!!!¾ ½&£!?!??°???" roared Captain Whistler—weakly it is true, and huskily, but with gathering volume as his sticky wits ceased to whirl. "!&£&/£/!" He gasped, he blinked, and then, as the full realisation smote him, he lifted shaking arms to heaven and set roaring his soul in one hoarse blast: "!!!!&/£—!!?????&—&£!!/?2/3 3/4 1/3!? Thieves! Murderers! Help!" (6)

The comic romance between Hugh Donovan and Patricia Standish in *The Eight of Swords* in some ways looks forward to that of Alan Campbell and Kathryn Campbell in *The Case of the Constant Suicides*. Of course, whereas Hugh and Patricia fall in love at first sight, Alan and Kathryn do no such thing—both professors of history, they spend the better part of a train ride to Scotland arguing over esoteric points of seventeenth-century British history. But the light-hearted comic tone is the same, and Carr here genuinely approaches Wodehousian humour in portraying these two slightly pompous but warm-hearted and loveable figures. The murder takes a firm backseat to their and other characters' antics, and the book is the better for it.

Death-Watch introduces an interesting trend in several of the early and middle Fell novels: the building up of a seemingly impregnable case against someone other than the actual murderer. Here Hadley is genuinely convinced of the guilt of Eleanor Carver, and in "The Case for the Prosecution" (chapter seventeen) presents an eloquent but coldly rational case that seems to account for nearly all the phenomena. At its conclusion it is said:

> He rose, went to the fireplace, and knocked out his pipe on the marble edge. Hadley took pride in himself as a relentless logician who was not above a crackle of drama. Smiling grimly, he leaned his elbow on the mantelpiece and looked at them.
> "Any questions, gentlemen?" he enquired.

Questions there are; for in the next chapter, "The Case for the Defence", Fell systematically and completely dismantles Hadley's reconstruction, leaving him confused, angry, and demoralised. To his credit Hadley accepts defeat and pursues the actual murderer. *The Crooked Hinge*, another remarkably rich novel, plays a variation on the idea: here Fell constructs a highly plausible case against Lady Farnleigh that he knew to be false, in order to coerce the real murderer into a confession. This novel, like *Hag's Nook*, contains at its conclusion a letter from the murderer that, in its arrogance and pomposity, is meant to condemn him in our eyes; but again Carr's handling lacks subtlety. It is the only failing in a novel that rivals *The Mad Hatter Mystery* in narrative tensity, vivid characterisation, and fiendish ingenuity. The atmosphere here, however, is entirely dark, with scarcely a glint of humour.

Of *The Three Coffins* it is also difficult to speak with restraint. Aside from the extraordinarily acute "Locked-Room Lecture" (to be studied in detail in another chapter), the novel presents what is perhaps Carr's cleverest locked-room scenario. This is one of several—perhaps many—Carr novels that one ought to read twice in succession: the first to be bamboozled, the second to see how it was done. It is to be argued which reading will be the more satisfying. Here the solution shows that our initial conception of the crime and its aftermath was not merely erroneous, but almost mathematically the exact opposite of the truth.

It is my feeling that *The Arabian Nights Murder* is not merely Carr's best pure detective story, but very likely the greatest pure detective story ever written. (It is not necessarily Carr's best novel—a distinction we shall examine later.) No more complex puzzle has ever been devised in mystery fiction; the mere fact that it requires four detectives—Detective-Inspector John Carruthers, Assistant Commissioner Sir Herbert Armstrong, Hadley, and Fell—to solve it points to the staggering complexity of the core problem. Carruthers begins the investigation at the Wade Museum in London, where a man has been found dead in a carriage with false whiskers and a cookbook in his hand (that cookbook could serve as the definition of the term "red herring"). After being completely bewildered by the case and the confused stories of its many characters—all young men and women, but each realised crisply and distinctly—Carruthers turns the matter over to Armstrong, who appears to clear up one aspect of the case only to leave another in further confusion; finally Hadley takes over, and appears to solve the case to his satisfaction, attributing the murder of Raymond Penderel to Gregory Mannering. It is at this point that Fell, to whom the three have been relating the case in an all-night session at his home, remarks placidly:

"Now let me say what I do believe. I think Hadley's reconstruction of the crime was quite correct, except in one small and possibly trifling detail. That detail was that Gregory did not, in fact, kill Penderel." (Epilogue)

This is not intended as sarcasm, even of a mild variety: it is the literal truth. It is not that Hadley's entire reconstruction is wrong; it is right in every particular except the actual hand that committed the crime.

There are so many good things in this novel—the narration of the case in the three distinct voices of the police officers; the wildly bizarre setting and appurtenances of the case, derived perhaps from *The Corpse in the Waxworks* but handled without the oppressively dark atmosphere of that work; the Chinese-box nature of the situation, as each solution leads to additional puzzles—that it is difficult to single out any one feature. Perhaps we should focus on the most riotously funny character in all Carr, the utterly unworldly scholar Dr. William Augustus Illingworth, who speaks to Armstrong at length about his unintentional involvement in the case. This whole subnarrative of Illingworth is what gives the novel its unique air of crazy hilarity. For sustained comic genius Carr has here rivalled and perhaps even surpassed Wodehouse. Illingworth's entry into Armstrong's office must be quoted at length:

...First, you see, he had taken a box of matches out of his pocket; and in trying to get one out, he had yanked the box and sent a shower of matches into my face. *That* was all right. Then he had picked up one and struck it to light my cigar. Where he said, "I beg your pardon!" was where his fingers shook so much that he softly dropped the lighted match down between my shirt and waistcoat. He said it was extraordinary how he came to do it, and I agreed. The things I also said while I pounded at my chest should never have been said in front of a clergyman. For a minute I was so wild that I was going to have him chucked out, but I got a grip on myself and only gave him a cold look.

"Dr. Illingworth," I said, when I could get my breath, "Dr. Illingworth, I have told you that I am not a blacksmith. Adopting your own conversational style, I may say that neither am I a goddam skyrocket. This is a match. Look at it. It is a useful article, applied to the proper surfaces, but my person is definitely not one of them. Now *I* will light *your* cigar, if you can be trusted with a cigar. Then, police-regulations or no police-regulations, you are going to have a drink. You need one."

"Thank you," he answered. "While I do not, of course, share the national weakness, and am myself a zealous worker in the cause of temperance, nevertheless, *true* temperance—in short, yes."

I poured him out a man-sized one, neat; he swallowed it without winking, and with an absolutely expressionless face.

"That was very refreshing," said Dr. Illingworth, gravely dropping the glass into the waste-paper-basket... (9)

This sort of thing goes on for four chapters; but Carr has a remarkable skill at suddenly changing the atmosphere from the grotesquely hilarious to the chillingly grim; and here it takes place when we learn that one of the young women in the case had an illegitimate child by Penderel—all at once several motives for murder arise, as we come to terms for the first time with the fact that a man has actually died. *The Arabian Nights Murder* is Carr's single longest non-historical detective story; and it is difficult to find a wasted word or to see how so convoluted a plot could have been executed more compactly.

The Fell novels after *The Crooked Hinge* are perhaps not worth studying individually: many of them are very fine, and all are unfailingly readable, but none presents quite the union of great qualities found in the best of the earlier ones. *The Man Who Could Not Shudder* displays perhaps the most stunning triple surprise ending in detective fiction; *Death Turns the Tables* excels in the portraiture of the implacable Judge Horace Ireton; in *Till Death Do Us Part* we feel genuine concern for both Dick Markham and his fiancée as she appears guilty of murder; *He Who Whispers* exhibits one of the most sadistic killers in all Carr's work, as at the end we see him inflict the most hideous mental torture upon his victim; and *In Spite of Thunder* is a breathless read that takes us not only to Switzerland but to a villa frequented by the Nazis where an old murder during Hitler's time must be cleared up before the modern crime can be dealt with.

There is perhaps not a single genuine failure in the Fell canon—except perhaps *Below Suspicion*, although the principal reason for its weakness is the odious Patrick Butler—even if the last three novels, *The House at Satan's Elbow*, *Panic in Box C*, and *Dark of the Moon*, are the products of Carr's tired old age. It is perhaps this consistency—found not even with the five Bencolin novels, to say nothing of the much more inconsistent Merrivale saga—that raises the Fell series to its height not only as Carr's best but as one of the best in all detective fiction. Fell is a huge character in more than the obvious sense: intellectually brilliant, he yet seems a combination of an absent-minded professor and a carnival entertainer. His supporting cast—notably Hadley, but many other non-recurring characters as well—only augments Fell's distinctiveness. In sum, it is the atmosphere of half-controlled lunacy, both in events and in narration, that makes the Fell novels unique; he does not need to perform the physical antics of a Henry Merrivale to achieve the heights of farcical comedy. It is as if everything Fell comes into contact with is bent slightly askew; and it is only he, with his self-parodically ponderous utterances, who can set it right again.

Works about Dr. Fell

A. Novels

Hag's Nook (1933).
The Mad Hatter Mystery (1933).
The Eight of Swords (1934).
The Blind Barber (1934).
Death-Watch (1935).
The Three Coffins (1935).
The Arabian Nights Murder (1936).
To Wake the Dead (1937).
The Crooked Hinge (1938).
The Problem of the Green Capsule (1939).
The Problem of the Wire Cage (1939).
The Man Who Could Not Shudder (1940).
The Case of the Constant Suicides (1941).
Death Turns the Tables (1941).
Till Death Do Us Part (1944).
He Who Whispers (1946).
The Sleeping Sphinx (1947).
Below Suspicion (1949).
The Dead Man's Knock (1958).
In Spite of Thunder (1960).
The House at Satan's Elbow (1965).
Panic in Box C (1966).
Dark of the Moon (1967).

B. Short Stories

"The Proverbial Murder" (before 1941).
"The Wrong Problem" (1938).
"The Locked Room" (1940).
"A Guest in the House" (or "The Incautious Burglar") (1940).
"King Arthur's Chair" (or "Invisible Hands") (1957).

[Fell is also featured in a number of radio plays.]

Sir Henry Merrivale

The Plague Court Murders (1934) is subtitled "A Chief-Inspector Masters Mystery": the designation may or may not be significant. It seems unlikely that Carr envisioned making Masters rather than Sir Henry Merrivale the focus of a whole series of novels; but the facts that Masters is constantly involved in the mystery, that the novel reproduces in chapter ten transcripts of actual testimony taken down as Masters interrogates witnesses (something Carr does very rarely in later works, and which here lends a marked police-procedural air to the work), and that Merrivale is not brought into the case until just about halfway through the book point to the possibility that Masters in this novel at least is meant to occupy a position of much greater equality to Merrivale than, say, Hadley does to Fell. Even if this is the case, however, the scenario does not persist in later works, and Merrivale takes center stage to an even greater degree than Fell. It is significant that Merrivale is never consulted in the manner of Dr. Fell in *The Blind Barber* or *The Arabian Nights Murder:* Merrivale could not conceive of being a mere "armchair detective"; his boisterous presence must be made evident in each of the novels in which he appears.

The central fact about Merrivale is that he was created after Dr. Fell; and we have conjectured that there may have been a certain element of compulsion in his creation, given that Carr, writing three or four novels a year in the first decade of his career, could not write them all about one detective. After discarding Bencolin, Carr in quick succession wrote novels featuring Patrick Rossiter (*Poison in Jest,* 1932), Fell (*Hag's Nook,* 1933), John Gaunt (*The Bowstring Murders,* 1933), and Merrivale (*The Plague Court Murders*). It seems clear that Carr was "fishing" for a detective or detectives who could sustain a lengthy series of novels; and Carr was probably wise in sticking to Fell and Merrivale, although Rossiter is an engaging enough character.

Merrivale may well, then, have been an afterthought, although clearly Carr grew fond of him as time passed. But the differences between Fell and Merrivale are not always easy to distinguish, especially as in the early novels Carr seems intentionally inclined to confuse them. There is certainly no difference in the type of situation each is involved in: the locked room or "impossible crime" predominates, and Fell's and Merrivale's methods of detecting it—insofar as either has definite methods or principles—seem roughly analogous. Moreover, certain mannerisms that become standard in each are often muddled in the early works. Fell's archetypal utterance,

"Archons of Athens!",[1] first occurs in *The Eight of Swords* (1934 [5]); but Merrivale surprisingly utters it in *The Unicorn Murders* (1935 [4]). Similarly, Fell in *Death-Watch* (1935) calls Hadley "my fathead" (15), a term later used almost exclusively by Merrivale. Then in *The Red Widow Murders* (1935) Merrivale usurps Fell's "Harrumph" (20). It may be thought that these verbal tropes are not important indicators of character, but the fact is that Carr rarely describes even his detectives, let alone other characters, in any more significant ways; we will find in a later chapter that Carr does not so much draw characters as caricatures.

We learn superficially more about Merrivale than we do about Fell, although in the end Merrivale merely becomes a gargantuan parody of himself as he acts more and more the conscious buffoon. He was born, we are told in *The Plague Court Murders*, in 1871 (5); this would make him nearly sixty when we first see him, as the Plague Court case is definitely dated to September 6, 1930, in the first chapter. He must be well past eighty if we assume that his last case, "All in a Maze" (1955), is set roughly at the time of its writing. But Carr does not make even the pretense of aging Merrivale; he remains precisely the same from first to last.

Merrivale has a genuine occupation—he is chief of the Military Intelligence Department in the War Office—and this role takes on actual importance in some of the early cases. There is a little difficulty in ascertaining how long he remains in this capacity: does he, for example, retain it through World War II, where such an office would have vast political and strategic significance? The evidence is ambiguous, largely because Carr developed the penchant of dating the events of the Merrivale novels several—sometimes many—years before their time of writing or publication. (Several Fell novels are also antedated in this fashion, and we shall supply some conjectural reasons for this phenomenon in a later chapter.) In *Death in Five Boxes* (1938) Merrivale is still noted as being head of Military Intelligence (7); this persists through *The Reader Is Warned* (1939 [8]) and *And So to Murder* (1940 [7]), but becomes muddy so early as *Nine—and Death Makes Ten* (1940):

> Max forebode to question further. What H.M.'s position at Whitehall had become, since the war, he did not know; but he believed that the old man still had twice the brains of any person who was apt to succeed him as chief of the Military Intelligence Department. (9)

Does this mean that Merrivale has already been succeeded? It is difficult to tell, for it is at this point that Carr begins backdating his novels. *Seeing Is Believing* (1941) is set in 1938, and *The Gilded Man* (1942) appears to be set prior to the war—certainly there is no mention of the war anywhere in it—so that the remark that Merrivale is "a very big wig at the War Office" (6) is not of much help. *She Died a Lady* (1943) is set in 1940, but no mention of Merrivale's War Office capacity is noted. *He Wouldn't Kill Patience* (1944), however, is clearly dated to September 6, 1940 (1), and Merrivale is called

the "War Office pundit" (3). *The Curse of the Bronze Lamp* (1945) is set
"ten years ago" (1), hence turns out to be one of Merrivale's earlier cases.
The bulk of *My Late Wives* (1946) is set just after the war, as is *The Skeleton
in the Clock* (1948), while *A Graveyard to Let* (1949) has a character attacking
the Labour party (3), hence is presumably set around 1948; but in none
of these three novels is Merrivale's occupation cited. He is called the "War
Office chap" (4) in *Night at the Mocking Widow* (1950), but this novel
is set anomalously in 1938 (1). *Behind the Crimson Blind* (1952) and *The
Cavalier's Cup* (1953) are probably set roughly at their time of writing, but
we learn nothing about Merrivale's function in either. Finally, in "All in
a Maze" (included in *The Men Who Explained Miracles*), Merrivale's official
function has altered:

> "I'm to go back to my own office, d'ye see? It used to be part of the War Office,
> before they messed everything about in the war. And I'm to be in charge of Central
> Office Eight of the Metropolitan Police."
> "Please," said Jenny in her soft voice, "but what is Central Office Eight?"
> "It's me," H.M. replied simply. "Anybody who calls it The Ministry of Miracles
> is going to get a thick ear. They had enough fun, curse 'em, with the late Ministry
> of Information. If anything rummy turns up at Scotland Yard—any loony case that
> doesn't make sense—they chuck it at my head."

In effect, Merrivale has usurped Colonel March's duties at the Department
of Queer Complaints. But what is ultimately significant about Merrivale's
cloudy involvement with the War Office during the war is that he almost
never becomes enmeshed in a situation actually utilising the War Office,
spies, or espionage. Interestingly enough, Carr claimed to enjoy spy stories
in principle; but the way he expressed it is worth noting:

> But any fondness for espionage needs no defense, not even the defense of a joke.
> When such a story has been carefully plotted, with strong motivation and a strong
> central situation to carry all the gunplay, it belongs as legitimately to the field of
> mystery as does *Trent's Last Case* or *The House of the Arrow*. The best espionage
> novels will explode a surprise ending after honorably displaying the clues, always
> the mark of good detective fiction since Poe invented it.[2]

In other words, spy stories for Carr can be good reads just like pure detective
stories; no mention is made of the possibilities for political or social
commentary in such works. Even in those few novels where Merrivale is
dimly involved in a legitimately official capacity, Carr goes out of his way
to avoid any political implications.

But before studying those novels as a group, let us backtrack and fill
in more biographical information on Merrivale. Our first encounter with
him in *The Plague Court Murders* is typical:

I thought again of that room high over Whitehall, which I had not seen since 1922.
I thought of the extremely lazy, extremely garrulous and slipshod figure who sat
grinning with sleepy eyes; his hands folded over his big stomach and his feet propped

up on the desk. His chief taste was for lurid reading-matter; his chief complaint that people would not treat him seriously. He was a qualified barrister and a qualified physician, and he spoke atrocious grammar. He was Sir Henry Merrivale, Baronet, and had been a fighting Socialist all his life. He was vastly conceited, and had an inexhaustible fund of bawdy stories. . . . (13)

What strikes us immediately about this description is the degree to which Carr is self-consciously trying to be funny; as with all such efforts (see *The Blind Barber*), it fails through excess. Carr never learnt better, and in as late as *My Late Wives* he tries to provoke a chuckle by passages like the following:

"I really am a meek sort of feller, my wench. Honest. I'm a man of mild language. I never use profanity, God damn it. Otherwise, so help me! I'd have told him to take his ruddy file and stick it. . ."
"What I mean is," coughed H.M., suddenly remembering his high-mindedness and assuming an air of piety, "that it wasn't a very nice thing to do; now was it?" (18)

Carr would never be mistaken for Wodehouse on the strength of something like this. Throughout the Carter Dickson novels Merrivale simply plays the blustering clown: he is constantly glaring at people with "indescribable malignancy", but of course we all know he is really an old softie. In his own way, therefore, he like Fell presents a deceptively harmless appearance, as two characters discuss him in *The Gilded Man*:

"So that," murmured Betty, "is the criminals' nemesis."
"Yes. You wouldn't think he was such a crafty old devil, would you?"
"No, I certainly shouldn't. Is he?"
"Yes. He's the old man. But in private life he practically challenges you to take him seriously." (9)

Like Fell, Merrivale is married; in *Night at the Mocking Widow* we learn that her name is Clementine, and receive the most elaborate description we ever get of her:

"Looky here!" H.M. said sternly. "I'll tell you. Clemmie gets bored with the south of France. She sends a cable tellin' me to expect her. Well, we go to the Ivy, or maybe Claridge's or the Savoy Grill—" H.M.'s tone was still deprecating—"and we begin having maybe four or five double whiskies. See what I mean?"
"Oh, yes! My husband and I—" Stella paused.
"And about the sixth one, when we both feel we've just been met at the Pearly Gates with a brass band, Clemmie will begin to look thoughtful. And she says to me, 'Henry, I've got a *wonderful* idea. How would it be,' she says, 'if we put a stuffed policeman sittin' on top of every chimney at Scotland Yard? And we did it in broad daylight, and nobody in the building saw it done?"
"And me, being full of whiskey and cussedness, I say, 'Clemmie, that's not bad at all. Gimme a few minutes to work out how we can do it.' We did it, too. And then there was the time we. . .But what I mean," persisted H.M., raising a finger

impressively as he preached his moral lesson, "you can't go on doin' that, can you? I got my dignity to think of." (16)

This is amusing enough, but Mrs. Merrivale must really love the south of France, as she is always there (as stated in *The Red Widow Murders* [11] and *The Judas Window* [9]). In most of the novels she is never mentioned, and Carr unintentionally betrays the utter irrelevancy of her existence in a passage in *The Skeleton in the Clock:*

> "Martin," she asked, "is H.M. married?"
> "Yes."
> "Have you ever met his wife?"
> "No." (17)

Well, we haven't either, and Carr has much explaining to do as to why he ever invented her. Merrivale has two daughters also, but they are mentioned even more fleetingly than their mother; the most we get is in "All in a Maze":

> "Well," glowered H.M., scratching the back of his neck, "I've got a house, and a wife, and two daughters, and two good-for-nothing sons-in-law I've had to support for eighteen years. So I expect you'd better move in too."

I now wish to consider those novels that feature some element requiring Merrivale's War Office functions. They are fewer than one might suppose. It is true that Merrivale in *Nine—and Death Makes Ten* (1940) makes an interesting speech about the true nature of spying:

> "Espionage, son, is far from being a joke in these days. It's wide and it's deep and it sinks under your feet—like that water out there. It runs much deeper than it ever did twenty-five years ago. Not picturesque like all the legends have made it, or always dealin' with very important issues. The proper enemy agent is an ordinary insignificant sort of person. The clerk, the small professional man, the young girl, the middle-aged woman. Not askin' for rewards, or even very brainy: but all fanatical idealists. You could shoot the lot of 'em without causing much of a flurry to G.H.Q. But each one of those little mites, individually, is a potential death's head." (9)

It is also true that the scenario—a passenger ship secretly carrying munitions across the Atlantic—suggests espionage, and indeed the brooding and anxiety-filled character of the setting, where each of the handful of passengers and crew knows that the ship could be bombed at any time if the nature of its cargo is discovered, is handled ably and with dramatic tensity. But as it happens, the actual murders (there are two of them) have nothing to do with espionage or the war effort; the bulk of the volume deals with how it is possible to flummox fingerprints such that they do not look like one's own. We can also skip *And So to Murder* (1940): here again, although we are in a film studio outside London where war propaganda films are being made, the war does not occupy much attention. A film containing

naval secrets is stolen, but ultimately recovered; and we are far more concerned
with the unsuccessful murder attempts on the fetching Monica Stanton than
on any attempted thievery of classified documents.

Merrivale's Intelligence work comes into play, curiously, in two novels
written well before World War II, *The Unicorn Murders* (1935) and *The
Punch and Judy Murders* (1936). Both are narrated in the first person by
Kenwood Blake, Merrivale's underling at Military Intelligence; he blunders
by accident into the first case, and is consciously summoned by Merrivale
into the second. He meets Evelyn Cheyne, another Intelligence agent, in
the first novel and predictably marries her in the second. In both works
we are concerned with a wily international criminal—Flamande in the first,
and someone named merely "L." in the second. No actual espionage is
involved here, either, but at least Merrivale's presence is for once legitimate,
unlike his intrusions into purely domestic crimes; the peculiar setting of
The Unicorn Murders—a French castle cut off by a flood from the outside
world, in which Flamande is known to be one of the guests—compels one
character to remark that there is "no possibility of routine police work"
(12); Merrivale and his cohorts must solve this for themselves.

Ken Blake is worth considering briefly, as he is a more persistent
protagonist than any in the Fell novels. We find him already in *The Plague
Court Murders*, hanging around Masters and Merrivale as he is coincidentally
Johnny-on-the-spot at the crime; he returns in *The Unicorn Murders* and
The Punch and Judy Murders; and after a hiatus of several books he reappears
in *The Judas Window*. What is interesting is that Blake, like Jeff Marle,
narrates these novels in the first person, and as a result he lives as a vibrant
personality far more than Carr's usual protagonists. When, in *The Unicorn
Murders,* a hocussing of evidence causes Blake himself to fall under suspicion
of murder, we become genuinely concerned and apprehensive of his plight.

Chief Inspector Humphrey Masters is also a more persistent colleague—
or, more frequently, hostile opponent—of Merrivale than Hadley is of Fell.
He appears in *The Plague Court Murders, The White Priory Murders, The
Red Widow Murders, The Peacock Feather Murders, Death in Five Boxes,
The Reader Is Warned, And So to Murder, Seeing Is Believing, He Wouldn't
Kill Patience, The Curse of the Bronze Lamp, My Late Wives, The Skeleton
in the Clock,* and *The Cavalier's Cup.* Masters is shrewd, canny, and a little
sly. Merrivale constantly maintains that Masters is trying to "do him in
the eye"; and although Masters always blandly denies the charge, it is clear
that he yearns for an intellectual conquest of Merrivale. It never comes.
But Masters is no fool, either. Even though he never makes a more vivid
appearance than in his first, in *The Plague Court Murders*, it is vastly amusing
to see him take a card from Merrivale's deck and practise some mystification
of his own in *The Red Widow Murders:*

[H.M.:] "Then you think you know who did this, and how it was done?"

Masters waved away Shorter, who was assisting the others into their coats. He walked with them to the door. A thin mist was still ghostly in Curzon Street, muffling the lamps, and Tairlaine shivered as it began to curl in.

"I'm rather certain I do," the chief inspector told them, "and one or two minor points—minor points, mind!—will clear up everything."

"And who's guilty?"

"Mr. Guy Brixham. Look here, Sir Henry," said Masters, beginning to grin, "shall I take *your* attitude, and drop a couple of hints as you would?"

"Well?"

"I know it," said Masters, "first, because I saw some mist—like that. And, second, because I've been in Mr. Guy Brixham's room, and found he owns a real Japanese dressing-gown....I'll bring you the proof in the morning. Good night, gentlemen. Mind the steps."

He bowed like a butler against the yellow light as the door closed. (10)

He is wrong, of course, but he is impressive for the moment. And it is rather heart-warming to see him admit his fondness of Merrivale in *The Curse of the Bronze Lamp,* when Sir Henry has disappeared and is feared dead:

"After last night, I tell you straight, I could almost believe in old Herihor myself. One minute the girl was there. The next she wasn't. And no joke about it, because I was there. I saw it happen. As for Sir Henry..."

Masters brooded. Then he lowered his voice.

"I wouldn't have him know it for a good deal, Mr. Farrell. But the fact is— I tell you straight!—I rather like the old devil." (17)

We have already cited the passage in *The Plague Court Murders* deeming Merrivale a "fighting Socialist"; a later passage emphasises the idea:

H.M., with a pint tankard in his hand and an admiring crowd about him, was throwing darts at a scarred board. In the intervals he was saying, "Gentlemen, we must not, we *will* not, as free British subjects, submit to the indignities perpetrated by the present Government in grindin' the faces of the working—" I stuck my head through the doorway of the bar-parlor and whistled. He stopped, disposed of the pint of bitter with a shark-like gulp, shook hands with everybody, and lumbered out pursued by cheers. (17)

This passage is comic, to be sure, but Carr seems to be urging us to laugh more at Merrivale than with him; given Carr's apparently lifelong conservatism, Merrivale's Socialism, when combined with the fact that "his baronetcy is two or three hundred years old" (*The White Priory Murders* [1]), appears intended to cast some doubt on Merrivale's sanity or, at least, his social decorum. Merrivale's Socialism is a harmless eccentricity, like Fell's penchant for drinking beer on every possible occasion.

In *Death in Five Boxes* it is said of one character that "she can't understand why you [Merrivale], who have one of the oldest baronetcies in the Peerage, and a string of academic degrees after your name, will lower yourself to use slovenly grammar so consistently" (15). This remark is curious for more than one reason; first, that "string of academic degrees" is never specified, so far as I know, and seems designed again merely to impress us with Merrivale's erudition or, at the very least, reputation; and second, Merrivale actually does not use bad grammar so much as somewhat plebeian colloquialisms, particularly Americanisms—by today's standards Merrivale's grammar is purer than that of many professional writers!

Another interesting remark on Merrivale is found in *The Skeleton in the Clock*, where the hoity-toity Lady Brayle comments:

"Constantly he consorts with low company. Never does it enter his head—" this was the real grievance—"that their station is in any way inferior to his. His childish vanity, which makes him seriously imagine he is a model of deportment like Lord Chesterfield, is infuriating. On his vile tempers and obscene language I need not dwell." (13)

The tone and context of these remarks make it transparently obvious that Lady Brayle's rigidly aristocratic code is being held up to ridicule. But all these disparate qualities of Merrivale's—on the one side his old baronetcy and academic degrees, on the other his language, actions, and "consorting with low company"—show that Merrivale himself is consciously flaunting the conventional standards of behaviour expected of the titled aristocracy. This sort of thing presumably humanises Merrivale in our eyes (just as Lord Peter Wimsey's first utterance, "Oh, damn!", is supposed to do the same), but Carr's portraiture—certainly in the later Merrivale novels—is simply too broad, obvious, and farcical for us to think of Merrivale as anything but a clown. Margery Allingham was vastly subtler when she saddled Albert Campion not with a dignified, Bunter-like manservant, but with the hilarious ex-convict Magersfontein Lugg.

We are also not much encouraged by Merrivale's principles of detection, or rather the lack of them; in this regard his stated views are even more nebulous than Fell's. In *The Red Widow Murders* Merrivale claims that he stumbled upon the solution by "a crazy association of ideas" (18); this suggests a profoundly intuitionist, even non- or anti-rational approach to detection. But Merrivale's habitual comment is that he solves cases merely by "sittin' and thinkin' ". The most elaborate expression of this somewhat unhelpful notion occurs in *The Unicorn Murders:*

[D'Andrieu:] "You realize that I have found the weapon?"
    "Oh, yes."
    "I found it in the possession of one of my guests, and I can offer a logical explanation of how the crime was committed?"
    "Well...now." H.M. rubbed his head. He seemed disturbed. "Logical, yes. I was afraid you were goin' to say that. Believe me, I've seen a heap of logical explanations in my time; I know a feller named Humphrey Masters who can give you logical explanations enough to freeze your reason; and the only trouble with 'em is that they're usually wrong."
    D'Andrieu was in his element again.

"We come again," he said, nodding, "to the difference between Latin and Anglo-
Saxon. You deplore logic, because it requires intensity and concentration of thought.
For example, what is your method?"
"Method? Oh, I dunno. I just sit and think." (14)

The open scepticism of rationality is to be noted; and yet, this "sittin' and
thinkin' " in practise works very similarly to Fell's attention to the small
detail. The passage just quoted from *The Red Widow Murders* continues:
"One little point—only one little point—has been confusin' the case from
the beginning. It's so damned simple, the trick of Bender's murder was so
simple, that we refused to look at the truth when it came up and kicked
us." That "little point" is something Fell's intellect would have seized upon
also. In *The Gilded Man* Merrivale emphasises that the solution to the crime
is simple and warns: "Don't be misled by trappings" (14). But we are never
told how to distinguish the simple core of the case from its distracting
trappings.

Merrivale's attitude to the rule of law and justice is cavalier, bordering
upon the anarchic. He is not callous to the fact of murder; in *The Peacock
Feather Murders* he adopts unwontedly sombre tones:

"Oh, I know," said H.M. despondently. "I get into some almighty messes, don't
I, with my sittin' and thinkin'? Cases get to be too human all of a sudden, don't
they? Real, living people gather up round you: you're not analyzin' X and Y: and
you feel as you'd feel at a party if you spat in the soup or slapped the hostess'
face. Do you think I enjoy this?" (18)

But this does not stop him from letting avowed murderers go free more
regularly, and with even less regard to the consequences, than Fell. It happens
first in *The Punch and Judy Murders*, as Merrivale lets the criminal go
because he is "an old friend" and adds in a letter:

"Besides, you're not so bad...You wouldn't fasten the crime on living people, who
could suffer, when it would have been easy. You only swore it was a dead man.
Worse things have been done. Worse things will be done again."

This is not very encouraging: there are surely few worse things than murder.
In one instance, however, Merrivale displays admirable compassion: in *She
Died a Lady* he willfully destroys evidence so that a man will never know
that his son, now dead in the war, committed the crimes.

Related to freeing murderers—or, rather, that of which it is a
component—is what Merrivale airily calls "flummoxing the law". In *A
Graveyard to Let* he openly declares: "How in the name of Esau are you
goin' to get justice unless you flummox the law?" (17). Here Merrivale at
least grants the logical possibility of such a thing as justice; very different
are his actions and utterances in *Behind the Crimson Blind*, where he lets
the engaging criminal go (there have only been jewel robberies and attempted
murders, no actual deaths) with the following justification:

"You yourself told me," continued H.M., "he never once cracked a private house. In other words, he never took a penny from anyone who could even remotely be affected by losin' it. What did he crack? *Only* big firms of jewellers and rich small banks, which—d'ye see?—were bound to be heavily protected by insurance. Ever think of that?"

"But, whoever shall lose, it is against the law!"

"Oh, absolutely," agreed H.M., leaning lazily back in the swing. Again that expression of serenity stole across his face. "It's against the law. It's shockin'. Big companies oughtn't ever to be nicked like that, ought they? And yet somehow, me being an old sinner, it fails to curdle my blood. It's too much like doin' down the bookies or the income tax. All three of 'em are fair game." (19)

This in itself is interesting in that it could be interpreted as a holdover from Merrivale's Socialism and anti-capitalism, although I suspect Carr had no such intention. But Merrivale goes on:

"And now," he said, "would you like to hear the real, personal, human-being reason why I wanted Bentley to escape?"

"Yes," snapped the Colonel, his face empurpling again. "If you can."

Whereupon, deplorable to relate, H.M.'s temper blew to pieces with a bang. He surged up, amid a heavy rattle of dishes.

"It was because I liked both of 'em," he roared. "That's all; that's enough. Especially I liked that little gal Paula. *You* talk about 'regrets' and 'dyin' days.' Cor! Before I'd let 'em break that gal's heart by arresting her husband, I'd have upset the government of hell and kicked Satan off the smoky throne! Don't come any moralist nonsense over me; it won't go down. Don't try any blatter about 'law' or 'justice'; we both know they don't exist, unless we go out and get 'em for ourselves. Now stick that where you like, but don't forget it!"

This sort of cynicism, or even nihilism, is something Fell never descended to; perhaps it is just as well that Merrivale bows out after two more cases— clearly he has lost any incentive to bring criminals to justice, and he cannot engage in a case purely for the exercise of his logical faculty because, as we have seen, he does not believe in logic or rationalism.

It is not very profitable to trace the course or history of the Merrivale novels: not one, I believe, is to be compared in scope or brilliance with the four or five best Fell novels, or even with the best of the Bencolin series, and in general there is simply a gradual decline in quality and readability. And yet, what makes several of these cases interesting and substantial is not their setting—for they nearly all take place in England, in large homes or country towns—but certain novel experiments in narrative technique. In this sense they are more varied in tone and atmosphere than the Fell cases. We have seen how the early Merrivale novels revive the use of the first-person narrator (Ken Blake) from the Bencolin series; several of the early novels—*The Plague Court Murders, The Unicorn Murders, The Punch and Judy Murders*—are staggeringly breathtaking reads with non-stop action and fiendishly convoluted construction. The first narrative twist comes in

The Peacock Feather Murders: the puzzle is uncommonly fine, but the interest stems from the fact that the protagonist is not some unrelated private citizen who wanders into the fray and tags along with the police investigation, but a policeman himself—Sergeant Bob Pollard, a somewhat bored young P.C. who yearns for some excitement on his beat. He gets it.

The Judas Window is a narrative *tour de force.* In the "Prologue" we see events through the eyes of Jimmy Answell; the rest of the book is narrated in the first person by Ken Blake, and focuses entirely upon the trial of Answell for murder. Merrivale is so convinced of Answell's innocence that he undertakes his defence personally, although he has not defended a case for years. Here is his initial act:

> He rose majestically—an effect which was somewhat marred by the fact that his gown caught on something, probably himself. It tore with a ripping noise so exactly like a raspberry that for one terrible second I thought he had given one. He squared himself. However rusty his legal talents had become, it was in cross-examination, where leading questions are permitted and almost anything within reason may be brought up, that his usual rough-and-tumble tactics would be most deadly. (3)

The bulk of the work is merely the actual testimony of the various witnesses at the trial, with prosecution and defence examining and cross-examining; far from producing tedium, however, the novel develops consuming interest both through Merrivale's shrewd questioning and through interludes where the background of the case is supplied. Erle Stanley Gardner allowed a courtroom scene only toward the end of his novels; Carr structures his entire novel around the courtroom drama (in this sense *The Judas Window* superficially resembles Philip Macdonald's *Persons Unknown* [1931],[3] although Macdonald's purpose is quite different), and pulls it off without allowing the reader's attention to lapse for a moment.

Another innovative narrative device is used in *She Died a Lady.* Here the case is presented as the written narrative of Dr. Luke Croxley, an elderly man who tells the tale a few months after the events. In a postscript, written by another character, it is announced that Croxley has died in the early part of the war; the stage is now set for the final revelation—that Croxley's son was the actual murderer. Suddenly the entire narrative takes on a different cast as Merrivale points out places in Croxley's manuscript where, unbeknown to its author, the son's guilt is evident. It might almost be said that Carr has written a sort of metafiction here, although Carr—with his extreme literary as well as political conservatism—would be the first to scorn the notion: whereas in other novels Carr as author consciously conceals clues in the fabric of his narrative, here Carr must adopt the persona of another man who unwittingly reveals clues. The final result is a deeply etched impression of both the elder and the younger Croxley—expecially the elder, as he makes valiant and desperate efforts to solve the case himself—and a sense of overwhelming pity for his own blindness.

The best of the Merrivale novels is probably *The Reader Is Warned.* There is no especially novel narrative technique here—save one we shall study in a later chapter—but Carr's brooding intensity and portrayal of character (genuine character, not mere caricature as with *The Arabian Nights Murder's* Dr. Illingworth) reach perhaps their heights here. Herman Pennik, who claims that he can not merely read minds but kill with the power of thought, is perhaps the most vividly realised character in all Carr; and it is his boundless and entirely sincere confidence in his own powers—and his apparently authentic displays of them—that make him a figure of acute fear and apprehension. The odious arrogance and self-righteousness of Pennik is powerfully sketched:

"With my heart and body and brain I have made a new and great power, gentlemen. I have plundered the treasure-house of the unknown. Dr. Sanders will tell you that there is no realm more mysterious, more incalculable, or less understood than the force called nervous shock; but I have found its secret. Before I have finished I shall have made bats and owls of their scientists, and shown their logic for puerility. But the gift must be used sparingly. It must be used for good. Yes. Always for good. Always, always, always." (7)

But the miracle is in the slow devolution of Pennik from an object of terror to an object of contempt: his mind-reading powers are carefully dismantled to mere shrewdness, his "Teleforce" (killing with thoughts) is shown to be a red herring, and in an almost tragic manner—Pennik, like the tragic hero, is cursed with a single flaw, the inability to endure confinement— he declines to a pitiable state after he is faced with the prospect of three months in jail:

Pennik's face looked queer and bloated because the man had been crying: crying like a child; crying until his eyelids were puffy and the whites of the eyes showed streaked with pink. He put up a hand to shield those eyes from the light. The corners of his mouth turned down—and he whimpered. (18)

The richness of this novel depends not only upon the elaborately crafted and executed puzzle and the powerful suggestion of supernaturalism, but in this almost cruelly meticulous delineation of character—both Pennik's and others' in the book. This particular achievement Carr rarely equalled.

The fact is that the Merrivale novels begin to decline—at least in consistency—at a fairly early stage. *Death in Five Boxes* (1938) is an entirely competent puzzle, but the murders are saddled upon a very minor character. With *Seeing Is Believing* (1941) Carr begins a practise of having Merrivale engaged in some grotesque or ludicrous activity, and very frequently this activity ends up dominating the actual mystery; here Merrivale plans to write his memoirs, and spends any free moment reeling off some risqué or outrageous anecdote. It is all moderately amusing, but as with so much of the Merrivale work Carr is simply trying too hard to be funny, and it sometimes backfires. The puzzle in *The Gilded Man* (1942) is considerably simpler than in many other Carr novels; this is not surprising, since the core of the plot is taken from the short story "The Incautious Burglar" (1940). This is interesting in itself in that the short story involves Dr. Fell, and is one more example of the interchangeability of Carr's two principal detectives. In any case, much of the action toward the end of *The Gilded Man* becomes centred around Merrivle's playing a conjurer—the Great Kafoozalum—at a fête held for children. This event is only tangentially related to the actual crime.

And So to Murder (1940) is the first Merrivale novel not to feature any murder at all, but only attempted murder; the novel is really a comic love story very similar to *The Case of the Constant Suicides*. This novel, however, still sustains interest, something that cannot be said for *The Curse of the Bronze Lamp* or *The Cavalier's Cup*, neither of which features murders, although in the former one is suspected for a long time until at the end the supposed victim magically reappears. (*A Graveyard to Let* and *Behind the Crimson Blind* also have no murders, but are entertaining light reads.) *Bronze Lamp* ushers in a tendency toward egregious overwriting, as Carr tries artificially to stimulate emotional interest by passages like the following:

> Whether Kit Farrell felt a breath or air, or whether it was H.M.'s reference to Masters, Kit never afterwards remembered. But he glanced round towards the library door. That door was open now.
>
> It wasn't Masters who stood in the aperture. Audrey Vane stood there, well back where the study lights hardly touched her. Once again, for a flash as brief as the flicker of a camera-shutter, Kit surprised on Audrey's face that look of blind and helpless rage. Once more he could hardly be sure he saw it, for Audrey backed away and closed the door.
>
> Cross-currents! Cross-currents! Cross-currents! (14)

Carr became very fond of this sort of triple repetition, although its significance escapes me. *The Cavalier's Cup* is dubiously distinguished for two shocking lapses of taste—a painfully stereotyped characterisation of a comic Italian music-master and, at the end, the depiction of a hitherto strait-laced young woman chasing a man about a lawn in her underwear. Carr evidently expects us to find this sort of thing genially amusing. There is also a lame attempt to defend the dramatic interest of non-murderous larceny, the attempted robbery of the jewelled Cavalier's Cup.

> "Let's face it. The thing does have an element of—well, of what some people would call the ridiculous. But does that make the problem any less difficult? If somebody had been murdered or seriously hurt, as Sir Henry asked me, we should be chewing our fingernails and trembling at shadows. Even though that hasn't happened, does it help us?
>
> "Put it in terms of the not-too-serious, if you like. Who got into that locked room? And how was it done? And why should the cup have been moved again? We're up against the essential detective problems of who, how, and why. Simply because there was no murder or near-murder, does that make the mystery one bit less baffling?" (14)

Less baffling, no; less interesting, very likely.

In *She Died a Lady* Merrivale, having broken his foot, is seen tearing around like a demon on an electric wheelchair. Here there is some genuine amusement, although inevitably of the slapstick variety. When Merrivale first appears in a small English town on his wheelchair, he meets opposition from an unexpected source—dogs.

> Upon the face of the man in the wheel-chair was now a lordly sneer. As though conscious of his prowess, he made the chair swerve left and right in graceful fashion like a master of the art of skating. Even then, Tom maintains, things would have been all right if it had not been for the dogs.
>
> Our dogs in Lyncombe, as a rule, are a mild-mannered lot. Motor-cars they understand. Wagons and bicycles they understand. But the spectacle of a joy-riding invalid, in a chair apparently equipped with a super-charger, was beyond comprehension and therefore maddening to the canine soul. As though conjured by magic, they came pouring over fences into the foray.
>
> The din of their barking rose deafeningly above the *pop-pop-pop* of the chair. The Andersons' Scotch terrier Willie was so excited that he turned a complete somersault, landing on his back. The Lanes' Airedale made a daring dash under the wheels. Roused from his scientific absorption, the man in the chair attempted reprisals. He leaned out and made a face at them. It was, indeed, a face so terrifying that the more timorous shied back again, barking frantically; but a so-called Manchester terrier sprang on the front of the chair and attempted to get his teeth in the steering-apparatus. (5)

This goes on for several more paragraphs, and it is all delightful. In *My Late Wives* Merrivale causes a ruckus in a pinball arcade; in *The Skeleton in the Clock* he is convinced that he is the reincarnation of a Cavalier poet; and in *Night at the Mocking Widow* more merriment is caused when dogs begin to chase a huge suitcase of Merrivale's equipped with wheels:

> The race was approaching that partly curving, smooth hump of rock. Below it, and a little way out, sat a tall straight-backed military-looking gentleman, his brush poised for some delicate touch on the canvas in front of him. Beside him stood two ladies, one of them Joan Bailey, who faced the street but could only stand petrified with mouths open.
>
> "*Goggles!*" shrieked the last war call.
>
> With one bound Goggles' long legs, as he ran almost beside it, carried him to the top of the suitcase. There he stood bewildered.
>
> But the suitcase, rocked by that left-hand jump, swerved its direction. It raced straight up to the top of the rock hump and burst open.
>
> A spotted dog flew in one direction. A bottle of Scotch whiskey flew in another direction. The suitcase, seeming to unfold huge and evil leather wings as it leaped amid a surge of H.M.'s clothes, knocked the back of Colonel Bailey's head, smacking his face against the wet canvas; whereupon suitcase, Colonel, and easel toppled onto the ground. (4)

This really is very funny and genuinely brings Wodehouse to mind; and Carr once again admirably displays his ability to switch the atmosphere from rollicking hilarity to oppressive grimness in a few sentences. But many of the Merrivale novels seem designed purely to provide a stage for his antics, and he rapidly declines into a self-caricature.

In the final analysis the twenty-two novels and one novelette of the Merrivale saga are distinctly more uneven than the Fell or Bencolin canons; even such a work as *The Reader Is Warned* only approaches, and does not equal, such masterworks as *The Corpse in the Waxworks, The Arabian Nights Murder*, and *The Crooked Hinge*. The Merrivale and Fell novels are roughly equal in number, but not in substance; with rare exceptions, characterisation is not as sharp, the puzzle not as intricate, and the detective himself not as interesting. Of Merrivale Carr wrote: "He's a composite...There's a lot of Churchill in him, and some other people I know in England, and possibly even a little of me."⁴ This would seem to imply that Merrivale might be closer to Carr's heart than Fell, but—judging from the evidence of the novels themselves, as well as the fact that the Merrivale saga began slightly later and ended well before the Fell saga—the reverse is probably the case. There are one or two complete failures among the Merrivale novels, none among Fell's; and yet, we can find enough worthy specimens to make even this corpus of Carr's work readable.

Works about Sir Henry Merrivale

A. Novels

The Plague Court Murders (1934).
The White Priory Murders (1934).
The Red Widow Murders (1935).
The Unicorn Murders (1935).
The Punch and Judy Murders (1935).
The Peacock Feather Murders (1937).
The Judas Window (1938).
Death in Five Boxes (1938).
The Reader Is Warned (1939).
And So to Murder (1940).
Nine—and Death Makes Ten (1940).
Seeing Is Believing (1941).
The Gilded Man (1942).
She Died a Lady (1943).
He Wouldn't Kill Patience (1944).
The Curse of the Bronze Lamp (1945).
My Late Wives (1946).
The Skeleton in the Clock (1948).
A Graveyard to Let (1949).
Night at the Mocking Widow (1950).
Behind the Crimson Blind (1952).

The Cavalier's Cup (1953).

B. Short Stories

"The House in Goblin Wood" (1947).
"Ministry of Miracles" (or "All in a Maze") (1955).

Other Detectives

At sporadic intervals throughout his career, Carr wrote works involving detectives other than his "big three" of Bencolin, Fell, and Merrivale. Often such detectives appear in only one or two novels or only in short stories; as a result, it is not possible to trace the evolution either of the detectives themselves (although, quite frankly, we have noted relatively little development even in Fell or Merrivale) or of Carr's writing in general. Still, a number of these novels are of intrinsic interest, several of them being just below the very first rank of his work.

We have seen that Carr's experimentation in the early thirties after his initial flurry of Bencolin novels led to the creation of several new detectives; Fell and Merrivale have already been dealt with, and we are left with Patrick Rossiter in *Poison in Jest* (1932) and John Gaunt in *The Bowstring Murders* (1933).

Poison in Jest, it will be recalled, is narrated in the first person by Jeff Marle, Bencolin's young disciple; Rossiter does not make his appearance until almost exactly halfway through the book. Actually, we have met him in the "Prologue" to the novel but are not aware of it, as he is not named there; but he throws out some magnificently tantalising suggestions as he reports reading Marle's account of the case:

"I've read this," he said at length, and tapped his fingers on the sheets. "I don't see that I need to explain much. You've got it all in here. That remark Clarissa made was a dead give-away, it's so damned obvious. And those things about the variations in poisons. The real origin of the obsession was clear all the time—so clear I'm surprised it didn't occur to you. Even I didn't have all the information you did when you wrote this. You had a glimmering of the truth. But you were simply applying your theory to the wrong person."

Rossiter himself makes a somewhat bumbling entry into the narrative proper:

I heard, from the interior, a muffled splintering noise, a series of thuds, and a crash. They were followed by an outburst of the most picturesque profanity (punctuated by the sounds of thrashing about) it has ever been my good fortune to hear. It dealt chiefly with the shockingly lascivious habits of staircases, and surged from the heart like a prayer. I hurried over, pulled the door open, and peered inside.

The sight was as extraordinary as the language. Grimy light filtered through a high window; the place smelt of dampness, decay, and old hay. Past a line of ghostly stalls, a man sat on the floor talking to a stairway. In one hand he held an ancient board bucket, and in the other what appeared to be a decomposed stocking. A carriage-rug, crusted with stiff dirt, hung across his shoulder.

"—and furthermore..." said the man querulously, "furthermore—"

"Excellent!" I said. "Why don't you get up?"

"Eh?" said the man, twisting his head around. "Oh, righto."

He sighed and began to haul himself to his rather surprising height, slapping dust from his coat with the stocking. A disreputable hat, brim turned down, was stuck on the back of his head, and from his lower lip dangled the small stump of a burnt-out cigarette. Then he seemed to forget his disaster. He looked round with an air of refreshed and naive interest, and the most good-humoured expression I have ever seen on a human face. (11)

Rossiter, later described as a "loopy Englishman" (11), has been summoned by another character to the dismal Pennsylvania home of Judge Quayle, where murders and attempted murders are occurring at every turn. In a sense Rossiter could be said to anticipate both Fell (general air of scatterbrained clownishness, and manners that consciously parody the fictional detective) and Merrivale (note the "picturesque profanity", a trademark of Sir Henry). And yet, his buffoonery fails to lift the impressively oppressive atmosphere of the work, something Carr rarely equalled in later novels. In part this is because Rossiter arrives on the scene before anyone has actually died—there have only been two attempted murders to this point. Once the murder (one of two) actually occurs, Rossiter's frivolity is shed like a cloak, and he achieves an intensity that rivals Bencolin's:

"I'm very much afraid the murderer isn't through."

Though I had been expecting this, the words struck me with a chill none the less.

"And why isn't he through?" demanded Rossiter, sitting up straight. "That's the hellish part of it. It's inescapable. It's so obvious—and so ghastly—I say, I'm tempted to wash my hands of the whole business. I'm tempted to take Jinny and get out of here..."

"Why?"

"Because if I stay," Rossiter said in a queer voice, "I shall have to tell them the truth."

I stared at him. The expression of the intoxicated crystal-gazer had come back; he seemed even more blundering and foolish, knocking fire from his cigarette all over the chair; but there was something in his hushed nervousness which made my throat dry and tight.

"You—you think you know?"

"I'm afraid so. Good Lord, why doesn't somebody else see it?" he cried and slapped the arm of the chair. "Why don't you see it? Why doesn't Sargent see it, or anybody except me? It's so dashed, infernally obvious! Why must *I* be the one? I can't do it. I'll be damned if I do it. And yet, sooner or later, I've got to." (17)

I think Carr could have made a successful series detective out of Rossiter;
even in this single work he is vividly realised. Although much of his
clownishness is a self-parodying pretence ("I'm not such a fool, really,"
he says—a little disingenuously—in the "Epilogue"), the gamut of emotions
he runs might have augured well for his subsequent development.

Carr instead chose, in *The Bowstring Murders*, to create John Gaunt.
Both he and the novel are spectacular failures. Oh, to be sure, he solves
the case—he makes the very impressive utterance that "I knew who the
murderer was before I had been in this house an hour" (13)—whereas the
poor reader cannot; but this is largely because the solution depends vitally
upon our knowing the exact plan of the house, which is not provided. It
is Carr's clearest violation of his own "fair play" convention. In any case,
Carr has decided that he will here make his detective as imposing as possible,
bypassing the reverse psychology of creating a foolish-looking detective to
augment the impressiveness of his final achievement. This sort of tactic
worked well for Bencolin, principally because he displayed a cynicism and
even misanthropy that made him flaunt his intellectual superiority with
a certain sardonic relish. Gaunt, however, comes off as merely pompous
and arrogant. Carr tries to lay the groundwork by having other characters
speak of him with awe before he ever arrives on the scene:

> He said abruptly: "They still tell tales about Gaunt, Frank. Medbury told me
> that one day he was sitting in his usual big wing chair at the club window, and
> all of a sudden he jumped up from his chair, went to the telephone, and rang up
> Vine Street. 'There's a heavy-set man with square spectacles, wearing a trench-coat
> and a green felt hat,' he told the magistrate, 'passing Waterloo Place just about now.
> You'd better hold him. You don't know it yet, but you'll want him for murder.'
> And sure enough, they found out later that the man had bashed in his wife's head,
> though they didn't find the body until two days afterwards....Then," said Sir George,
> scowling, "there was the London-Liverpool bank robbery; you remember it? They
> nabbed Partington and two of his gang, but they couldn't find the stolen bearer-
> bonds. It was stalemate. Then the Commissioner got a note, one line scrawled on
> the wrapping of a tobacco package: 'In the bedpost, you bloody fool. Gaunt.' And
> that's where Partington had hid the bonds. I know. The Commissioner told me so
> himself." (5)

Carr also makes the mistake of letting Gaunt lecture on at tedious length,
as in his attack on "scientific" detection:

> "Never put a clinical thermometer into a man's ear and attempt to get the
> temperature of his brain, you see. Let him alone, utterly and completely. Never
> encourage him to talk, and browbeat only those who are loquacious to begin with;
> then they will become more loquacious than ever. If he has prepared an intricate,
> spacious, well-constructed lie, it may be difficult to trap him. For the questioner,
> the fortunate point is that so few lies are well-constructed beforehand. They are spur-
> of-the-moment, and, even if they have been thought about beforehand, the liar cannot
> resist the temptation to *elaborate*. For example, if you sincerely want to go to dinner
> with somebody, and circumstances make it impossible, your apologies to that person

later are brief and cost you no effort. It is only when you wish heartily to avoid
the dinner and miss it deliberately that your apologies take the form of a lengthy
and detailed story. In other words, the betraying detail is the unnecessary detail."
(14)

Gaunt's name is presumably meant to suggest John of Gaunt (1340-1399),
although what relevance this historical association is supposed to have is
never clarified by Carr; it is one of the many things wrong with this confused
and shoddily written work.

We can take a brief look at *The Third Bullet* (1937), an entertaining
short novel featuring Colonel Marquis, Assistant Commissioner of
Metropolitan Police, who later was metamorphosed into Colonel March of
The Department of Queer Complaints (1940). Carr becomes so involved with
the details of the murder (a highly baffling and skilfully presented one)
that not much room is left to portray Marquis, who remains nebulous
throughout the work. He states at the beginning, "I am bored; bloody bored;
bored stiff and green", hence finds the case highly stimulating. Toward
the end note is made of his "deplorable fondness for flourish and gesture";
but this is equally a trait of Bencolin, Fell, Merrivale, and even Rossiter
and Gaunt. Indeed, most of Carr's characters exhibit such a penchant.

Fatal Descent (1939) was written by Carr under the Carter Dickson
pseudonym and in conjunction with John Rhode, longtime Detection Club
member. It is a thoroughly stimulating work, although perhaps its greatest
point of interest is how much might have been written by each of the
collaborators. In the absence of any documentary evidence available to me,
it appears that Rhode—although he received top billing—may have supplied
only the central idea (involving a somewhat technical point in electronics—
this sort of thing was a specialty of his); nearly all the writing seems to
be Carr's. From beginning to end there are typically Carrian turns of phrase
("He liked to see the young folks have a good time" [1], something Merrivale
repeats time and again; "There was a silence" [8], a statement that occurs
in nearly every Carr novel; "That's torn it" [17]), and the atmosphere of
boisterous comedy—very different from the almost Victorian stodginess of
most of Rhode's own writing—is highly reminiscent of the early Merrivale
and Fell novels. Here we have a detective rivalry in Chief Inspector David
Hornbeam and Police Surgeon Dr. Horatio Glass, who spend the entire
novel roundly abusing each other while trying to reach the solution before
the other. Again, we do not derive any especially distinct impression of
either figure, but with all the fun—even if one character affirms that "Even
a regrettably low view of the human race and a wide acquaintance with
such goings-on in films have not yet convinced me that a corpse is necessarily
funny" (14)—we do not seem to mind.

With *The Emperor's Snuff-Box* (1942) we are in an entirely different
atmosphere altogether. I see this as a novel in which Carr is forthrightly
attempting to answer his critics that he cannot engage human emotions
or draw real character. The opening scene—where Ned Atwood breaks into

his ex-wife's house in a small French town because he has heard she wishes to remarry—achieves an emotional intensity found nowhere else in Carr:

> In the dark, as clearly as though he could see her, he knew what she was doing. By the rustling sound, the creak of a spring, he could tell that she had caught up the heavy lace negligee that lay across the foot of the bed, and was starting to put it on. She had struggled into it, all except one sleeve, by the time he reached her.
>
> There was another fear, too. Eve had not failed to think of it. No woman—so her more worldly acquaintances had always assured her—ever forgets the first man in her physical life. She may think it forgotten, yet it remains. Eve was a human being; she had been alone for many months; and Ned Atwood, whatever else you might say, had a way with him. What if...?
>
> She struck out at him, fiercely but clumsily, as he caught her.
>
> "Let go! You're hurting me!"
>
> "Are you going to be good?"
>
> "No! Ned, the servants...!"
>
> "Nonsense. There's only old Mopsy."
>
> "Mopsy's gone. There's a new maid. And I don't trust her. I think she spies. Anyway, can't you *please* have the ordinary decency to..."
>
> "Are you going to be good?"
>
> "No!" (2)

All the characters stand out vividly—the pliant, easily victimised Eve Neill; the arrogant yet vulnerable Ned Atwood; the seemingly ingenuous yet hypocritical Toby Lawes. Even Maurice Lawes, who is murdered very early in the book, is etched harshly in one of the most fiercely cynical passages in all Carr:

> In those far-off days when newspapers had little to print and much paper to print it on, his death created a stir in the English press. True, few people even knew who he was, let alone why he had got his knighthood, until somebody mysteriously murdered him. Then everything about him became of interest. A knighthood, they discovered, had been the reward for his humanitarian activities in the old days. He had been interested in slum clearance, interested in prison reform, interested in seamen's betterment.
>
> *Who's Who* listed his hobbies as "collecting and human nature." He was one of those contradictory characters who, a few years later, were to bring England almost to ruin. Though he gave large sums to charity, and was always badgering the authorities about spending for betterment, he himself lived abroad to avoid the iniquity of paying income tax. Short, tubby, rather deaf, with a mustache and little tuft of chin beard, he also lived in a world of his own. But his qualities as a popular man, a kindly man, a pleasant man in his own household, received their full tribute. And it was a deserved tribute. Maurice Lawes really was just what he pretended to be. (4)

Much of this is a trifle blunt, and yet it succeeds. Interestingly enough, Dr. Dermot Kinross, the amateur detective, is a devotee of "criminal psychology" (6), something Carr has elsewhere heaped with scorn; perhaps this is why he never recurs in another work. *The Emperor's Snuff-Box* is among the most popular of Carr's works, especially with those who may tire of the prodigious ingenuity of his more elaborate "impossible crimes"; and although Carr continued to stoke the emotional fires high in later works—both the detective stories and the historical mysteries—he never achieved so concentrated an impression as here.

And now we come to Patrick Butler.[1] To say that Butler is conceited, pretentious, and arrogant is not sufficient; for the alarming and mortifying thing is that Carr cannot help liking him. It is as if Carr is saying, "Yes, he is all these things—tut, tut!—but he's still a fine fellow, isn't he?" Butler's mastery over females is particularly thorough (and here is one of many instances where Carr reveals the most profound ignorance of female psychology); note this passage from *Below Suspicion* (1949):

He was a product of Westminster and Christ Church, Oxford. But often, very deliberately, he would inflect his speech with a trace of Dublin accent which the English called a brogue; they [women] loved it and fell for it. (1)

And again:

("By George," he thought, "she's falling for me!" His female clients often did, and it was damned awkward.) (1)

Damned awkward. How Carr could have portrayed this repulsive character—who joins Philip Macdonald's Anthony Gethryn, S. S. Van Dine's Philo Vance, and Ngaio Marsh's Roderick Alleyn as the most odious detectives in literature (a result, in every instance, of the fact that their creators have fallen in love with them)—without an iota of humour or self-parody escapes me utterly. Butler's trademark utterance is "I am never wrong"; he says it throughout *Below Suspicion* and *Patrick Butler for the Defence* (1956). In both novels he comes close to making a mistake, but does not actually do so. Indeed, in the latter novel Butler's near-mistake is precisely his doubting at one point that he is ever wrong!

Below Suspicion is based upon the case of Florence Bravo, a sweet and innocent-seeming woman of the middle nineteenth century who was hanged for murder. To this day there is still doubt as to the true resolution of the case; Carr himself later wrote a foreword to a nonfictional account of it, John Williams' *Suddenly at the Priory* (1957). Carr has, of course, set the events in the twentieth century, and otherwise changed facts and details; but unlike *The Murder of Sir Edmund Godfrey* and his historical mysteries, it was his prerogative to do so here.

The most interesting aspect of *Below Suspicion* is that it involves both Butler and Dr. Fell (and also David Hadley toward the end). Fell generally takes a back seat to the action, and Butler becomes the protagonist through whose eyes we see the events; in spite of this (or perhaps because of it), Fell remains—and is intended to remain—the more impressive figure. Carr makes sure that Fell is never truly bested by Butler; even so small a detail as the fact that Butler's collection of works on crime was "almost as large" (9) as Fell's suggests Fell's ultimate superiority.

We must admit that the portrait of Butler is somewhat modified and softened in *Patrick Butler for the Defence*. In the first place it is interesting that Butler is said to have been involved in several other cases in the interval between this novel and *Below Suspicion*, as one character notes:

"Ever since that witchcraft affair, six or seven years ago, he's had a whole batch of cases which could be turned into proper detective-stories: the evidence fully displayed, the conclusions logical." (1)

This certainly seems to suggest that Carr intended to write more works about Butler, but in fact I do not think this is the case: the passage is probably merely meant to show that Butler has had considerable experience in detection. Other characters discuss the accusation that Butler cannot solve a case without Fell (3), and in a later passage Butler reveals rare insecurity on the subject:

"No, by God!" roared Butler, and sprang to his feet. "They're not going to laugh at me. They say I can't succeed at a murder mystery unless I've got Gideon Fell to back me. Don't they?" (10)

But aside from this Butler is about as insufferable as ever. What makes this novel worthwhile is the really remarkable metamorphosis of the hoity-toity Lady Pamela de Saxe from a completely brainless aristocrat (merely an act) to a clever, shrewd, and determined woman. One of the most intense emotional scenes in Carr—rivalling the opening scene of *The Emperor's Snuff-Box*— is where Pamela and Helen Dean argue bitterly about Hugh Prentice, whom Pamela genuinely loves but whom Helen, his fiancée, only pretends to love. When Pamela suddenly sheds her pretentious aristocratic accent with the blunt "Oh, come off it" (16), it is like a slap in the face.

Let us backtrack to *The Nine Wrong Answers* (1952), Carr's remaining non-series detective novel. It is worth quoting in full the significant portion of the dedication: "It has been called 'a novel for the curious' because there seems no other way of classifying it. It is a novel of character combined with one of very fast action, yet always underneath—without police investigation—runs a fair-play duel of wits between reader and writer." In this, Carr's most formally radical or unconventional mystery novel, the "fair play" convention persists as a sort of bedrock principle that can never be abandoned. But *The Nine Wrong Answers*—an extreme amplification and elaboration of the radio play "Will You Make a Bet with Death?" (1942; included in *The Door to Doom and Other Detections*)—is really a novel-length *conte cruel*, where we witness the harrowing experience of a man, Bill Dawson, who blunders into a bet with an evil old man, Gaylord Hurst, that the latter cannot murder him within six months. Gaylord Hurst is one of the great villains in Carr: if Carr had a single strength as a portrayer of character, it is his ability to depict loathsome and hateful figures, and Hurst is near the top of the list. For all Carr's detestation of the term, this work must be called a novel of suspense; and yet, the mere suspense of whether Dawson will survive Hurst's fiendish plot is in the end submerged into an entirely sound and fully realised fair play murder mystery, and this novel gains a compact unity not found in many of Carr's later works. It may be his best detective novel since the great feats of the thirties.

The relative paucity of the works studied in this chapter suggests that Carr was not especially comfortable writing pure detective stories (as opposed to historical mysteries) without a series character; all the novels considered here are interludes, diversions, or experiments. But at least three of them— *Poison in Jest, The Emperor's Snuff-Box,* and *The Nine Wrong Answers*— are equal or superior to all but the very best of Carr's series novels. It is precisely because Carr does not have a series character to fall back on that he is compelled in these works to draw all characters with clearer or broader strokes; in large part he was successful at so doing, and the best of these books gain their strength from this circumstance.

Works about detectives other than Dr. Fell or Sir Henry Merrivale

Poison in Jest (1932).
The Bowstring Murders (1933).
The Third Bullet (1937).
Fatal Descent (1939; with John Rhode).
The Emperor's Snuff-Box (1942).
Below Suspicion (1949).
The Nine Wrong Answers (1952).
Patrick Butler for the Defence (1956).

The Historical Mysteries

Deadly Hall (1971) opens with a patently autobiographical passage:

"I'm afraid I must still ask, my boy, what you intend to do."

"Live abroad for a while, I think. With a base in Paris, but visiting London as often as possible."

"Of course," Ira Rutledge said drily, "there's no real reason why you *should* work."

"Oh, I intend to work, sir, though some mightn't call it that."

"Just as you please. What do you want to do?"

"I want to write historical romances, as I always have. Swashbuckling stuff, not altogether free of gadzookses or the like, but at least historically accurate. France and England are ideal backgrounds for that. There's one other kind of novel I'd rather like to try, though I don't think I ever can."

"Indeed? And what is that?"

"Detective stories, about who killed whom and why. There's always a market for blood and thunder, and I love it!"

"Now there," Uncle Gil had interjected with some heartiness, "you're really speaking my language. Our friend Ira wouldn't touch a criminal case if they accused his own son of murder, and yet it's what *I* love. By all means write historical romances, provided you don't turn out the oversugared confectionary we get so much of. Why not write detective stories too?"

"Because I don't think I've got enough sheer ingenuity. You need a first-class, brand-new idea, with all the tricks of presenting it. Whereas the historical can be managed. I'm probably going to make a hash of it. But I think I can write readable English, and I'm game for all necessary research." (1)

What is interesting about this passage is the notion, firstly, that historical novels are his first love, and, secondly, that he yearns to write detective stories but feels they are beyond the scope of his ingenuity. How accurately this passage actually reflects Carr's feelings at the beginning of his career, I have no idea (as for the second point, perhaps Carr was still recalling that bored undergraduate who so easily guessed the solution of one of his earliest detective tales); the actual course of Carr's career, of course, was exactly the reverse, where many detective novels were written before the bulk of his historical mysteries came to be conceived. But we have already made note of the exceptions—*Devil Kinsmere* (1934) and *The Murder of Sir Edmund Godfrey* (1936) were written relatively early in Carr's career—and also the likelihood that Conan Doyle's historical novels, read during Carr's work on the Doyle biography (1949), led to the resurgence of his interest in (or at least his sense of the potential success of) historical fiction.

History frequently plays a significant part in the pure detective novels also. Many of them feature a crime that occurred years before the bulk of the action—a crime that must either be cleared up before the entire case can be laid to rest, or that seems an uncanny precursor to the modern crime. Certainly the oppressive weight of the past is very evident in *Hag's Nook* and *The Mad Hatter Mystery*, the latter set within the very confines of the hoary Tower of London. *The Crooked Hinge* (1938) draws upon an attempted murder aboard *The Titanic* in 1912 (where, as Carr frequently notes, Jacques "Thinking Machine" Futrelle perished). "Persons or Things Unknown" (1938) deals with the explication of a crime in the seventeenth century. *The Man Who Could Not Shudder* (1940) is set in 1937, but the murder here seems inexplicably identical to one that took place in 1920. "The Gentleman from Paris" (1950) is a celebrated story set in the middle nineteenth century involving Edgar Allan Poe. In *The Dead Man's Knock* (1958) documents for an unwritten locked-room novel by Wilkie Collins in 1869 provide clues to a murder committed in 1948; this anticipates Collins's actual entry as an amateur detective in *The Hungry Goblin* (1972). Perhaps *The House at Satan's Elbow* (1965) puts the seal on this historical tendency in the detective novels when it is remarked: "Whatever may be happening here, it had its origin in the past" (8).

In terms of the historical mysteries themselves, it is worth examining both their setting and their dates of occurrence; some significant patterns will emerge:

Work	Setting	Date
Devil Kinsmere (1934)/*Most Secret* (1964)	England/France	1670
The Murder of Sir Edmund Godfrey (1936)	London	1678
The Bride of Newgate (1950)	London	1815
The Devil in Velvet (1955)	London	1675
Captain Cut-Throat (1955)	France	1805
Fear Is the Same (1956)	London	1795
Fire, Burn! (1957)	London	1829
Scandal at High Chimneys (1959)	London	1865
The Witch of the Low-Tide (1961)	England	1907
The Demoniacs (1962)	London	1757
Papa Là-bas (1968)	New Orleans	1858
The Ghosts' High Noon (1969)	New Orleans	1912
Deadly Hall (1971)	New Orleans	1927
The Hungry Goblin (1972)	London	1869

Of the first seven novels, three are set in the England of Charles II and four in Napoleonic Europe; we have already noted the possible influence of Doyle in this vein, although of course late Stuart England was an area of especial interest to Carr, and he was close to a specialist in it. Indeed, *Devil Kinsmere* (1934) neatly joins these two eras by having a figure in

1815 tell the story of his grandfather, Roderick Kinsmere, as he remembered hearing it from Kinsmere himself. Only one novel is set in the eighteenth century; two more in Victorian England, one in the ante-bellum South; and three in the early twentieth century. There is a gradual but unsystematic trend toward increasing recency in dates; Douglas G. Greene has remarked on the anomaly that in *Deadly Hall* "the events begin only four days before the events of Carr's first novel, *It Walks by Night*, [but] more than forty years have passed, and thus *Deadly Hall* should be considered a historical novel."[1] I shall have reason for slightly qualifying this basically true assessment, but it can be noted that *Deadly Hall* and, in a very slight way, *The Ghosts' High Noon* are the only novels of this group that draw upon Carr's firsthand experience as opposed to book-learning.

The Murder of Sir Edmund Godfrey has been unhesitatingly inserted into this sequence because, though technically a work of nonfiction, it utilises fictional techniques very close to those in the actual historical novels. But whether we regard it as fiction or nonfiction, it is unquestionably one of Carr's finest works. Written in the midst of Carr's most productive period of fiction-writing, it has after a somewhat slow beginning all the vigour and pungency of his best detective fiction. And yet, the dynamic tension of this work rests precisely upon the fact that it is neither fiction nor nonfiction—or that it is both at the same time.

In the first place, Carr makes no pretensions to being a true historian (perhaps he was thinking—a little harshly—of himself when he wrote of the protagonist of *The Crooked Hinge*: "He was too indolent for real scholarship, yet too restless-minded and intellectually alert to let it alone" [1]):

This record does not presume to be history, except insofar as it tries to be true. To write good history is the noblest work of man, and cannot be managed here: the intent is only to amuse with a detective story built on facts. ("Preface")

Earlier Carr had stated bluntly that he has discovered "no new facts...I have only tried to draw a few new deductions from the evidence, and construct a theory which shall explain *all* the contradictory facts" ("Preface"). What Carr is referring to is the fact that the solution to the actual murder he proposes was already outlined in a brief article by J. G. Muddiman, "The Mystery of Sir E. B. Godfrey";[2] but Carr—as well as the somewhat uncharitable reviewer of *The Murder of Sir Edmund Godfrey* in the *Times Literary Supplement,* who remarked: "Those already familiar with the controversy will find that Mr. Carr's 348 pages add nothing of substance to the half-dozen in which Mr. J. G. Muddiman first propounded this solution twelve years ago"—is being entirely unfair to his own achievements. Not only has he fleshed out the events and vivified the historical characters, but he brings many pieces of evidence not considered by Muddiman into the story, and points out several places where Muddiman is demonstrably wrong in the interpretation of details.

Still, although Carr goes out of his way to assert the historical veracity of all he records—to the point of failing to say anything about a certain meeting involving some figures in the case and the Earl of Shaftesbury, because historical evidence of what happened there is lacking—he cannot refrain from injecting novelistic elements into the work, especially as regards the possible thought-processes of those involved. Consider the poignant vignette of Samuel Atkins, falsely accused of the crime:

It seemed to Samuel Atkins that he had grown very much older in one week. He was not now concerned with little Captain Charles, who took your money and betrayed you; he was concerned with larger, and more perplexing and maddening things. It was not that he much minded, one way or the other, but he would not be put upon. It was the mere bigness and overbearing calm cheat of this business, as though a tapster should swear you had not paid a reckoning when you had paid it, that determined him to fight: the calm fashion in which they told you you had better swear away your master's life, and no nonsense about it. God rot 'em, anyhow! thought the mouse, and began to nibble at his bonds. Ay, fight: but how prove he was not in Somerset House on the Monday night, when they all swore he was? How did a man prove where he was on such-and-such a date, unless he had some cause to remem—

Samuel Atkins stopped writhing in his manacles, and in the gall of the cold: for the darkness seemed to have a window in it. He saw a trim yacht riding at Greenwich, against the bleak low shore in October. He saw a cabin with wine-bottles on the table, and the laughing faces of women half-boozy, and the captain a-chuckle, and himself shouting out toasts. He felt himself being lowered like a sack into the wherry, as foxed as ever a man was, while the rowers strained against the tide. He remembered that: just as it had come into his mind, in fear, when they first arrested him; and the night of that debauch had been the night of that debauch had been the night of Monday, the 14th of October.

. . .

He could think of the whole world raising its hands in horror at such debauchery; but he lay back and cried a little nevertheless, for he knew now that he was not going to be hanged after all. (4)

It is obvious that Carr was drawn to this case because it seemed naturally suited for fiction: "The fact remains that only in very rare cases can real life be fashioned into the tidy, clipped maze of fiction" ("Preface").

But Carr does more than merely propound a solution to this still unsolved case; he is careful to point out its historical significance:

Again, this killing on Primrose Hill (this mere murder) is so much a part and texture of the whole age, so entwined in its political history, that we must glance first at a different sort of Dirty Work which was leading up to it in the year 1678. Does history seem too important a business to devote to the end of one small broken body in a ditch? Is the devil evoked in all his majesty merely to preside over the theft of twopence? Yet it is possible to argue that this death in a teacup helped most of all to bring about the huge political quarrels of the later seventeenth century, the sharp lines of Whig and Tory, the battle that almost swept away James the Second before he had even ascended the throne. ("Preface")

Later Carr suggests that Charles II's dissolution of Parliament in early 1679 and the subsequent elections were of great historical importance: "For the first time in English history, there was an election fought out along party lines as we know them now" (6). None of this, of course, is any great breakthrough in historical thinking, but Carr is to be praised for including it; again he is too humble when he sums up his achievement in this work: "For the mountain has laboured, and brought forth—a thriller" ("Preface"). The last chapter—"An Ending for Connoisseurs in Murder"—considers in detail twelve different theories to explain the crime. It is a miracle of detective reasoning.

The later fortunes of *The Murder of Sir Edmund Godfrey* are of interest. The *New York Times Book Review* praised Carr's work, although remarking that "It is not a swift-moving tale". The *Times Literary Supplement* grudgingly acknowledged that "the general reader could have no more lucid guide through the maze of the Popish Plot". John Kenyon, one of the most distinguished modern historians of Stuart England, concludes that Carr's work

is not to be despised. It contains some bad history and some very doubtful characterization, but it sets out the facts as they are known, and gives an exhaustive review of the possible culprits.[3]

In an appendix on the murder of Godfrey, Kenyon reports Muddiman's and Carr's view that the Earl of Pembroke murdered Godfrey because Godfrey was the judge in a case involving Pembroke earlier in 1678; but Kenyon ultimately rejects this theory, resorting to the notion that Godfrey was killed by an "underworld" gang. Otherwise Kenyon follows Carr's reasoning on the subject closely.

The most recent writer on the subject, Stephen Knight in *The Killing of Justice Godfrey* (1984), offers some new insights. Several new pieces of evidence discovered long after Carr wrote now cast doubt upon his solution of the case. Medical evidence in a document discovered in 1976 seems to prove that Godfrey was not kept in captivity for several days, as Carr believed, but died on the day he disappeared. More significantly, new documents show that Godfrey was a member of Peyton's Gang, a group of fanatical republicans. But they felt that Godfrey's allegiance to them was wavering in 1678, and so wished to test him: would he indict his friend, the Catholic Edward Coleman, falsely accused of plotting to assassinate the king? Knight writes: "If he betrayed the government, he could expect a judicial death. If he betrayed the Gang it would be furtive execution by hired killers."[4] (But I wonder why, if Godfrey did betray the Gang—as in fact he did, on Knight's reconstruction—it would not have been sufficient to denounce Godfrey as a Papist sympathiser?)

In any case, Carr (following Muddiman) does commit one demonstrable error: Carr believed that Godfrey fled abroad in the summer of 1678 to escape Pembroke's wrath for convicting him of murder (he was freed on benefit of clergy); but Godfrey's trip actually occurred in 1677, before Pembroke's trial. Curiously, however, Knight concludes that the hot-headed Pembroke was actually the Peyton Gang's "hit-man" for Godfrey—thus Carr got the right man but for the wrong reason! Unlike the Poe who "solved" the murder of Mary Rogers in "The Mystery of Marie Rogêt" but learned to his embarrassment that his solution was disproven by new facts, Carr never learned that his masterful case against the Earl of Pembroke would ultimately prove inaccurate. And yet, whether one accepts or rejects Knight's reconstruction (and there are some problems with it), one cannot help concluding that he has not sufficiently acknowledged Carr's work in the writing of his own tract. Certainly Carr's remains by far the more enthralling read, and the best account of the case based on the evidence available to him at the time.

An early passage in *The Murder of Sir Edmund Godfrey* is of some interest in connexion with Carr's later work:

These wide-eyed men and women of the seventeenth century—with their childlike curiosity, their hilarity, their *naiveté*, their fondness for toys or gauds, their plump oaths and plump women—they are live, like rowdy adolescents, and preoccupied with much the same sort of thoughts. ("Preface")

A similar remark is made in the afterword to *The Devil in Velvet:* "It [the Restoration] was a combination of the adolescent and the sophisticated" ("Notes for the Curious"). This appears to be the sum total of Carr's view of the seventeenth century, and does not provide much of a justification for Carr's writing historical mysteries at all. Merely to fictionalise history is a slim motive for writing. And yet, Carr repeats frequently that this is his sole aim, as in *The Murder of Sir Edmund Godfrey*, where he admits to wishing to make "these people walk and talk like recognisable human beings" ("Preface"). In *The Bride of Newgate* Carr confesses that he is "one who, after dark, likes still to repeople the old streets with the old ghosts" ("Notes for the Curious").

What we miss in most of Carr's historical novels—indeed, what is present only in *The Murder of Sir Edmund Godfrey*—is a rationale or aesthetic purpose, higher than that of entertainment, for the writing of these works. Some of them are lively and engaging, and the historical atmosphere and details are almost always handled with accuracy and flair; but in the end these stories remain just stories, with no broader conclusions drawn from them. Now and again a somewhat more serious message emerges. In *Captain Cut-Throat* it is said: "The future of several countries for the next fifty years may depend on what can be discovered at Boulogne in the next few days" (7). Indeed, if Carr can be said to have any sort of philosophy of history, it is this notion that single individuals and actions, rather than broad and impersonal socio-economic conditions, are the moving forces in history. It is the guiding principle behind most of Carr's undistinguished and overly melodramatic historical tales of his college years, in one of which it is written: "Because of L'Aubley, Marie Antoinette will go to the guillotine."[5]

In *Devil Kinsmere* we read:

> This is my grandfather's story, true enough, but it is also a much bigger story. It is, as you must have guessed, in some measure the story of the Secret Treaty of Dover. Therefore it must be larger than an account of a murdered man in a tavern, even though your only interest lies in the question of who killed him. (10)

This indicates the most significant and refreshing difference between the historical mysteries and the pure detective tales—the degree to which the actual murder is frequently overshadowed or submerged in other events. Oftentimes—as in *The Demoniacs*—the murder is not even of any particular interest, and little time is devoted to it. Again, however, *Devil Kinsmere* and *Most Secret* are nearly alone in making explicit some overriding political consideration that casts the actual murder into the shade—or, rather, that shows that the murder is a mere component of it. Political considerations of a sort are involved in *Papa Là-bas*, where many Southerners are made to express their support of slavery. The problem here is that Carr seems to be on the Southerners' side on the issue. One character says: "I can't be as shocked by slavery as people at home [in England] think I ought to be" (14). Although this character turns out to be the murderer, at this point he is a sympathetic figure. A later discussion is of interest:

> "Do I hear *you* saying slavery is wrong? *You?* Is Saul also among the prophets?"
> "I do not say slavery is wrong, as I do not say owning any property is wrong. I say merely that it may cease to be economically sound."
> "What are you talking about?"
> "I myself was once part-owner of a sugar plantation down the river. You are a plantation-owner. So is General Ede; so are several of our friends. What I say may be true only of Louisiana. But consider:
> "The work of your field-hands, particularly on the levee or in irrigation-ditches, is hard and dangerous. Many die or are incapacitated there; others die from yellowjack, cholera, snake-bite, and kindred ills we are all prey to. A good field-hand represents an investment of twelve to fifteen hundred dollars; lose him, and you lose your whole investment. If instead of using slaves you had hired the many Italian or Irish immigrants who for small pay are accustomed to labours far more dangerous, surely you would have found it cheaper in the long run?" (17)

The extremely tasteless and offensive remarks made here—slaves as "property", the approval of the use of cheap immigrant labour for hazardous work—does not seem intended to portray these two characters as evil or selfish: both are figures the reader has identified with up to this point, and the principal speaker is the amateur detective who solves the case. Could

Carr actually be subscribing to these views? Given his conservative politics, anything is possible.

Devil Kinsmere and *Most Secret* is the second occasion where we have an early and a later draft of a major work; the first, of course, being *Grand Guignol* and *It Walks by Night*. (Some short stories are rewrites of others, and some short stories and radio plays were rewritten as novels; but we have only these two instances of different versions of lengthy works.) Unlike the first pair, however, where the two versions were written within a year of each other, *Most Secret* is separated from *Devil Kinsmere* by an interval of thirty years. Again, I have no idea why Carr chose this particular time to rewrite this novel; perhaps he was running out of his 120 prepared plots. In any case, the rewrite has been done with considerable skill; perhaps a comparison of the very first paragraph of the "Editor's Note" in each volume is sufficient:

Devil Kinsmere:
    To anybody who reads this rowdy chronicle, it will shortly be apparent that Major Kinsmere (rest his soul) was one of the most genial old liars who ever glorified his family name. This is the pronouncement of my friend Mr. N. R. Nevlin, who has assisted me in preparing the record; so that I am in no danger of libelling somebody's ancestor, and getting sued for it.

Most Secret:
    Well, how much truth is in it? Anyone who reads the ensuing narrative may wonder whether Colonel Kinsmere (rest his soul) was not glorifying his grandfather by building the sort of vague legend found among many families into a lyric edifice of lies. This is the verdict of one of his descendants, Mr. Herbert Darlington, who has assisted me in preparing the record, so that in suggesting it I am in no danger of getting myself sued for libelling somebody's ancestor.

The first is a little stiff and formal; the second not merely more fluid, but both more expansive and more compact at key points. This sort of rewriting is carried on throughout the novel; and yet, even so *Devil Kinsmere* perhaps retains a freshness that ought not to relegate it to mere academic interest; it ought to be reprinted.

    Other demonstrable changes include an elaboration of the romance of Roderick Kinsmere and Dolly Landis (although their quarrel in chapter thirteen of *Devil Kinsmere* is rather more charming and witty than the more compressed version in *Most Secret*); the painting of one of the villains, Captain Harker, in a crueller light by his being seen striking and verbally abusing Dolly; and a somewhat more unceremonious treatment of the principal villain, Salvation Gaines (called, less interestingly, Jeremiah Gaines in *Devil Kinsmere*). *Most Secret* has been tightened by the omission of a tableau of the Thames River in chapter eleven. Carr, however, curiously retains almost unchanged the rather static second chapter, a description of London in 1670 (one wonders whether this is intended as a dim parody of Macaulay's great third chapter of the *History of England*, a systematic and richly detailed account of England in 1685), and also chapter nine, a tableau of the King's Theatre prior to a performance of *Julius Caesar;* although here at least Carr in both versions has engagingly utilised the rare second-person narration:

> Never expect, as you enter, to see anything like our modern theatre of 1815. There will be no drop curtain, as you observe; no floats or footlights to shine on it; such things have not yet been invented. Merely a raised platform of a stage, with double doors at the back and a smaller door flanking them on either side; above the stage, on ropes so that they may be raised or lowered, two chandeliers with crowns of candles. (*Most Secret* [9])

Three historical works—*The Devil in Velvet, Fear Is the Same,* and *Fire, Burn!*—involve modern people going back in time to participate in events up to two and a half centuries before. Technically this would, I suppose, make them novels of fantasy or the supernatural, but it is cumbrous to consider them so. In *The Devil in Velvet* the Devil literally appears to Nicholas Fenton in 1925 and offers him the chance to go back in time; we are evidently to regard this incident as actually occurring, but Carr wisely anticipates our not surprising incredulity by having Fenton himself express scepticism:

> "Did you actually sell your soul, Professor Fenton?"
> "Actually, no." His dry chuckle was barely audible. "In the first place, I cannot quite credit the reality of the devil. He might have been only a hoaxing friend, with a talent for stage effect. I should not put it past Parkinson of Caius, for example."
> (1)

In *Fear Is the Same* Lord Philip Clavering and Jennifer Baird are hurled back in time, evidently to enact a crime in 1795 that is identical to a crime in which they have become enmeshed in their own time:

> "Oh, God," Jenny said. "This is *my* fault."
> "Jenny, stop talking nonsense! Come closer to me!"
> "But it is *my* fault. I cried out and said, 'Oh, if only we could be out of this! If only we could go back a hundred and fifty years in time, and forget it!' You must listen to me, Phil. This isn't a fit of the horrors; I swear it isn't! For just then a little voice—inside my head; I don't know from where—whispered to me and said, *Would it be any different, if you did go back?*
> "Then I think there was a clap of thunder, or a roaring in my ears. The next thing I knew, I was sitting in this house, before a fire, in a room I'd never seen before. It's taken me a long time to understand, but I think I see now.
> "Don't *you* understand, darling? I don't know whether it's punishment for some wrong or sin, or only whether a wish is granted to teach you a lesson. But we've been carried back in time, just as I prayed. We've been allowed to retain only small bits and pieces of memory. We've got to enact the same horrible story, just as it was in the other life. Only—we don't know what it is." (3)

This anomalous situation leads to Clavering's brilliantly sardonic utterance later on: "What an irony it is, madam, that a man can't remember the future!" (15). In *Fire, Burn!* John Cheviot gets into a taxi in the modern age and gets out in 1829:

To this day he swears that he had no cold premonition, no warning that a bit of the dark world had pierced through and pinioned him, when the cab drew up and stopped almost at the place where it should have stopped. (1)

It might be thought that this lack of explanation—or, as in *The Devil in Velvet*, lack of plausible explanation—of these time-travelling feats is a failing; but Carr is not writing science fiction and does not have to make any scientific justification for this shuttling back and forth in time. As in some works of fantasy—E. R. Eddison's *The Worm Ouroboros*, for example, which transports us for no apparent reason to Mercury at the beginning of the work—we are willing to allow Carr this initial premise simply to follow its consequences.

The principal consequence, of course, is that the modern-day characters retain at least some of their twentieth-century memories and attitudes; Fenton in *The Devil in Velvet* makes the Devil agree to this condition (" 'Only one thing more,' said Fenton, who was sweating. 'Though I shall be in the body of this Sir Nicholas, I must retain my own mind, my own knowledge, memory, and experience, just as they are in this year 1925' " [1]). The result is that the characters themselves—rather than Carr as omniscient narrator—can comment on the startling differences in both large and small matters between modern times and the times into which they have been flung. This is perhaps handled best in *The Devil in Velvet*, which is one of Carr's best novels. Nick Fenton has enormous difficulty convincing his servants—who are amazed that he does not constantly beat them—that he really wants a bath every day, and can never convince them to leave the windows open at night; night air, they are certain, can kill. At one point he mutters to himself: "Really, these people seem to have no inhibitions whatever" (2), echoing Carr's own sentiments about the seventeenth century as expressed in *The Murder of Sir Edmund Godfrey*. But Fenton does not remain unaffected by the era in which he finds himself: at a late stage he himself ponders, "My error lay in believing that, by travelling back into the seventeenth century, I should become for the most part a detached observer, all but a ghost" (19), and earlier it is said of him, "Slightly, very slightly, the fastidious ex-don was coarsening to meet the mood of the time in which he now lived" (11). *The Devil in Velvet*, in its flawless recapturing of late Stuart England, rousing action, and this slow metamorphosis of a twentieth-century personality into a seventeenth-century one, is one of Carr's masterworks.

Fear Is the Same is another fine work, and reaches great poignancy when Jenny Baird prays to God to be released from a time in which she manifestly does not belong:

"O, Thou," it was a trembling through her, "bid us go from this cage in which we are held. Lead us back to our own space and time. Set us free from this dirt, and cruelty, and snobbishness. Was it not marked, only a moment ago, how the worst of men was called worthy because he was the grandson of a duke, and no man laughed, or even smiled?

"Is my lover, my husband, forever to be beaten to his knees? He stands up again; he defeats them, and I am glad. But there is much blood on his head; he is changing every hour before my eyes, and I am afraid. Let him go! And, if I be considered at all worthy, let me go too." (18)

The most dramatic moment in the novel comes when Clavering defeats two men simultaneously in a duel:

"Tell you something," he muttered in that low, groping voice. "In all ages, everything changes. Manners, customs, speech, views on life, even morals—all change. But fear is the same. Only fear is the same." (18)

In *Fire, Burn!* there is a suggestion that, as with Nick Fenton, John Cheviot's secret wish to go back in time somehow led to his actually doing so:

"Come, now!" crackled a satiric voice in his own brain. "Isn't this only the other part of your dream, the secret dreams all men hide and cherish? Didn't you want to see, in action, the first Scotland Yard in history? When the mob was a tiger, when gangs were more murderous, when the police were hated and attacked as interferers with personal liberty? When puzzling crimes, of house-breaking or murder, could be solved only by a blunder of luck or the whisper of the informer?

"Murder, let's admit," whispered that same satiric voice, "is always sordid; usually dull; not at all the stuff of novels. Still! Didn't you want to amaze them by solving some such mystery, with fingerprints or ballistics or modern deduction? In your heart, now, don't you want to astonish them with what can be done?" (1)

Again, one of the high points of this novel is where Cheviot's lover Flora, Lady Drayton, fails to understand some of the modern-day attitudes he has brought with him to Regency London:

"To be open with you, my dear, there is much I don't understand. Of you. Sometimes you might be a man from another world. I don't understand why you insist so much on 'your work.' " Perplexity made her bite her lip. "A gentleman does not work, or at least need not. Never, never, my father said! No, don't protest!— For why need I understand?" (16)

Of Carr's two other novels about the Napoleonic era, *The Bride of Newgate* and *Captain Cut-Throat*, the former is by far superior; in its vivid characterisation, vigorous narration, and real emotional involvement, it may be the best of the historical mysteries. The tale opens grippingly, as we see Richard Darwent in Newgate Prison the night before he is scheduled to be executed for a murder he did not commit. Thinking there is no hope, he cynically accepts Lady Caroline Ross's equally cynical offer of marriage—

she must be married before the age of twenty-five or else forfeit her inheritance. To her horror, Darwent is not executed, and the convoluted plot is under way. The gradual transformation of Caroline from the type of insolent aristocrat to a warm, sensitive woman—who falls in love with the man she has married out of convenience—is a miracle of character portrayal. Her sentiments at learning that Darwent has apparently died in a fight are expressed with poignancy and eloquence:

> Through her dulled mind came one resolution: that she would accept no sympathy, even from a close friend. As soon as she achieved complete calmness, in a minute or two, she would go out of these muffling curtains. She would walk quietly upstairs, and lock herself in her room for days or weeks or months. Let the flapping crows, ill-meaning carrion like Townsend or well-meaning carrion like Jemmy, say what they liked.
>
> Yes, and let the world say what it liked! That was Dick's view; it should become hers.
>
> Whereupon a very small thing, as small things will, almost upset her dry-eyed resolution.
>
> Outside the curtains, in the dining room, silence had become an intolerable weight. Caroline heard the small, soft rattle as Alfred gently put down the saber on the sideboard. She felt she could almost hear Alfred's blunted mind move. Thoughtfully, with intense reserve, Alfred spoke.
>
> "He was a werry brave man, the governor." (19)

This scene is almost matched in emotional intensity by the death of Dolly Spencer, Darwent's previous lover. And yet, the one flaw in this novel is an elaborately neat resolution in accordance with the "happy ending" principle: the murdered man is an odious blackmailer and the murderer a sympathetic character who goes free; Darwent comes to the conclusion that he never really loved Dolly, thereby freeing him to transfer his emotions to Caroline; Darwent's friend Tillotson Lewis is stabbed three times in a fight and left for dead, but at the last we hear that he still lives; and finally, although it appeared that Caroline, either accidentally or deliberately, pushed Dolly down the stairs and thereby caused or hastened her death, a fortuitous letter by the doctor frees Caroline of all complicity in the matter. It is as if Carr does not really want to face up to all the emotional fireworks he has aroused; and this artificially happy conclusion strikes up as more than a little meretricious.

Scandal at High Chimneys is presented as a pseudo-sequel to *Fire, Burn!*: in the earlier novel Richard Mayne, a Commissioner of Police, played a significant role; in the later novel he is said to be "a very old man" (9). In his very lengthy "Notes for the Curious" to this novel, Carr remarks that "these events are seen through the eyes of Clive Strickland, who is a man of his time and has not the gift of prophecy", explicitly distinguishing this work from his three previous time-travel historical novels. The result is that the reader must conclude for himself the differences between the mid-Victorian era and our own day.

Much fighting goes on in the novels dealing with the seventeenth, eighteenth, and nineteenth centuries. Curiously, in light of the fact that these are not at all series novels like most of his detective tales, there is an almost mechanical repetition of certain types of incidents: each work contains a love affair and each features either a formal duel or general fisticuffs. The one that concludes *Fear Is the Same* is probably the most dramatically effective, and many of the sword duels allow Carr to unleash his prodigious technical knowledge of fencing.

The three novels dealing with the early twentieth century—*The Witch of the Low-Tide, The Ghosts' High Noon,* and *Deadly Hall*—are perhaps the least satisfying of all the historical novels, for the simple fact that Carr does not do an especially good job at capturing the atmosphere of the period. *The Witch of the Low-Tide* is a perfectly entertaining murder mystery (this is the only historical novel that genuinely and exclusively focuses upon the crime), but—aside from repeated references to the recently published *Mystery of the Yellow Room* by Gaston Leroux—we would have no especial awareness that this novel is supposed to take place in 1907. There are so few references to any social or political events of the Edwardian age that this work hardly deserves to be called an historical novel at all.

Of *The Ghosts' High Noon* and *Deadly Hall,* written very late in Carr's career, when he was clearly no longer the writer he once was, it is difficult to find anything good to say. Here again the sheer recency of the setting works against Carr, and we simply receive no strong impression that these two novels are set fifty and forty years, respectively, before their dates of writing. The problem is not so much that there is no sense of the antiquity of these periods as that Carr's pure detective novels themselves make relatively few references to contemporary events or take cognisance of recent social and cultural trends. The last few Dr. Fell novels grudgingly mention television in a few isolated passages, but this is about all we get. Carr thus has an added burden in segregating his avowed historical novels from his detective novels, which immediately date themselves by resolutely conforming to conventions of mystery writing out of the thirties. In both *The Ghosts' High Noon* and *Deadly Hall* Carr could draw upon his own memories: the former has a brief vignette of Washington, D.C., in 1912, and the latter is set in 1927 (albeit in New Orleans), a time Carr could surely remember distinctly. This would seem to make *Deadly Hall* not so much an historical novel as a sort of pseudo-memoir; if Carr had set this novel in a place he had actually known at the time, this effect might have been augmented, much to the novel's benefit. As it is, both these works—as well as *The Hungry Goblin*—fail through sluggish action, lack of subtlety in characterisation, excessive histrionics, and simply bad writing. No one would be the poorer for not reading these works.

Carr fortunately avoids the error of many historical novelists of including cameos of as many famous individuals of the time as possible. Although most of the characters in these novels are either of the aristocracy or at least well-to-do, and although some works deal with the highest political figures of the day, Carr is restrained in allowing actual glimpses of the great. The depiction of calm, philosophical, and self-deprecating Charles II in *Devil Kinsmere* and *Most Secret* is one of the many charms of these two works. In *Captain Cut-Throat,* although the shadow of Napoleon hangs over the entire novel (it is set in 1805, like Thomas Hardy's *The Trumpet-Major,* as Napoleon is contemplating an invasion of England), the Emperor himself appears only on the very last page. The eternally drunk and slightly mad Rev. Laurence Sterne is an engaging minor character in *The Demoniacs.* Wilkie Collins, of course, is the amateur detective in *The Hungry Goblin,* but he appears only intermittently.

Given the fact that most of Carr's historical novels take place before the advent of modern methods of detection and police procedure—much of the interest of *Fire, Burn!* is the depiction of these methods just coming into existence—Carr can allow his amateur detectives freedom to investigate in a much more plausible manner than in his pure detective novels. In many instances the protagonists themselves, accused or suspected of murder, must solve the case. Even here, however, there are some anomalies and implausibilities. In *Papa Là-bas* a senator usurps the investigation from the police officer in charge. Wilkie Collins in *The Hungry Goblin* archly tells how he became involved in the matter:

"Ah, you guessed? I thought you would. At Colonel Henderson's suggestion, accompanying the colonel and Chief Inspector Gobb of the Detective Branch at Scotland Yard, this morning I paid a visit to Hampstead. Colonel Henderson thinks he has found an affair in which I should be of assistance. I am immodest enough to think so too, though perhaps not for the reason he does. And so, come what may, I am to be an amateur detective." (9)

The lawyer Gilbert Bethune in *Deadly Hall* is a somewhat interesting figure. At one point there is reference to his "Mephistophelian eyebrows" (12); a later passage elaborates:

Momentarily Uncle Gil had looked less like amiable, beardless Mephistopheles than like a Grand Inquisitor preparing to order torture. (15)

Of whom is this reminiscent? Surely it is Henri Bencolin. I think this parallel is intentional, given the fact that the novel takes place only days before Bencolin's first great case as recorded in *It Walks by Night.*

Carr's historical mysteries are noble experiments, and many of them are highly successful. The mere fact that he must take some time away from the simple murder mystery to set the stage and characters means that for once the crime is not the exclusive rationale of the novel. All the historical novels up to *Most Secret* (1964) can be recommended for their narrative drive, lively characters, precise recreation of their historical periods, and, of course, for the ceaseless cleverness of the puzzle. Carr's "Notes for the Curious" at the end of each novel (something he may well have derived from Conan Doyle, who has notes appended to *Micah Clarke* and *The Refugees*) supply the historical sources for the work, and they reveal Carr to be a sound and careful historian: he went back to primary documents of each period (diaries, letters, contemporary treatises) and augmented them with the best modern scholarship available to him. It is true that he parades historical erudition a little too self-consciously at times, but on the whole his synthesis is seamless and seemingly effortless. Carr has set for himself a high challenge in these works: the bounds of historical fact must in no way be broken, and yet an entirely fictitious murder mystery and fictitious characters must be inserted into the fabric of historical reality. It is a challenge Carr met fully in all save his very last works.

Historical Mysteries

A. Novels

Devil Kinsmere (1934).
The Murder of Sir Edmund Godfrey (1936).
The Bride of Newgate (1950).
The Devil in Velvet (1951).
Captain Cut-Throat (1955).
Fear Is the Same (1956).
Fire, Burn! (1957)
Scandal at High Chimneys (1959).
The Witch of the Low-Tide (1961).
The Demoniacs (1962).
Most Secret (1964).
Papa Là-bas (1968).
The Ghosts' High Noon (1969).
Deadly Hall (1971).
The Hungry Goblin (1972).

B. Short Stories

"The Red Heels" (1926).
"The Dim Queen" (1926).
"The Blue Garden" (1926).
"The Inn of the Seven Swords" (1927).
"The Dark Banner" (1928).
"The Other Hangman" (1935).
"Persons or Things Unknown" (1950).
"The Gentleman from Paris" (1950).
"The Black Cabinet" (1951).

Short Stories and Radio Plays

For a writer of seventy-one novels, John Dickson Carr wrote surprisingly few short stories—a total of forty-seven. Of these, thirteen must be called juvenilia—his college writings (both detective and historical tales) in *The Haverfordian;* six are collaborations with Adrian Conan Doyle; and one is a round-robin story. This leaves only twenty-seven stories, which can be handily included in three slim collections, *The Department of Queer Complaints* (1940), *The Third Bullet and Other Stories* (1954), and *The Men Who Explained Miracles* (1963). Even including the collaborative *Exploits of Sherlock Holmes* (1954) and the posthumous compilation by Douglas G. Greene, *The Door to Doom and Other Detections* (1980), the output of Carr's short fiction remains amazingly small.[1] Margery Allingham wrote nearly as many stories as Carr, although her novels number well under half as many; while Agatha Christie's two and a half dozen volumes of short stories dwarf Carr's into insignificance—numerically, at least.

The simple fact is that Carr is not a good short story writer. To say this need not, paradoxically, imply a criticism—not entirely, at any rate. It is precisely because Carr had certain definite strengths as a writer that he failed at the short story. We have suggested these strengths in our previous discussions: the elaborately convoluted nature of the plot, often involving competing reconstructions of the crime; multiple murders in Carr's early work; the fact that Carr wrote *howdunits* as well as *whodunits,* in which clues must be dropped surreptitiously over the course of a work—all these qualities are antithetical to short story technique.

It is also the case that Carr had certain weaknesses that prevented him from being a consistently good short story writer. Carr cannot draw character with a few bold strokes, in the manner of Margery Allingham or P. D. James; when he tries to do so, his characters become mere caricatures, as in "The Locked Room":

> She was what is called an outdoor girl, with a sturdy and well-shaped body, and a square but very attractive face. Her dark-brown hair hung in a long bob. She had light-hazel eyes in a tanned, earnest face. Her mouth might have been too broad, but she showed fine teeth when she laughed. If she was not exactly pretty, health and vigor gave her a strong attractiveness which was better than that. (*The Third Bullet and Other Stories*)

Carr, in order to draw character at all effectively, required a cumulative description available only in the novel form. What is more, Carr too often makes the mistake of involving actual murder in his stories. Dorothy L. Sayers, notwithstanding the occasional prolixity of her novels, wrote many excellent short stories precisely because she dealt with such lesser crimes as larceny, fraud, and the like. She knew that murder, being the most heinous and significant of crimes, required a lengthy space for both the exposition of the scenario and the eventual capturing of the perpetrator; in any shorter compass, the fact of murder—the brute fact that someone has died by violence—becomes trivialised. Carr already falls under this danger because of the cerebral and puzzle-like nature of his situations, where the corpse is regarded unemotionally as a mere cog in the machine, and the problem is exacerbated in his short stories.

It is not, therefore, surprising that Carr's best short stories are not, on the whole, his pure detective stories but his *contes cruels*, his tales of the supernatural, and his suspense-action stories.

We have already remarked briefly on the four Henri Bencolin short stories dating to Carr's college years; in spite of the youth of the author, they may be among the best of his short fiction—in particular "The Shadow of the Goat" (1927), even though here Bencolin appears to know the solution before the entire scenario is laid. Carr's characterisation in these tales really is crisp and vigorous, and the focus is kept almost exclusively on the seemingly impossible nature of the crime; once the smokescreen of misdirection is dispelled, the solution is seen to be a very simple one, hence satisfyingly encompassed in a short story.

Early in his career Carr experimented with the supernatural, and his two pulp stories "The Man Who Was Dead" (later rewritten as "New Murders for Old") and "The Door to Doom" are pleasantly shuddersome in the *Grand Guignol* manner. It is somewhat curious that the latter tale was published in a "weird menace" pulp (*Horror Stories*), since magazines of that genre generally featured tales that appeared supernatural on the surface but were ultimately explained in natural terms. We have an example of such a tale in "Terror's Dark Tower" (1935), a marvellously evocative story with a stupendous surprise ending; the very ingenuity of the natural solution precludes the deflation and disappointment inherent in many stories of this type. We shall study the whole phenomenon of the natural and the supernatural in Carr in a later chapter.

Aside from *The Exploits of Sherlock Holmes*, Carr's stories in *The Department of Queer Complaints* (surely one of his most inspired titles and conceptions) are his only tales to be conceived as a series. This is not to say that there is any interlinking or sequentiality to these tales, but they are far more a unity than the random stories involving Dr. Fell. Here the hero is Colonel March. To what degree he is meant to be an adaptation of the Colonel Marquis of *The Third Bullet* (1937) is not entirely clear; there may in fact be no similarity save the name. Physically, at least, the two are widely different: Colonel Marquis is described as "a long, stringy man" while March is "a large, amiable man (weight seventeen stone)" ("The New Invisible Man"). The wittiest description of both the colonel and his odd department is in "The Crime in Nobody's Room":

> "I know you, Colonel," said Conyers, with a crooked grin. "You're head of the Ragbag Department, D-3. Some call it the Crazy House."
> Colonel March nodded seriously. He wore a dark overcoat, and had a top-hat pushed back on his large head; this, with his florid complexion, sandy moustache, and bland blue eye, gave him something of the look of a stout colonel in a comic paper. He was smoking a large-bowled pipe with the effect of seeming to sniff smoke from the bowl rather than draw it through the stem. He appeared to be enjoying himself.
> "It's a compliment," he assured them. "After all, somebody has got to sift all the queer complaints. If somebody comes in and reports (say) that the Borough of Stepney is being terrorized by a blue pig, I've got to decide whether it's a piece of lunacy, or a mistake, or a hoax, or a serious crime. Otherwise good men would only waste their time. You'd be surprised how many such complaints there are."

These stories are all lightly entertaining, with their air of farcical grotesquerie. "The Footprint in the Sky" is one of Carr's many variations of the scenario whereby one set of tracks is seen in the snow (or sand) leading to the victim and none returning; the solution to this tale was already anticipated in a passage in *The Problem of the Wire Cage* (1939).

Strangely enough, the unity of *The Department of Queer Complaints* is marred by the inclusion of four stories not involving March; several of these are tales of the supernatural. What is even more odd, two further March stories about the Department of Queer Complaints, although written about the time of the others, were not collected until *The Man Who Explained Miracles*. I am utterly at a loss to explain this situation. One of these stories, "The Empty Flat" (1939), is of some interest, not so much intrinsically as in its relation to two of Carr's best novels. The vignette of two competing scholars who initially find themselves at loggerheads but quickly fall in love is repeated at vastly greater length and richness in *The Case of the Constant Suicides;* the core of the plot is identical to that of *The Reader Is Warned* (1939), and I am unable to say which work has chronological priority. It hardly need be remarked that the novel develops the plot more elaborately and skilfully than the story.

The four stories appended to *The Department of Queer Complaints* deserve some attention. Two—"New Murders for Old" and "Blind Man's Hood"—are definitely supernatural; a third, "Persons or Things Unknown", dimly anticipates the historical mysteries as an historian talks of a murder very early in the reign of Charles II. The fourth—"The Other Hangman"— is in some ways the most interesting of the lot, although quite frankly it is not a good story. It is really a *conte cruel,* but it is a stylistic experiment in that Carr attempted to write the entire tale in the diction of an old Pennsylvania judge who colloquially recounts a grim murder decades in the past:

It was in '92 or '93; anyway, it was the year they put the first telephone in the court house, and you could talk as far as Pittsburgh except when the wires blew down. Considering it was the county seat, we were mighty proud of our town (population 3,500). The hustlers were always bragging about how thriving and growing our town was, and we had just got to the point of enthusiasm where every ten years we were certain the census taker must have forgotten half our population. Old Mark Sturgis, who owned the *Bugle Gazette* then, carried on something awful in an editorial when they printed in the almanac that we had a population of only 3,265. We were all pretty riled about it, naturally.

This is quite stiff and self-conscious: Carr's notions of stylistic purity and formality could never allow him to write in a genuinely colloquial vein, and it is just as well that he did not try this experiment again.

Of the five Gideon Fell stories, only two—"The Wrong Problem" (1938) and "Invisible Hands" (1957)—are especially memorable. The latter unveils one of Carr's most fiendishly clever "impossible crime" scenarios, and in a remarkably compressed space presents all the pertinent clues in the best fair play manner. "The Wrong Problem" is brilliant for an entirely different reason. The central plot (parts of which have been drawn from "Terror's Dark Tower") is certainly clever and well-executed, but what grips our attention is the narrative voice. Nearly the entire tale is taken up with a man's recounting to Fell and Hadley an old murder case in which he was involved, and the quietly brooding and pensive tone of his narration is a triumph of atmosphere. In effect, this story is a mood piece in the form of a detective puzzle.

It is peculiar that Carr involved Sir Henry Merrivale in only one short story—"The House in Goblin Wood" (1947)—and one novelette, "All in a Maze" (1955). The latter we have studied earlier; it is certainly a rousing piece of work. "The House in Goblin Wood" concludes with one of the grisliest images in all Carr's work, but it seems artificial and contrived. Merrivale is as clownish as ever: he slips on a banana peel on the steps of his club and bellows out "such a torrent of profanity, such a flood of invective and vile obscenities, as has seldom before blasted the holy calm of Pall Mall". But we have heard this sort of thing too many times before.

"The Clue of the Red Wig" (1940) appears to be the only occasion where Carr used a female detective—the vivacious, seemingly empty-headed, but ultimately shrewd and hardnosed Frenchwoman Jacqueline Dubois, a journalist for the London *Daily Record*. The story itself is relatively undistinguished, and Carr's attempts to portray Jacqueline as slightly crazed become rapidly tiresome; but the puzzle, as always, is clever.

In *The Men Who Explained Miracles* Carr grouped two stories written at wide intervals—"Strictly Diplomatic" (1939) and "The Black Cabinet" (1951)—under the heading "Secret Service Stories". In reality they have very little to do with each other. The first is an entertaining spy story—perhaps the only genuine tale of espionage in Carr's work, several of the Merrivale novels notwithstanding. The other is an historical mystery concerning the attempted murder of the Emperor Napoleon II in 1858. Like some of his early college historical tales, it is overly melodramatic, and further marred by a contrived surprise ending. Carr's other historical detective tale, the windy and meandering "Gentleman from Paris" (1950), is also of no especial note.

The collaborations with Adrian Conan Doyle, *The Exploits of Sherlock Holmes*, are worth a little notice. There are twelve stories in the volume, but Carr fell ill during the latter stages of the collaboration and the last six are entirely the work of Doyle. Of the first six, a publisher's note informs us that "The Adventure of the Wax Gamblers" and "The Adventure of the Highgate Miracle" are almost entirely by Carr, "The Adventure of the Black Baronet" and "The Adventure of the Sealed Room" almost entirely by Doyle, and "The Adventure of the Seven Clocks" and "The Adventure of the Gold Hunter" genuine collaborations. This in itself is a little odd, because "The Adventure of the Sealed Room" strikes me as the most authentically Carrian: aside from the obvious circumstance that the tale involves a locked room, there are several phrases found in many of Carr's other works, notably the curious expression "superstitious dread" (to be studied in a later chapter).

Whatever the situation, the majority of the stories are attempts to write up those cases that Dr. Watson cryptically alludes to in the course of the Sherlock Holmes saga. This idea is in itself a clever one, but the execution occasionally goes awry. "The Adventure of the Seven Clocks" is founded upon a remark in "A Scandal in Bohemia": "From time to time I heard some vague account of his doings; of his summons to Odessa in the case of the Trepoff murder." The ordinary signification of the words would imply the murder of someone named Trepoff in Odessa; in fact, the story concerns the attempt by an anarchist named Trepoff to murder someone else, but he is prevented and ultimately killed in a gun-battle with Holmes and Watson themselves. This sort of contrived air dogs all these stories; although in one instance Carr makes the implausible work to his benefit. The nucleus of "The Adventure of the Highgate Miracle" is found in Conan Doyle's "Thor Bridge" (in *The Casebook of Sherlock Holmes*): "Among these unfinished tales is that of Mr. James Phillimore, who, stepping back into his own house to get his umbrella, was never more seen in this world." Carr himself could have come up with this teasing plot-suggestion, and this tale is perhaps the most engaging of them all.

The trouble with serious pastiche—as opposed to parody, something Carr did brilliantly in two hilarious Sherlockian send-ups, the stage plays "The Adventure of the Conk-Singleton Papers" and "The Adventure of the Paradol Chamber"—is that any sort of creativeness or originality is by definition ruled out. Pastiches must be rigidly faithful to their originals in spirit, tone, and mannerism, and to a genuinely creative artist like Carr such constraints become highly limiting. The only writers who can work comfortably with pastiche are those who (like August Derleth) have nothing of their own to say.[2] Carr tries admirably to conform to Conan Doyle's fundamentally different methodology of detection, but lapses into originality almost in spite of himself. Conan Doyle, for example, has very few locked-room or "impossible crime" situations in the Sherlock Holmes tales, but Carr cannot resist writing several stories of this type. The attempts to imitate Holmes' or Watson's habitual utterances become after a time increasingly hollow and wooden.

It can hardly be denied that Carr's short stories are as a whole quite undistinguished. And yet, the fact that he rewrote his stories several times over or used the nucleus of some short story plots in novels (we have noted elsewhere how "The Incautious Burglar" was transformed into *The Gilded Man*) need not mean that Carr was running out of ideas. On the one hand, Carr perhaps felt that a given conception had not been used to fullest advantage in a tale, and successive rewriting would be his way of perfecting the idea; on the other hand—and this I think is the more probable—Carr simply did not want to waste his elaborate plots in the narrow and confined focus of the short story when they could be (and were) so much more richly realised in a novel. The fact that Carr wrote no short stories in the last twenty years of his life seems to prove that short story writing was never a priority with him; it is even conceivable that some tales—like the collaborations with Adrian Conan Doyle, published in such lucrative "slick" markets as *Life* and *Collier's*—were written principally to make money. This fact alone—if it is true—need not militate against a story's quality, but may indicate that the short story form was not one to which Carr naturally inclined. On the whole, this body of his work is his most insubstantial, uneven, and disappointing.

Of Carr's radio plays, however, precisely the opposite is true—they are some of the most vivid and thrilling works in his entire *oeuvre*. I myself have had access only to the six radio plays published in *The Door to Doom* and the nine in *The Dead Sleep Lightly* (1983); it is to be hoped that Carr's six dozen or so other radio plays will soon be made available. Even these fifteen offer considerable riches.

We have already remarked that one of them, "Will You Make a Bet with Death?" (1942), was radically transformed into the novel *The Nine Wrong Answers*;[3] although the novel version is clearly the more substantial, the radio play provides a condensed potency also. The same may be said for "Will You Walk into My Parlor?" (1943), whose basic idea was used in the radio play "Vampire Tower" (1944), then fleshed out in *Till Death Do Us Part* (1944).

The most effective radio play of Carr's I have read is "The Dead Sleep Lightly" (1943), a magnificently shuddersome tale whose supernatural overtones we shall study in a later chapter. It typifies, however, the generous helping of the seemingly supernatural that Carr evidently included in many of his radio plays; and although here the natural explanation is more than a little contrived, the atmosphere of weirdness is authentic while it lasts.

"The Dead Sleep Lightly" is one of several radio plays to involve Dr. Fell, and here we not merely are presented with a particularly effective example of Fell's scatterbrained temperament but, for the first and only time, see Fell endowed with a manservant, the dour Cockney Hoskins:

HOSKINS: You're not going out of the house tonight, sir?

DR. FELL (*with dignity*): And why not, my good custodian?

HOSKINS: 'Cos you oughtn't to be out at any time, that's why. You haven't got the foggiest idea where you're going; you concentrate across the street against a red light; you walk off Underground platforms onto trains that ain't there...

DR. FELL (*with still more dignity*): If you are implying, my good Hoskins, that I occasionally suffer from a slight...a very slight...absent-mindedness...

HOSKINS (*awed*): Absent-mindedness, sir?

DR. FELL: That was the word.

HOSKINS: So help me, sir, when you was solving that Vickerly case, you came home cold sober and stood for twenty minutes trying to open the front door with a corkscrew. (*The Dead Sleep Lightly*)

This inevitably leads to the comic radio plays, of which we have one example in "White Tiger Passage" (1955). One section—recording a phone conversation as the journalist Bill Stacey and his sweetheart Jenny Holden seek to get to the bottom of a murder mystery—will suffice:

MAVIS (*on filter*) Grayson's Hotel.

BILL (*becoming the stuffy official*): Good afternoon, madam.

MAVIS (*suddenly lyrical*): Good afternoon, good afternoon, good afternoon! And isn't it a *lovely* afternoon in the early evening?

BILL (*taken aback*): I beg your pardon?

MAVIS: Granted! And you have *such* an attractive voice. Why don't you come over and have tea with me?

BILL: I can't help feeling, madam, there must be some mistake. But I wish more switchboard operators were like you.

JENNY (*fierce whisper*): Bill Stacey, this is the absolute end! Must you make improper advances to every woman you meet?

BILL (*incautiously loudly*): But I'm not making improper advances!

MAVIS: Aren't you? What a pity! As a matter of fact, I'm not the switchboard operator. I'm a guest. But whenever this mouldy old foyer is empty, I've longed and longed to sit down and make rude remarks to anyone who rings up. But I can't make rude remarks to *you*, my pet. (*The Dead Sleep Lightly*)

Many of Carr's radio plays are adaptations of stories by other writers; "The Devil's Manuscript" (1944) is adapted from Ambrose Bierce's "The Suitable Surroundings". Here Carr has followed the basic skeleton of Bierce's story—whose premise rests upon a slightly mad author's contention that a ghost story he has written, if read in the "suitable surroundings", can actually kill—but updated it and made it much more of a crime story than a horror story: a doctor who arrives at a deserted house where a couple has found a man evidently dead from reading the manuscript urges the pair to remember the details of the setting, "because you may have to testify"; this detail is entirely absent in Bierce. Carr has also changed the setting from America to England, and enhances this change by so subtle a thing as altering a minor character's last name from Breede (American) to Brede

(English). Carr adapted many classic horror tales into radio plays (although this one is non-supernatural), and he did so with obvious relish.

Again, the fact that many of Carr's radio plays are adapted from other works of his own or works by others need not be held against him; for the radio plays gain a sense of freshness because of the radically different medium and attendant constraints involved. Narrative description must be held to a minimum; characterisation must be accomplished by blunt stage instructions to his "voices" ("Fielding is in his late forties, with a deep, slow-speaking voice, smooth and almost affable yet faintly sinister: a semi-educated voice with a certain amount of false deference") and by the dialogue itself: Carr's characters are inevitably sketched boldly and a little crudely, but subtlety is not to be sought or perhaps even desired here. Although the number of scenes had to be kept to a minimum to prevent fragmentation and confusion, Carr introduces some structural complexity with modest flashbacks and other variations. The publication of Carr's complete radio plays would be a landmark.

I have studied the short stories and radio plays separately—even though many involve his principal detectives or are historical mysteries—not only because of their general qualitative but also their fundamental structural and tonal difference from the novels. Carr must adopt radically different methods of plot-weaving, characterisation, and mood-creation in these shorter works; that he so signally failed in short fiction may be an indication that his type of puzzle-story is inherently inapplicable in a shorter compass. Carr is at his best when he is at his most bewilderingly complex; and complexity invariably involves length, not only for the mere exposition of the plot but because the solution of some elaborate puzzle cannot be too compressed lest the reader feel cheated. In a short story there is not enough space for the reader to develop that gnawing sense of confusion and bafflement that Carr can generate at novel length.

But we treasure a few of the short stories—as we treasure the majority of the radio plays—for offering in a compact way many of the same qualities of ingenuity, quasi-supernatural shudders, and atmosphere that we find so abundantly in the novels.

Short Stories and Radio Plays

The Department of Queer Complaints (1940).
The Third Bullet and Other Stories (1954).
The Exploits of Sherlock Holmes (with Adrian Conan Doyle) (1954).
The Men Who Explained Miracles (1963).
The Door to Doom and Other Detections, ed. Douglas G. Greene (1980).
The Dead Sleep Lightly, ed. Douglas G. Greene (1983).

[For a complete list of Carr's short stories, see Bibliography, Section A.6.]

PART II

Philosophy

In the sort of puzzle-story written by Carr for the bulk of his career, it is difficult to include philosophical reflexions of any depth or substance. Perhaps Carr took note of Philo Vance's pompous lecturing on literature and philosophy in the novels of S. S. Van Dine, or Dorothy L. Sayers' subtle but scarcely concealed class consciousness in the Lord Peter Wimsey cases; whatever the situation, Carr in his fiction rarely even mentions topics connected with philosophy, politics, religion, or social life, and the fact that he wrote very few nonfiction articles on these subjects means that his view of the world must be inferred and fleshed out from the most glancing and oblique mentions. I have no doubt that Carr had pronounced views on many philosophical and social issues; perhaps his letters will reveal them. But judging solely on what he published, we do not come away with the impression that Carr was either a very subtle or very flexible thinker.

Carr's views on religion are of some interest. Late in his career he claimed wryly that he was a "backwoods Presbyterian";[1] no particular religious upbringing is mentioned by Robert Lewis Taylor in his *New Yorker* article, so we can presume that Carr either received none or that it made little impression upon him. What is interesting, however, is the frequency in the early works with which religion and religious people come off as buffoons or as positively evil. So early as " 'As Drink the Dead...' " (1926), one character claims that a cup that has killed without any poison found in it was subject to "the will of God", to which von Arnheim remarks airily, "The will of God...if you wish it."[2] Of course, a natural explanation is later discovered. In both "The Ends of Justice" (1927) and *The Eight of Swords* (1934) we see bishops who engage in detection ("a churchman turned detective,"[3] it is cynically remarked in the short story). We have seen that the figure in *The Eight of Swords* is parodied in a relatively genial manner ("...the old man was a stout fellow, even if he did happen to be a bishop" [2], one character remarks); quite otherwise is the portrayal of Bishop Wolfe in "The Ends of Justice". In this, one of the bitterest of Carr's tales (an amazing production for a twenty-year-old), the entire story really rests upon the fact that the bishop has—in good faith, admittedly—fastened the guilt on the wrong party. Bencolin, hearing the bishop's recitation of the case, perceives the error in his reasoning and feels there is still time to save the accused, now already in prison and about to be executed. An intense confrontation follows:

They stood up, opposite each other, clergyman and detective, each vaguely visible, but the hatred that sprang between them lit each face like fire.

"Bishop Wolfe," Bencolin said quietly, "Pilate was more merciful than *you*."

Then he went out into the blue-shadowed lawn, striding up the terrace with Sir John after him.[4]

But in fact they are too late; the accused has already been executed. The bishop can only speak in pious hypocrisy:

"It is God's will," he said piously. "The ways of the Lord are dark, and His servants can only follow humbly. This thing, which seems so tragic, is but another manifestation of divine intervention for good. We must pray for Fellowes' soul."

Bencolin did not laugh. He did not feel like laughing. But he made a sound that was something like passionate fury, and his hand dropped from the window, and he turned.

"Oh, Bishop," he said, "when will you learn? When will you learn?"[5]

Carr in later years was rarely as brutal as this; and one cannot help wondering whether, for all his admiration of G. K. Chesterton, there may not be in this vicious portrayal a hint of annoyance at the unrelenting sermonising of Father Brown.

A somewhat lighter view of religion is taken in *Devil Kinsmere* (1934). At the outset it is remarked with ill-concealed disingenuousness of Roderick Insmere, "Of religious education he had, I regret to say, little" (1). Later Bygones Abraham makes a lengthy speech on the matter (a passage curiously not reproduced in *Most Secret*):

"I don't claim to know the right or wrong of it [religion], not being a praying man myself. Religions in general is very much like meat-pies: you're never sure what's in 'em till it disagrees with you. Personally, I don't see why the Romish faith ain't just as good at saving souls, or even a *soupçon* better, than one that's subject to change every time the board o' clergymen needs an excuse for throwing somebody out of office. And I know it's an uncommon sight better than the Puritan." (8)

This scorn of sour-faced Puritans reaches its height in the contemptuous portrayal of Jeremiah Gaines (Salvation Gaines in *Most Secret*), the odious insincerity of whose pious mouthings is patently obvious. Carr's relative sympathy with Roman Catholicism might be expected from a Tory, although I suspect that he, like Bygones Abraham, was not "a praying man".

Aunt Elspat Campbell's religious views are held up to polite ridicule in *The Case of the Constant Suicides* (1941):

Aunt Elspat wanted to know what his religion was.

Colin said he didn't know, but that it didn't matter a damn *what* his religion was.

Aunt Elspat intimated, on the contrary, that it mattered very much indeed, adding remarks which left her listeners in no doubt about her views touching Colin's destination in the afterlife. This, to Alan, was the hardest part of Elspat's discourse to put up with. Her notions of theology were childish. Her knowledge of Church history would have been considered inaccurate even by the late Bishop Burnet. (8)

Elspat is presumably a Scotch Presbyterian, so evidently Carr felt that, as a co-religionist, she was fair game. But it becomes the more amusing when, in a brilliantly satiric stroke, Dr. Fell and Charles Swan undergo "a great spiritual experience" (12) as they drink the potent Campbell whiskey after a fine meal.

I am not, however, sure what we are to make of Sir Henry Merrivale's backhanded defence of Christianity in *The Plague Court Murders* (1934):

> "Y'know, that half-cracked young feller would have concealed that crucifix from you quicker and deeper than he'd have concealed a crime. He would honestly have considered himself shamed if you had thought that he, the intellectual snipe, carried it because he reverenced it or thought it holy: which he would say he didn't at all...And that's the dancin', topsy-turvy puzzle of people nowadays. They'll sneer at a great thing like the Christian Church, but they'll believe in astrology. They won't believe the clergyman who says there's something in the heavens; but they will believe the rather less mild statement that you can read the future there like an electric sign. They think there's something old-fashioned and provincial about believing too thoroughly in God, but they will concede you any number of deadly earthbound spirits: because the latter can be defended by scientific jargon." (19)

This appears to be more an attack on modern social attitudes than anything; if Carr is praising anything here, it is the sincerity with which a belief—any belief—is held, something Carr evidently finds absent in the iconoclastic younger generation. But this passage provides a good enough transition to the treatment of spiritualism in Carr's work. The number of fake mediums and other claimants to knowledge from beyond the grave is very great in Carr; even Pennik of *The Reader Is Warned* (1939) has the hollow aura of the spiritualist, although the powers he claims are even greater. A snide reference in *The Plague Court Murders* to "the wrong kind of Conan Doyle's books" (4) may indicate Carr's early disappointment—even sense of betrayal—at his mentor's increasing devotion to spiritualism in his later years; but by the time he came to write Conan Doyle's biography, he had adopted a much different attitude. It was not, of course, that Carr ascribed to Conan Doyle's beliefs; he explicitly remarks to the contrary in *The Life of Sir Arthur Conan Doyle:*

> The writer of this biography is not a Spiritualist. Spiritualism is not a subject on which he yet feels qualified to pass an opinion. But the religious views of the biographer, it may be suggested, should not make a farthing's worth of difference to his task. He must try to present, however imperfectly, a living image of the only man in question: what *he* said, what *he* thought, what *he* believed. (21)

But he makes a valiant defence—not entirely successful, to my mind, and even a little sophistical—of Conan Doyle's views and at least deals with them objectively and non-judgmentally.

Carr's religious views, therefore, were decidedly those of a sceptic and an agnostic; but he was no evangelical atheist, and perhaps he inclined towards Christianity or even Roman Catholicism in accordance with his notions of tradition and hostility to what he saw was the radical nihilism and rootlessness of the modern age.

If there is any systematic and unchanging belief in Carr's philosophical outlook, it is his political conservatism. Many of the sympathetic characters in his work are self-confessed reactionaries, and even his detectives take occasion to lash out at socialism and liberalism. We have seen that the vehemence of Carr's views led him ultimately to leave England with the advent of the Labour government in 1945. Curiously enough, in 1942 he had satirised a character in *The Emperor's Snuff-Box* because "he...lived abroad to avoid the iniquity of paying income tax" (4); but it appears that Carr left England for a reason very similar to this.

Some late novels feature characters who transparently mirror Carr's political views. Alan Grantham, protagonist of *Dark of the Moon* (1967), laments over his disagreement with Camilla Bruce, a woman he fancies:

"There is no subject calling for an opinion," he said, "where we don't collide head-on. Camilla's a mathematician, mathematics being my pet abomination. Politically she's a liberal concerned with social welfare; I'm a reactionary conservative who couldn't care less. She's got some fairly far-out views on letters and art; I see no virtue in butchering the English language or spoiling canvas with a nightmare. The best we achieve is an armed truce; wait and see." (2)

But such disagreements turn out, in Carr's rosy world of romance, to be illusory, as Camilla admits toward the end:

"I don't like Joyce a bit; I absolutely loathe Proust; I can't bow down before *any* of the sacred cows. I'm as conservative as you are or more so, politically speaking; only I lack your nerve at opposing popular trends and telling the intellectuals to go to hell. Apart from mathematics and science, and I *won't* give in on those, there's nothing you've ever preached with which deep down inside me I haven't thoroughly agreed!" (18)

We will pass over in silence the implication that Joyce "butchered the English language"; we will find in a later chapter that Carr's literary stance is very nearly as primitive as his political.

Jim Blake in *The Ghosts' High Noon* (1969) objects to the prospect of a political assignment for a newspaper:

"But why, of all things, a political assignment for *me?* Both Wilson and Roosevelt claim to be progressives. I'm a conservative, even a reactionary, insofar as I'm anything at all; I distrust progressives and hate reformers. In the name of sanity, Colonel, why a political assignment for *me?*" (1)

None of these comments, it will be noted, amount to a critique of liberalism or even a defence of conservatism—in this sense they are still less well-reasoned (or at least less well-expressed) than his views on literature. It is all mere assertion and emotion. Nowhere does Carr really say what is wrong with liberalism; presumably there is some vague notion that liberals butt their noses into other people's business, or something of the sort.

Not much more can be learned when we study those characters whose politics Carr satirises or ridicules. We have seen how Merrivale, early in his career, had Socialist pretensions, but this seems designed merely to enhance his image as an aristocratic goofball. There is a brief and contentless attack on the Labour party in *A Graveyard to Let* (1949 [3]), and the caricature of Elaine Cheeseman, a Labour member of Parliament, in *The Cavalier's Cup* (1953) is contemptuous in the extreme. The most elaborate portrayal, however, is of Gabriel White in *The Third Bullet* (1937):

"So you want to know what I believe in?" he demanded. "I believe in a new world, an enlightened world, a world free from the muddle we have made of this. I want a world of light and progress, that a man can breathe decently in; a world without violence of war; a world, in that fine phrase of Wells's, 'waste, austere and wonderful.' That's all I want, and it's little enough."

This is bad enough—if Carr wanted to depict White as a complete ass, he has certainly succeeded. But it gets worse:

"And how would you bring this about?"
"First," said White, "all capitalists would be taken out and hanged. Those who opposed us, of course, would merely be shot. But capitalists would be hanged, because they have brought about this muddle and made us their tools. I say it again: we are tools, tools, tools, tools."

Our reaction to this is not, as Carr would like, "What a buffon White is!" but "What a buffoon the author is!" This sort of clumsy caricature goes far in revealing Carr's own insecurity: he cannot portray political (or any other) views opposed to his without making them grotesquely ridiculous. Carr is very anxious throughout his work that the reader like and approve of just those characters he likes and approves of, and hate those he hates. It was beyond his powers to portray sympathetically a figure whose beliefs he opposes.

If Carr's political views seem crude and undeveloped, his social philosophy is of a little more interest. In spite of his lifelong conservatism, it does not appear that Carr was as committed to rigid class distinctions as one might expect. It is true that throughout his novels—especially in the Bencolin series—there is much praise of aristocracy; but in other works members of the aristocracy are sharply criticised. Both the praise and the criticism focus on very specific issues, and are best revealed by quotation. Of Bencolin it is said in "The Murder in Number Four" (1928):

You noticed not a little of the aristocrat in the back-thrown head, the slow, graceful speech, the faint and dominant contempt with which he faced Miss Mertz.[6]

But let us recall that Bencolin is not actually an aristocrat: his superiority—in language and manner—derives principally from his intellect. Recall also that some of Carr's most vicious satire is directed toward Lady Pamela de Saxe in *Patrick Butler for the Defence* (1956) precisely because she affects a mindless conformity to the empty conventions of aristocratic behaviour. But when a figure in *It Walks by Night* (1930) utters the following lament to the dying aristocracy, we can feel Carr's support of his sentiments:

"You will not know, you will not understand, what it means to some of us when the last of the aristocrats pass one by one from the world. It is like the blowing out of candles, in a *château*, one by one, until all the house is dark. God in heaven! It strikes home! It leaves us lost!" (8)

Here the idea is that an aristocracy is necessary to a civilisation as a model of conduct—it is *aristocracy* in the literal sense of the term, rule by the naturally superior. Much sympathy is extended to old Colonel Martel in *The Corpse in the Waxworks* (1932) because he embodies all the *true* qualities of the aristocrat: natural dignity (without pomposity or pretentiousness), inflexible honesty, and indomitable courage even when his world is falling apart in front of his eyes. Contrast this portrait with that of the wealthy American Arbor in *The Mad Hatter Mystery* (1933):

If Mr. Arbor could not be called a type, he was at least among a certain class of Americans who had always irritated Rampole, and who can only be described as Overcultured. They try to see everything and know everything in as correct a fashion as possible. They go to the right places at exactly the right time. Their pale, assured knowledge of the arts is like their well-groomed houses and their well-groomed selves. When a new Atlantic liner is launched, they discover the proper place to sit in the dining-room, and sit there. They avoid errors, and never drink too much. (8)

This is the sort of aristocrat Carr cannot abide—the one who plays it safe, who does everything according to hackneyed convention, who fundamentally lacks courage. It is exactly by defying the accepted standards of aristocratic behaviour that Merrivale causes such perturbation amongst the upper classes. Perhaps the fundamental term here is *courage*: all his detectives have it (when Merrivale is seriously injured in *Nine—and Death Makes Ten* [1940], he remarks with sombre dignity: "It's a scar of honour, son. The first I've had in the way of business for twenty-five years" [18]), and all the protagonists of his historical mysteries have it also.

The portrayal of Arbor brings to mind another frequent feature of Carr's work—the withering scorn directed toward boorish or uncouth Americans. Perhaps Carr, as an Anglo-American who had seen much of the Continent, felt the need to separate himself as far as possible from such types; note the depiction of Sid Golton in *It Walks by Night:*

"I'm gonna pop *you,*" said the newcomer, opening his eyes and pointing a finger at the policeman with a curiously intent look. "Sure as hell I'm gonna pop you 'fyou don't getaway! Now you lemme 'lone in this chair...." He relapsed again.

"Who is this?" I asked Bencolin. The detective was studying him with narrowed eyes.

"I have seen him before, with Saligny," Bencolin replied, shrugging. "His name is Golton, or something of the sort. An American, naturally." (3)

Such figures recur with some regularity in the early works, but toward the end of his career, as he spent more time in his native land, he began to soften. Already in *A Graveyard to Let* (1949), and later again in *Dark of the Moon* (1967), we have charming digressions on baseball; and in *Panic in Box C* (1966) the brash Americanism of Lieutenant Spinelli (the same name, curiously, as a gangster in *The Eight of Swords*) offers a piquant contrast to the stateliness of Dr. Fell:

"I've got to simmer down," he declared. "I'm going nuts, I tell you; my mind's dissolving like an aspirin in water. I've got to get hold of myself, damn my ornery hide, before the D.A. thinks I'm even more of a wild man than Flo does. So, while I shuffle around with ways of working the trick, we'll just ask ourselves: *who* could have done it?" (9)

This is a little overdone, perhaps (we could have done without Flo), but effective enough. Still, Americans in Carr's eyes are generally the type of stupidity, unsophistication, and crassness.

The fact of the matter is that every single one of Carr's novels deals with characters belonging to the upper-middle class or actual upper class (even Richard Darwent in *The Bride of Newgate,* although we initially see him on the brink of a humiliating death, proves to be well-born); and right to the end we still find the ubiquitous servants who quietly tend to everything while the principals are free to engage in whatever histrionics they wish. It is this feature that most clearly "dates" Carr's work: it does not appear that he was capable (or, at least, desirous) of writing an entire novel or tale around a lower-class character; such characters appear now and again, and several are presented as admirable in themselves and loyal to their betters, but they are never the focus of attention.

But if anything positive can be said of Carr in this particular, it is that his treatment of servants is not—or at least not always—as brutally demeaning as that of the supreme middle-class snob Dorothy L. Sayers. It is true that passages like the following from *Hag's Nook* (1933) are not encouraging:

Mr. Budge, the butler, was making his customary rounds at the Hall to see that all the windows were fastened before he retired to his respectable bachelor bed. Mr. Budge was aware that all the windows were fastened, had been fastened every night during the fifteen years of his officiation, and would continue so until the great red-brick house should fall or Get Took By Americans—which latter fate Mrs.

Bundle, the housekeeper, always uttered in a direful voice, as though she were telling a terrible ghost story. None the less, Mr. Budge was darkly suspicious of housemaids. He felt that, when his back was turned, every housemaid had an overpowering desire to sneak about, opening windows, so that tramps could get in. His imagination never got so far as burglars, which was just as well. (6)

A later chapter (15) centres entirely on Budge in the same condescendingly bantering way; and yet, in the end Budge shows great daring and courage (note that quality again) in confronting the murderer, even though he is shot and injured in the process. Much satire is directed toward Mina Constable in *The Reader Is Warned* (1939) at her inability to cope without servants:

"Whatever happens," she said, "thanks anyway. You've been very decent to me, both of you. And you, Hilary: I don't know what I'd have done without you. Cooking the meals! And even washing the dishes!"
"A terrible job," said Hilary dryly. "A perfectly back-breaking job. It quite wore me out. What on earth do you do when you're off on one of these heathenish trips of yours and there isn't anybody to wash the dishes?"
"Oh, I pay somebody to do it," said Mina with a certain vagueness. "Saves time and trouble, you see." (9)

Two novels are actually based in part upon the supposed invisibility of servants in a murder case. We are all aware of S. S. Van Dine's magisterial dictum that "A servant must not be chosen by the author as the culprit"— a remark he explains with the astonishingly snobbish "The culprit must be a decidedly worth-while person",[7] as no servant, evidently, can ever be! Carr agrees with this utterance,[8] but bends it in interesting ways. Merrivale in *The Curse of the Bronze Lamp* (1945) notes:

"Didn't it ever strike any of you," he went on, "that in these big houses there are servants, like the kitchen-staff and the between-maid, never even *seen* by any guest? And that a gal masqueradin' as one of 'em could easily keep out of the way of anybody who might recognize her?" (19)

This is because part of the "miracle" in this case is that a character seemed to disappear into thin air by donning the costume of a maidservant. In *Below Suspicion* (1949) Fell explains to Patrick Butler the meaning of that peculiar phrase:

"In a detective story"—Dr. Fell puffed at the cigar—"no person is above suspicion. But there are several types who are below it. Any person serving as a detective, for instance. Any minor character. Any servant: because a servant, who may only enter to say 'The Archbishop awaits' is a wooden mask without a character to be read." (17)

Again, the application of this notion has a direct bearing on the outcome. In all this there is but the faintest trace of satire directed at the whole idea of servants as not being somehow real people; but let us at least give Carr the credit for being aware of the issue.

If the attempt to ascertain a political or social philosophy—let alone a metaphysics—in Carr's work is a fruitless undertaking, it is not merely because Carr deals with such issues only in passing; in a broader sense Carr really goes out of his way to avoid them. An encapsulated example occurs in the radio play "The Black Minute" (1940), which begins well by portraying an elderly scientist, Sir Francis Church, having come under the influence of a spiritualist. His discussion of the matter with Fell seems to promise a meaningful debate on philosophy and ethics:

SIR FRANCIS (with concentrated bitterness): . . . The police persecute Riven. Even the spiritualists persecute him. And therefore I am to turn away from the pioneer. I'm to get down on my knees like another scientist and deny that the earth moves. Well, I won't do it. I know what I know. I've never been afraid of ridicule in my life, and I'm not afraid of it now. (This seems to have exhausted him. His voice grows fretful.) Things are hard sometimes. Very hard on a man. We must have a creed, Fell. Even you must have a creed. What do you affirm?
DR. FELL: I affirm—
SIR FRANCIS: Yes?
DR. FELL (in a sharper, clearer tone): I affirm that I just heard somebody scream. (The Dead Sleep Lightly)

It is as if Carr cannot face up to the seriousness of the issues he had raised, and he lapses into sensationalism. This particular discussion is never resumed or resolved.

The most significant way in which Carr has avoided giving broader meaning to his work is his failure to make use of World War II, the only important conflict (save, of course, the Vietnam War) which Carr actually lived through. Merrivale and others can wax nostalgic about their involvement in World War I—something Carr could surely remember only dimly—but although World War II began when Carr was at the absolute height of his powers, he never made it the focus of any major work. The most interesting phenomenon here is how Carr, in the majority of those novels written during the war, sets them just before the start of that conflict. Let us study each of these novels systematically.

The Reader Is Warned (1939) was no doubt written at least a year before the war, but it contains one rather flippant mention of Hitler:

"Well, a little thought-reading is one thing," he said, as though arguing that boys will be boys. "But to crack a man's bones and skull with thought, like a death-ray, is coming it too strong. Think! Think what it would mean if it were true. Hitler, for instance. Hitler suddenly claps his hands to his head and says, 'Mein Gott!' or 'Mein Kampf!' or whatever it is he's always saying, and falls over as dead as Bismarck. I argued. I said, 'Well, could you kill Hitler, for instance?" (9)

Later, when Pennik is on trial, he is accused to being a Nazi (17).

The date of *The Problem of the Wire Cage* (1939), similarly written before the war, can be fixed to 1935.[9]

And So to Murder (1940) uses the war as a fairly significant backdrop, as we are at the set of a film studio near London engaged in an anti-Nazi film, *Spies at Sea,* and there is a suspicion of sabotage when a bottle of water is replaced with sulphuric acid; but in the end—although again a German character is suspected of Nazi affiliations (8)—the plot has nothing to do with espionage.

The Man Who Could Not Shudder (1940) is the first work written during the war to be consciously backdated; it is set in 1937 (1). The final chapter leaps ahead to September 1939, since a significant character has now died aboard a luxury liner sunk by the Germans, allowing the story to be told.

Nine—and Death Makes Ten (1940) opens grippingly aboard a ship carrying munitions across the Atlantic, but again the case ends up not involving the war in any significant fashion.

The Case of the Constant Suicides (1941) takes place in 1940 (13), and yet everything is still functioning rosily in Scotland, without such things as blackout curtains for windows or air-raid sirens.

Seeing Is Believing (1941) is definitely dated to 1938 (2).

Death Turns the Tables (1941) is set in 1936 (2).

The Gilded Man (1942) appears to take place before the war, as no reference to war activity is made.

The Emperor's Snuff-Box (1942) must also be set in pre-war France, although no date is specified.

The events of *She Died a Lady* (1943) take place in May 1940; Luke Croxley has written his account some months later, before dying "during the night of the first air-raid on Bristol" (19) in November 1940. Here there are some poignant reflexions on the commencement of the war:

> You remember that warm Sunday morning, with the September sunshine over everything, when the announcement came over the radio? I was alone in the house, in my dressing-gown. That voice, saying, "We are at war," seemed to fill every part of the house. My first thought was: "Well, here it is again," in a kind of blankness; and then: "Will Tom have to go?"
>
> For a while I sat and looked at my shoes. Laura, Tom's mother, died while I was in the last one. They played *If You Were the Only Girl in the World,* and it makes my eyes sting sometimes when I hear that tune. (1)

The war background here as well as in *He Wouldn't Kill Patience* (1944) is very prevalent, although in both cases only as a sort of disturbing backdrop. The latter novel is definitely dated to September 6, 1940 (1).

Till Death Do Us Part (1944) is set "a year or so before the beginning of Hitler's war" (1).

The Curse of the Bronze Lamp (1945) is set "ten years ago" (later more specifically to 1934-35 [1]).

In *He Who Whispers* (1946), evidently the first novel written after the war, "peace had crept back unwillingly to Europe" (1). Again there are some brief words on the general reaction to the advent of peace:

People didn't celebrate that victory hysterically, as for some reason or other the newspapers liked to make out. What the news-reels showed was only a bubble on the huge surface of the town. Like himself, Miles Hammond thought, most people were a little apathetic because they could not yet think of it as real.

But something awoke, deep down inside human beings' hearts, when the cricket results crept back into the papers and the bunks began to disappear from the Underground. (1)

This is clearly derived from Carr's personal experience; we only wish there were more of it.

My Late Wives (1946) is prototypical in that its opening chapter is set in 1934; the novel then leaps forward to just after "the end of Hitler's war" (2). There is a brief and inconsequential reference to the atom bomb (6).

In *The Sleeping Sphinx* (1947) "the war's been over for a year and three months" (1).

We have already noted the peculiarly archaistic *Night at the Mocking Widow* (1950), set in 1938.

All this does not amount to much: out of fifteen novels (beginning with *And So to Murder*) written during or just after the war, only two or three feature the war even as a significant element of background. Doubtless when Carr as a boy came up with his 120 plots, he did not bargain upon a second world cataclysm like the one that came to a close while he was still in elementary school. The fact is that Carr's puzzle-stories are not adaptable to a war setting, and so he chose the simple expedient of avoiding the conflict while it was occurring and pretending it had never occurred once it was over.

On those few occasions when Carr makes an attempt at significant political or social commentary, he usually fails through lack of penetrating insight. In his sociological explication of the witch-cult in *Below Suspicion*, Carr is in no danger of being mistaken for Max Weber:

"Witchcraft!" Lucia said, and shivered. "The worship of Satan! But—*nowadays?*"
"Nowadays," assented Dr. Fell, "more than ever."
"Why?"
"Because the world is in chaos. Because, after the late affair of Adolf Hitler, many persons believe that decent standards of behaviour cannot exist. Horrors no longer offend. As for religion, observe that politics have taken its place. We have seen little girls, fifteen years old, screaming-drunk in Leicester Square. Decent men are gleeful about trickery and deceit, because their lives compel them to be. This will all change, I grant you! Meanwhile, there is the witch-cult." (13)

Of Carr's historical novels Douglas G. Greene has noted that "it was in such books that he could most clearly express his attitudes toward the world."[10] But the unfortunate fact is that Carr does not seem to have had any interesting attitudes to express. When Nick Fenton goes back in time in *The Devil in Velvet* (1951), his failure to miss modern things is surely Carr's:

> "How strange," he reflected, "have been the minds of authors I have read, setting a character back hundreds of years in time! I think their learning is not wide enough. For they never allow the poor devil to have a good time. He must fret and fume because progress—accursed progress, and thrice-damned machinery—have not come to wreck men's lives.
>
> "He is infuriated by the lack of telephones and motorcars. I felt no need of them when I studied, in rural Somerset, for some dreary degree or other. Our author, through his hero, is appalled at the sanitation, the harsh laws, the power of King or Parliament. Yet, in my heart, I confess these matters trouble me not at all." (10)

But what this really tells us about Carr the thinker is not clear.

In truth, only a single novel—*The Sleeping Sphinx* (1947)—is genuinely based on a social conflict. Much of the tragic confusion in this work is caused by an old family doctor's fanatical desire to avoid scandal, to the point that he tries to convince a young woman that she may be insane. Fell chides him at the end.

> "You talk," cried Dr. Shepton, "as though—" He stopped. "Prosecution!" he added. "You talk as though—"
>
> "Yes?" prompted Dr. Fell.
>
> "As though," he spoke in a quavering voice, "I wanted to harm Celia in some way!"
>
> "Forgive me," said Dr. Fell. "I know you don't. And you were misled. Blame the girl, if you like, for telling lies. But in God's name let us have an end of these hush-hush methods which nearly did send her out of her mind and drove her to telling lies!" (19)

The emotional intensity of this novel is augmented by this authentic clash of wills. But it is a lone example in Carr's work.

Douglas G. Greene detects a significant philosophical issue inherent in the whole of Carr's detective writing:

> Why, then, must the puzzle be solved if not for law or justice? Because the mystery threatens the happiness of the protagonists and more fundamentally because it questions the rationality of the universe. The locked rooms, disappearances and other miracle crimes with their hints of black magic challenge our belief in rational cause and effect. If we don't carry the comparison too far, Carr's detectives act almost as exorcists; they dispel the devils and demonstrate that the seemingly supernatural events were created by human means for human motives.[11]

I strongly contest this entire interpretation, but it can be more fruitfully and pertinently treated when we discuss the role of the supernatural in Carr's work.

There can hardly be a doubt that Carr went out of his way to avoid dealing with significant social, political, or philosophical issues in his novels. In large part this derives from his very narrow theory of literature, which we shall study elsewhere; but it is also a result of the very nature of Carr's conception of detective writing, and it is to that rich topic that we now turn.

The Theory and Practise
of Detective Writing

Carr was a voluminous theorist of the detective story. Aside from such things as an introduction to a proposed anthology of mystery classics, a section on "Story Development" in *The Mystery Writer's Handbook* (1956), his acid review of Raymond Chandler's *The Simple Art of Murder,* and a speech on the history of the field delivered in 1968, we have more than ninety review columns in *Ellery Queen's Mystery Magazine* from 1969 to 1976, and a few more in *Harper's* at a slightly earlier date. All this material might make an interesting collection, although much of it tends to go over the same ground; indeed, perhaps all we really need to read in order to understand Carr's views on the purpose of the detective story is the magnificent seventeenth chapter of *The Three Coffins* (1935), titled "The Locked-Room Lecture".

This is surely a remarkable piece of writing, and Carr—quite unwittingly—anticipates some very avant-garde techniques of metafiction by having his characters realise that they are merely characters in a book:

"I will now lecture," said Dr. Fell, inexorably, "on the general mechanics and development of the situation which is known in detective fiction as the 'hermetically sealed chamber.' Harrumph. All those opposing can skip this chapter. Harrumph. To begin with, gentlemen! Having been improving my mind with sensational fiction for the last forty years, I can say—"

"But, if you're going to analyze impossible situations," interrupted Pettis, "why discuss detective fiction?"

"Because," said the doctor, frankly, "we're in a detective story, and we don't fool the reader by pretending we're not. Let's not invent elaborate excuses to drag in a discussion of detective stories. Let's candidly glory in the noblest pursuits possible to characters in a book."

That Carr would so readily destroy the illusion of realism with this pseudo-authorial intrusion means that what he (through Fell) is about to say is of enormous importance to him. And so it is. Fell's remarks about his (or Carr's) preferences in detective fiction may be the single most valuable utterance Carr ever made:

"I like my murders to be frequent, gory, and grotesque. I like some vividness of colour and imagination flashing out of my plot, since I cannot find a story enthralling solely on the grounds that it sounds as though it might really have happened. All these things, I admit, are happy, cheerful, rational prejudices, and entail no criticism of more tepid (or more able) work."

Fell goes on for several paragraphs attacking the charge of the "improbability" of the locked-room murder, stating that all detective stories that conceal the identity of the murder would be open to this charge. At this point we must bring in another piece of evidence. In defending Gaston Leroux's *The Mystery of the Yellow Room*, Carr wrote: "Any critic dull enough to call this story improbable would apply the same term to folklore or Arthurian romance."[1] I am not sure that the revolutionary nature of this statement—or of Carr's entire position—has been fully appreciated; for what Carr in effect is claiming is that the detective story does not belong to the domain of realism but to that of fantasy.

There can be no doubt that Carr really ascribes to this daring view. Bencolin in *The Lost Gallows* (1931) defends his reading of a sensational detective novel, *The Murders at Whispering House*, in terms very similar to Fell's:

"My fine nightmare is not bounded by any dull probability, nor yet by the discouraging fact that it really happened. The detective never errs, which is exactly what I want. I could never understand why writers wanted to make their detectives human beings, patient workers, liable to error, but through sheer doggedness—*bah!* The reason, of course, is that they have not the wit to create a really clever character, and so they must try to bulldoze us with makeshifts..."

"How long," I asked, "is this sermonizing to continue?"

"...in brief, life lacks all the fascination, the drama, the tidy working out of plot which I find here. In reply to your last question, I may say that you had better go on up to bed. I want to finish my tale." (9)

Truth is *not* stranger than fiction, Bencolin (with Carr) dares to say. Recall *The Murder of Sir Edmund Godfrey* (1936): "The fact remains that only in very rare cases can real life be fashioned into the tidy, clipped image of fiction" ("Preface"). I am not sure whether Carr really wants to say that *all* fiction is fantasy; it is quite possible. In any case, what such a position does is to free Carr from obvious attacks on the "improbability" of his complex and neatly fitting scenarios. "Realism" will in fact be involved, but—as in all good fantasy—it will be a means, not an end: a means to convey the emotions of shock, bewilderment, and horror that are Carr's true aims. H. P. Lovecraft enunciated perfectly the subordinate role of realism in fantasy:

In writing a weird story I always try very carefully to achieve the right mood and atmosphere, and place the emphasis where it belongs...Inconceivable events and conditions have a special handicap to overcome, and this can be accomplished only through the maintenance of a careful realism in every phase of the story *except* that touching on the one given marvel. This marvel must be treated very impressively and deliberately—with a careful emotional "build-up"—else it will seem flat and unconvincing. Being the principal thing in the story, its mere existence should overshadow the characters and events. But the characters and events must be consistent and natural except where they touch the single marvel.[2]

Whereas Lovecraft, in referring to the "single marvel", was speaking of some supernatural or supernormal event, Carr would apply the same dictum toward the "impossible" nature of the crime.

Carr's critical stance is in direct contrast to that of Raymond Chandler, who in the first sentence of his essay "The Simple Art of Murder" (1944) declared: "Fiction in any form has always intended to be realistic."[3] Carr spent much effort in later years heaping abuse on Chandler's position, but I am not entirely sure that he really understood what Chandler was talking about. In part this was Chandler's own fault. In "The Simple Art of Murder" there is a fundamental confusion between realism as referring to setting and incident (what Fell scornfully calls "a story...[that] might really have happened") and realism as referring to truth to human emotions. Carr is right to attack Chandler on the first point:

> His thesis is that murder must become realistic. It must be taken out of the Venetian vase and dropped into the alley. It must be handled by men who understand it, who use the Luger and the Colt for real reasons, undismayed by violence, all raw-head and bloody-bones.[4]

The fallacy in this part of Chandler's argument is that a "hard-boiled" story is just as unrealistic as any English drawing-room murder mystery. In any case, Carr has explicitly disavowed this sort of realism—except in a subordinate role—in his own work. But Carr had a more difficult time answering Chandler's second point:

> It [the traditional detective story] was second-grade literature because it was not about the things that could make first-grade literature. If it started out to be about real people..., they must very soon do unreal things in order to form the artificial pattern required by the plot. When they did unreal things, they ceased to be real themselves. They became puppets and cardboard lovers and papier mache villains and detectives of exquisite and impossible gentility.[5]

Carr does not so much address this issue—that the detective story does not engage our emotions or say anything significant about human existence—as ignore it. It appears that Carr felt the detective story could *never* say anything significant about life. In 1946 Carr wrote an introduction to a proposed anthology of classic detective novels; when published years later in *Ellery Queen's Mystery Magazine*, it was called "The Grandest Game in the World". This title, though not Carr's, is appropriate, since he considered the detective story merely a "game":

> It is a hoodwinking contest, a duel between author and reader. "I dare you," says the reader, "to produce a solution which I can't anticipate." "Right!" says the author, chuckling over the consciousness of some new and legitimate dirty trick concealed up his sleeve. And then they are at it—pull-devil, pull-murderer—with

the reader alert for every dropped clue, every betraying speech, every contradiction that may mean guilt.[6]

Carr has, therefore, wilfully relinquished any value to the detective story beyond entertainment and the bamboozling of the reader. We shall later discover that this is his view of fiction as a whole.

Carr is also emphatic on what features of the detective story should be paramount. "My concern is with who and how; seldom with why."[7] Elsewhere he praises those authors who concentrate "on *who* or *how* rather than not-very-appealing *why*".[8] It is curious how often this litany is uttered. Even in the historical mysteries it holds true. Wilkie Collins in *The Hungry Goblin* (1972) states at one point: "You prophesied endless trouble with *who* and *why*. Still greater bewilderment, I hereby swear, will arise from *how*" (7). There seem to be some exceptions to the downplaying of *why* (motive) and the elevation of *how* (method) and *who* (identity), but they prove illusory. In *To Wake the Dead* (1937) Fell speculates:

> We all know, in any murder case, the questions *who, how,* and *why*. Of these three, the most revealing, but usually by far the most puzzling, is *why*. I don't mean merely the actual motive for the crime itself. I mean the why of certain other actions, eccentricities of behaviour, which centre round the performance of the crime. They torment us at the time: a hat placed on a statue, a poker removed from the scene of the crime when by all reason it should not have been removed. (17)

But here the *why* seems to be really a facet or subset of *how:* once we understand the method, the causes for various characters' seemingly anomalous behaviour will fall into place. Similarly, in *The Mystery Writer's Handbook* Carr appears to establish a hierarchy of *why, how,* and *who;* but here the *why* seems restricted to supplying a plausible motive so that a murder is not committed "without due cause".[9] It is a sort of tepid bow to realism so that the mystery can have some reason for existence.

Judging solely from his work, we can scarcely doubt that *how* was preeminent in Carr's thinking; he has certainly come up with more bizarre ways of killing people than any other detective writer. The minimising of motive, however, does have considerable drawbacks. In many novels so much attention is devoted to the fantastic or "impossible" nature of the crime that we never receive sufficient evidence as to why the victim should have been killed in the first place. To be sure, Carr, in his adherence to the "fair play" convention, drops hints regarding motive, but frequently these hints are so minuscule that they come as a surprise when they are explained at the end. In any case, since the method of Carr's murders is so intricate and recherché, it can ordinarily be fastened upon a single individual: only the murderer could have had the means or opportunity to commit so peculiar a crime. Once this method is ascertained, the motive is a mere afterthought. In many of Carr's concluding solutions to the crime, we suddenly receive an elaborate description of the "true" nature of the murderer's character; a description frequently considerably at variance with our impression of this figure as developed through the course of the work, and something for which we are frequently not sufficiently prepared. Carr, through Fell, expressed concern that the reader might be disappointed with the explained method of the crime:

"Why are we dubious when we hear the explanation of the locked room? Not in the least because we are incredulous, but simply because in some vague way we are *disappointed*. And from that feeling it is only natural to take an unfair step farther, and call the whole business incredible or impossible or flatly ridiculous...

"You see, the effect is so magical that we somehow expect the cause to be magical also. When we see that it isn't wizardry, we call it tomfoolery. Which is hardly fair play." (*The Three Coffins* [17])

But Carr need not have worried on this score, for his elucidations of his "impossible" crimes are highly engaging; but what Carr has failed to notice is that he oftentimes violates not fictional probability but human probability in suddenly transforming normal-seeming characters without suitable forewarning into crazed monsters.

It is interesting to see how this disinclination to be concerned with "not-very-appealing *why*" affects even Carr's critical judgment; it accounts for his extraordinary preference for those works by A. B. Cox written under the Anthony Berkeley pseudonym (routine detective stories for the most part) over the remarkable *Malice Aforethought* and *Before the Fact* written as Francis Iles; of the latter he says:

Among aesthetes, who shudder at detective fiction, it has become the fashion to praise these "psychological" studies for superior characterization, and to exalt Francis Iles as though Anthony Berkeley had never existed. The true reason they say this lies deeper. Having no ingenuity of their own, they resent ingenuity in others and bitterly decry it as they decry the element of surprise.[10]

What Carr overlooks is that there are other, subtler types of "ingenuity" and "surprise" aside from the obvious kind; but Carr's hostility to the "psychological" detective tale—in spite of such of his own works as *Poison in Jest* (1932) or *The Crooked Hinge* (1938), which Fell declared (a little oddly) to be "an almost purely psychological puzzle" (7)—was such as to blind even his critical acumen.

The preeminence of *how* over *who* and *why* has, I believe, another unfortunate consequence. In conjunction with Carr's stated objective to "hoodwink" the reader, this concentration on an unguessable method of murder necessarily entails a rather callous lack of concern over the victim. In his early novels Carr had no compunction killing off two or three characters; in *The Bowstring Murders* (1933) two are murdered within minutes of each other. In order to preserve the "game"-like quality of the work, Carr was obliged to choose as his victims characters who were either odious in themselves or whom no one liked in any case; in this way the reader's attention would not be cluttered with any sense of horror or pity over the death of a human being, and the puzzle could operate in an environment of pure intellection. We have seen how the unpopularity or insignificance of the victim was a key to the maintenance of the comic tone of *The Eight of Swords* (1934) and *The Blind Barber* (1934), but in truth nearly all his novels feature such victims. Of the murdered man in *Night at the Mocking Widow* (1950) it is said: "Few attended the funeral, since Cordy had almost no friends and his death was regarded secretly as good riddance" (18). Carr is rarely as crass or obvious as this; but aside from a few early works, few tears are shed over the many victims in Carr's novels and tales.

Central to Carr's conception of the detective story as a game between writer and reader is the notion of "fair play". *"Once the evidence has been fairly presented, there are very few things which are not permissible,"*[11] Carr writes with italic emphasis. We have seen that there are extremely few instances where Carr even approaches the violation of this sacrosanct principle. What this rule really signifies is a battle of wits—and here is another reason why messy emotionalism must be avoided: it would interfere with the rational presentation of clues. Occasionally Carr is quite explicit in challenging the reader to guess the outcome, as in *The Plague Court Murders* (1934):

...it is as well to be very careful of what I say; not to exaggerate or mislead—at least, any more than *we* were misled—so that you may have a fair opportunity to put your wits to work on a puzzle apparently impossible of solution. (6)

But in fact such a challenge is implicit in all Carr's work.

And yet, Carr's addiction to the "fair play" convention can lead to some unexpected awkwardnesses in narration. Carr is so concerned with presenting clues fairly that he occasionally mars the narrative flow with startling authorial intrusions—intrusions much less amusing or studied than the "Locked-Room Lecture". Even so brilliant a work as *The Three Coffins* opens with an exceedingly clumsy caveat:

We must be very careful about the evidence when it is not given at first-hand. And in this case the reader must be told at the outset, to avoid useless confusion, on whose evidence he can absolutely rely. That is to say, it must be assumed that *somebody* is telling the truth—else there is no legitimate mystery, and, in fact, no story at all.

Therefore it must be stated that Mr. Stuart Mills at Professor Grimaud's house was not lying, was not omitting or adding anything, but telling the whole business exactly as he saw it in every case. Also it must be stated that the three independent witnesses of Cagliostro Street (Messrs. Short and Blackwin, and Police-constable Withers) were telling the exact truth. (1)

It is as if Carr felt he must direct traffic in this way so as to give the reader an honest shot at the solution. There are two problems with this: first, the fact that Carr has to state that "X is telling the truth" is an admission of his own failure as a novelist in conveying this character's veracity through the actual narrative; and second, Carr cannot really believe that the majority of his readers will make the effort to solve the mystery themselves—it is too fatiguing an exercise, and we are in truth reading only for the pleasurable sensation of momentary bafflement and ultimate enlightenment. But Carr persists in this sort of thing. *The Crooked Hinge* is also marred with a peculiar footnote:

> Newspaper-readers may remember, in the bitter debate which followed tragedy in the Farnleigh case, that this point [whether Kennet Murray was telling the truth] was often brought up by amateurs. Having myself once wasted time on many futile theories in an attempt to solve the mystery, I feel that I had better clear it up here. The honesty and good faith of Kennet Murray may be accepted as a fact. The evidence he possessed, with regard to establishing the identity of the real heir, was genuine evidence; and, it may be recalled, was later used to establish the truth.—J.D.C. (2)

This is slightly cleverer than *The Three Coffins* in that Carr maintains the illusion of the case's reality; but it is really unnecessary. There is no reason why the reader should not think that Kennet Murray might be lying—this would add an interesting wrinkle to the case. Carr evidently felt, however, that it would create too many possible resolutions, so he shepherds the reader away from this prospect.

In a few works these authorial intrusions are handled a little more interestingly. *She Died a Lady* (1943) is presented as the first-person narrative of Dr. Luke Croxley, and so his statement in an early chapter—"And, as I can see now, what he said was quite true" (6)—is plausible because it is put in the mouth of a character (not the author) as he is reflecting upon the case some months after the events.

In two novels Carr actually flaunts his intrusion in the interests of fair play, and the works become structured with great ingenuity around these authorial directives. The very title of *The Reader Is Warned* (1939) signals the author's throwing down the gauntlet to the reader. Here the narrative is in the third person, but the protagonist, Dr. John Sanders, appears to have had access to the written account of the case, for he supplies three footnotes to the novel, each ending with "The reader is warned". Here is the first:

> In looking over these notes of what I said, I think it only fair to add that Constable was not killed by any mechanical device which operated in the absence of the guilty person. The presence of the guilty person was necessary to make the method succeed. The reader is warned.—J.S. (6)

The second footnote (11) declares that no accomplice was involved (here again Sanders is speaking for Carr: "The crime shall be the work of one person"[12]); the third footnote is somewhat unhelpful:

The motive for murder, though fully indicated in the text, is not obvious on the surface; and it involves, indeed, a legal point. Anyone interested in solving the problem may be advised to look carefully below the surface. The reader is warned.—J.S. (16)

This is more cryptic than the passage it is designed to elucidate. Nevertheless, the whole device works well here because it is harmoniously integrated into the course of the narrative.

The Nine Wrong Answers (1952) is still more ingenious in this regard. Here there are nine footnotes, each ending with "Discard answer number..."; a summary of them is as follows:

1. There was no conspiracy against Bill Dawson to enmesh him in the case (1);

2. Larry Hurst really was murdered, and did not commit suicide or fake his death (5);

3. Either Gaylord Hurst or his evil-looking manservant Hatto really intended to kill Dawson—they were not putting on an act (8);

4. Marjorie Blair is not someone else in disguise (9);

5. Bill was really in love with Marjorie and no one else (13);

6. There was only one criminal, although he or she had an unwitting accomplice (14);

7. Gaylord Hurst did not kill himself but was murdered (21);

8. Ronnie Wentworth is not the murderer (21);

9. The reader is reminded that all footnotes were intended to be taken literally, "meaning no more or no less than they say" (22).

One footnote leaps out at us by its startling difference from the others. It was an aesthetic mistake for Carr to have pointed out in footnote five the true state of affairs between Marjorie and Bill: not only is this fact only marginally germane to the case, but it is again something that Carr as novelist should have been content to have conveyed through the narrative and not in a blunt authorial footnote. Aside from this, however, these nine "wrong" answers (resolved by the final chapter, "The Nine Right Answers") are perhaps the most delightfully clever structural formula ever devised by Carr. He is at his most daring here: by explicitly alerting the reader to erroneous solutions, he runs an even greater risk of having the real solution guessed than in other works. And yet, he need not have worried: even within this confined space Carr, like Houdini, manages to escape the reader's grasp.

The principal means by which Carr limited his field of play in detective writing was, of course, his nearly exclusive concentration on the "impossible crime", of which the locked room is a central subset. And yet, this self-restriction proved to be a great source of strength: not only did Carr contrive a seemingly endless series of ever-refreshing variations on this apparently narrow subgenre, but his works are the more satisfying precisely because only one solution can possibly take account of all the bizarre features of the case. Carr learnt well what Poe's C. Auguste Dupin, at the very outset of formal detective fiction, said in "The Murders in the Rue Morgue":

"It appears to me that this mystery is considered insoluble, for the very reason which should cause it to be regarded as easy of solution—I mean for the *outré* character of its features...They [the police] have fallen into the gross but common error of confounding the unusual with the abstruse. But it is by these deviations from the plane of the ordinary, that reason feels its way, if at all, in its search for the true."[13]

In his first major case Bencolin echoes Dupin almost exactly:

"It has been in the past my good or bad fortune to be concerned only in cases of an outlandish nature; cases whose very impossible character admitted of just one solution."[14]

Hadley says the same thing at greater length in *The Arabian Nights Murder* (1936):

There was never a case, I believe, in which you find so much opportunity to exercise pure logic as in this one. That's because there are so many oddities. Logic, gentlemen, is not lost among oddities; it is at its best there. For an *ordinary* circumstance or puzzle, there may be a dozen explanations, so that the detective may choose the wrong one and throw his whole case off at the start. But for a very outlandish circumstance there is usually only one possible explanation; the odder the circumstance may be, the more narrow becomes the list of motives which produced it. (18)

Gasquet in *The Unicorn Murders* (1935) states that "It would be a logical fallacy to say that there could be *two* explanations to the impossible" (14); and although Merrivale appears to demur (perhaps more at the tone of the statement than at its substance), it is something Carr appears to accept. We have studied several novels where a nearly impregnable case was assembled against an innocent party, but proved illusory because it did not take account of *all* the evidence. It is as if someone were to put together some complicated piece of machinery but have a few apparently insignificant pieces left over: the machine might operate after a fashion, but would not do so as it was meant to do. Such erroneous reconstructions could be either very close to the truth except in some small particular (as in *The Arabian Nights Murder*) or entirely erroneous (as in *The Crooked Hinge*). Here again we must marvel at Carr's ingenuity at contriving such a scenario: in these works he has not only left enough real clues to point to the guilty party, but enough false ones to point to an innocent one. The structural complexity required for such a feat is dizzying.

It is greatly to Carr's credit that, in devising so many "impossible" crimes, he did not shy away from coming to terms with *why* such a situation should come about. Recall Hadley's remark in *The Eight of Swords*: "You are in your element with the sort of fantastic lunacy of a case which doesn't come our away once in a dozen years, ordinarily" (3). Such cases appear to come rather more frequently than that to Bencolin, Fell, and Merrivale, and it is Sir Henry who, in *The White Priory Murders* (1934), confronts the situation directly:

"The first thing is to determine the murderer's *motive*. I don't mean his motive for murder, but for creating an impossible situation. That's very important, son, because it's the best kind of clue *to* the motive for murder. Why'd he do it? Nobody but a loony is goin' to indulge in a lot of unreasonable hocus-pocus just to have some fun with the police. And there are enough motives for Tait's murder flyin' about already without our needin' to explain the mess by simply saying that the murderer is crazy. Well, then, what reasons could there have been?" (12)

Merrivale goes on to enumerate three possible motives for creating the "impossible" scenario:

1. The murder is designed to look like suicide;
2. The murder is designed to look like a supernatural manifestation;
3. The "impossible" situation is the result of accident.

In *The Peacock Feather Murders* (1937) the discussion is resumed, and a fourth motive is added:

4. If the method of murder cannot be ascertained, there can be no conviction in a trial. (19)

This feature was already noted in *The Plague Court Murders*, where Masters says with some exasperation: "Do you realize it won't do us an ounce of good even to fasten on somebody we think is the murderer, if we can't show how the murderer did it? We shouldn't dare go to court, even" (9). Here is yet one more reason for the priority of *how* over *who*. In *Seeing Is Believing* (1941) Masters believes he knows both *who* and *why*, but the *how* (here, how a real knife was substituted for a toy rubber one) still baffles him:

"We've got here evidence of motive: that's good. We've got here," he tapped an official form, "the statement of the chemist, Lewis L. Lewis: that's better. We've got here, after some downright fine staff-work by Inspector Agnew," continued Masters, who believes in keeping in well with the local police, "evidence of the purchase of the knife in Gloucester. That's still better."...

"...But, sir, the case isn't complete. It's all very well to say, 'Write out your warrant.' We can't make out one, and the chief constable can't sign it, until we can know how the ruddy knife was used, and how the person in question managed to exchange it with the toy one in full view of all the other witnesses." (17)

Masters is understandably annoyed when Merrivale remarks to this last point: "Oh, that?"

In any case, most of Carr's "impossible" situations can no doubt be accounted for in one of these four ways (pseudo-suicide, pseudo-supernatural, accident, inability to convict); indeed, accident seems to predominate, since the others requite so careful a crafting of events on the part of the murderer that there is a great chance that the "impossible" crime might not come off. And yet, Carr's works are filled with such architects of murder. In *To Wake the Dead* Fell states ponderously: "These two murders are the work of one person: anything else, my boy, would be artistically wrong: and I have an unpleasant feeling that someone behind the scenes is managing matters with great artistry" (3). What makes this murderer-as-artist effect highly improbable is that human beings and human events rarely dovetail so neatly for all the cleverness and intelligence of the mind behind them. Carr was wise to make accident the primary cause of seemingly impossible crimes.

As for the locked room itself, Carr's first speculation on it occurs in *The Plague Court Murders,* where Merrivale clearly shows its connexion to the impossible crime in general:

"Y'see, fatheads, the fundamental trouble with the locked-room situation is that it generally ain't reasonable. I don't mean that it can't be worked, any more than you'd deny one of Houdini's escapes; oh, far from it. I mean that, under ordinary circumstances, no real murderer would think of indulging in all the elaborate hocus-pocus we're required to believe at the end of the story." (14)

In "The Locked-Room Lecture" in *The Three Coffins* Fell dissects seven different types of locked-room situations, being careful to note that these (unlike Poe's "Murders in the Rue Morgue") involve "a hermetically sealed room which really is hermetically sealed"; they are as follows:

1. "It is not murder, but a series of coincidences ending in an accident which looks like murder."
2. "It is murder, but the victim is impelled to kill himself or crash into an accidental death."
3. "It is murder, by a mechanical device already planted in the room..."
4. "It is suicide, which is intended to look like murder."
5. "It is suicide, which derives its problem from illusion and impersonation."
6. "It is a murder which, although committed by somebody outside the room at the time, nevertheless seems to have been committed by somebody who must have been inside."
7. "The victim is presumed to be dead long before he actually is."

It would be tedious and unprofitable to try to categorise Carr's locked-room situations as belonging to one or the other of these types. Carr attributes the first to Leroux's *The Mystery of the Yellow Room* and the last to Israel Zangwill's *The Big Bow Mystery,* and it is interesting that there do not appear to be any instances where Carr used either of these devices in the precise manner stated—he must have had great respect for these two famous predecessors, the former of which Fell pronounces "the best detective story ever written". The miraculous vanishment of the criminal in *The Mystery of the Yellow Room*—a separate "impossible" situation from the locked-room problem in this work—is borrowed after a fashion in *The Curse of the Bronze Lamp* (1945).

Fell then goes on to list various ways to tamper with locks, bolts, and hinges to create a locked room or the illusion of a locked room; and we see that many of Carr's works fall into this category as well, from the vacuum cleaner used to seal the room in *He Wouldn't Kill Patience* to the thread and thumbtacks used in *Till Death Do Us Part.*

Much more could presumably be done in cataloguing Carr's various uses of the locked room or impossible crime, but these notes sufficiently suggest how exhaustively Carr mined this multifaceted device, to the point that he could have his greatest detective halt the action of a novel to theorise about it.

The baffling nature of Carr's crimes is augmented by the repeated theatricality and intentional mystification of his detectives. One of the greatest comic moments in Carr occurs in the otherwise dark *Corpse in the Waxworks* (1932), where Marle expresses infuriation at some cryptic utterances by Bencolin:

> In a whisper, as though to test incredible words, he repeated: "Selling tickets. . . . If her father. . ."
> His lips moved soundlessly. With a spasmodic motion he rose to his feet, rumpling his hair, staring ahead.
> "What's the matter? What—?" I demanded, and paused as he made a fierce gesture. But still he did not see me. He took a few steps up and down, in and out of the shadows. Once he let out an incredulous bleat of laughter, but he checked himself. I heard him mutter, "Alibi. . .that's the alibi," and again: "I wonder who the jeweller is? We've got to find the jeweller. . ."
> "*Look here!*"
> "Ah yes! But," he argued, turning and addressing me with an appearance of easy good sense, "if you had one, it would be inevitable. You have got to consider the wall. What else could you use, that would do it?"
> "How about bromo-seltzer?" I suggested. " 'Twas brillig, and the slithy toves did gyre and gimble in the webe.' Go to hell, will you?" (11)

This is worth nearly all of Merrivale's shenanigans put together. It is tantalising hints of this sort that make Carr's work so pleasurable to read a second time, when we can understand references that on first reading seem either cretinous or half-mad. Where did Carr derive this device? It might be thought to have come to Chesterton, whose Father Brown was so fond of paradox; and an earlier remark about Bencolin ("The man struck me as being slightly out of his head, and therefore I knew he was closest on the track of discovery" [3]) is indeed very Chestertonian. But I suspect the trick really came from Sherlock Holmes. In *The Life of Sir Arthur Conan Doyle* (1949) Carr writes at length about Conan Doyle's use of the "enigmatic clue":

> It is customary to say that Conan Doyle derived one device from Poe, or another from Gaboriau, or a third device from somebody else. This obscures what he really did do: he invented the enigmatic clue. We find it running far back through the stories, notably illustrated by a passage which has been repeated over and over:
> "Is there any point to which you would wish to draw my attention?"
> "To the curious incident of the dog in the night-time."
> "The dog did nothing in the night-time."

"That was the curious incident."

Call this 'Sherlockismus'; call it any fancy name; the fact remains that it is a clue, and a thundering good clue at that. It is the trick by which the detective—while giving you perfectly fair opportunity to guess—nevertheless makes you wonder what in sanity's name he is talking about. The creator of Sherlock Holmes invented it; and nobody except the great G. K. Chesterton, whose Father Brown stories were so deeply influenced by the device, has ever done it half so well. (19)

As early as *Grand Guignol* (1929), Carr imitates or even parodies the "dog in the night-time" trope:

[Bencolin:] "Then that question of a weapon in his pockets—it was curious—"
"But we found no weapon in his pocket!" I protested.
"Ah, that was the curious thing."[15]

In any case, all Carr's detectives exhibit a fondness for mystification of this kind. Fell actually defends himself frequently from the charge, as in *The Man Who Could Not Shudder* (1940):

"See here. I don't wish to make mysteries. But then I am not making the mysteries. You are."
"As how?"
"By words. By the wrong implications. By your manner of stating the facts, or what you believe to be the facts." (17)

This is interesting in that it is really Carr's method of baffling the reader: he states facts in such a way that they carry the "wrong implication". The critical moment in *It Walks by Night* (1930), for example, is here:

Bencolin gently raised his hand. She shivered, looked slowly out across the *salon*, and then said, "There goes Raoul now, into the card-room."
She nodded towards the small door at the far end of the room, through which a broad back was disappearing; then the door closed. I saw no more than that, for I happened to be looking at my wrist-watch. I looked at it twice, absently, before I noted that the hour was eleven-thirty. (2)

What escapes us at the time is that this is *not* Raoul going into the card-room, but the murderer impersonating him; but Carr seems to emphasise the secondary point regarding the time of night, and we miss the fact that the figure in question is not Raoul but only someone who, from behind, looks like him.

If Fell cannot be accused as often as Hadley and others believe of genuine mystification (in *Till Death Do Us Part* it is said: "The Gargantuan doctor was not trying to be mystifying; he had merely slipped ahead into some obscure mental calculation, and forgotten all about what had been on his mind a few minutes before" [13]), Merrivale revels in it, as he states bluntly in *Night at the Mocking Widow:*

The bookseller, who now carried his broad-brimmed hat in his hand, ran his fingers through tufts of whitish hair.

"I have often wondered, merely as a matter of psychology, why you will never give a straight answer to a straight question. Do you enjoy mystifying people?"

H.M.'s eyes came into focus.

"Sure I do!" he retorted, with unusual candor. "Who wouldn't? Wouldn't you? But I never do it, son, when there's danger to the person concerned." (14)

Carr's use of detective mystification is perhaps unexcelled in the field; and in a very real way it augments or even creates that sense of almost intolerable frustration and bafflement that every reader feels when enmeshed in one of his "impossible" crimes.

Some interesting statistical surveys could be done on a writer so prolific as Carr. If we consider the first fifty-two detective novels of his career, from *It Walks by Night* (1930) to *The Cavalier's Cup* (1953), excluding the historical mysteries and including *The Burning Court* (1937), we can detect certain definite trends in his writing.

Let us first examine the number of murders (or, more generally, deaths) that occur in the novels. In Carr's early years he was very prodigal in killing off characters, and the first eighteen novels (1930-36) contain thirty-eight deaths, or slightly more than two per book. Five contain three, and only three contain a single murder; one of these, however, is *The Arabian Nights Murder*, and this is another testament to the staggering complexity of the work, where the entire plot hangs around a single killing. Of the next eighteen books (1937-41) we have only thirty deaths, and only one where so many as three are murdered; in this group is the first work (*And So to Murder*) where no one is murdered. The next group of sixteen books (1942-53) contain only twenty-four deaths, and this including the four murders of *My Late Wives* (1946), three of which occur in rapid succession in the first chapter, which is really the prologue to the novel proper. In four works of this period there are no murders.

The settings of these novels are not quite so diverse. A full forty are set in Great Britain (including the Scotland of *The Case of the Constant Suicides*), five in France (only three Bencolin novels, however), three in America (this number would increase in later works when Carr returned to his native country), and four elsewhere (two aboard ship, one in the Rhine valley, one in Tangier). The fifty that take place on land are divided roughly equally between city (twenty-three) and country or small town (twenty-seven). *Night at the Mocking Widow* opens a little coyly with the remark:

When murder occurs in an English village, which it does far more frequently than is known by those who have not troubled to study the history of crime, people usually feel the shock worse because of the village's intense respectability. (1)

This is little more than a makeshift excuse for Carr's continuing predilection for setting his crimes in hoary mansions or country towns; although we have noted how many of the Fell novels take place not merely in the city but actually in public places.

As both a theoretician and practising artist in detection Carr had much of interest to say. It is entirely possible that he, through his detectives and other characters, has more to say on the nature and parameters of detective fiction in his novels than in his essays and reviews. If his conception of the detective story as a game or battle of wits was limiting in depriving the field of any broader human significance, he nonetheless persisted in it throughout his career and was certainly as successful as anyone in embodying his views in one great work after another. His hostility to those types of literature that do not involve fast-paced action relegated him to the status of a major writer in a very minor field; and his unrelenting concentration on the "impossible crime" still further limited his scope. But no one can deny that what he chose to do he did supremely well.

The Supernatural

What separates Carr from most other mystery writers, and what gives his own detective stories their distinctive flavour and atmosphere, is their suggestion of the supernatural. We can see this in the very titles of some of Carr's novels, titles that could serve perfectly for works of Gothic fiction: *It Walks by Night, Castle Skull, Hag's Nook, To Wake the Dead, The Man Who Could Not Shudder, He Who Whispers, The Witch of the Low-Tide,* or—more pulpishly—*The Curse of the Bronze Lamp.* As we reflect on it, several of these titles actually have little to do with the content of the novels, and indicate that Carr chose them precisely for their eerie suggestiveness. Carr had a lifelong fascination with the supernatural in fact and in fiction; it is no surprise that Dr. Fell wrote a treatise on the subject.

Carr was very well read in weird fiction. In so early a work as the comic story "The Deficiency Expert" (1927), a character remarks: "This is a newspaper; we ain't running any Weird Tales magazine!"[1] This nod to the greatest of the horror pulps (then relatively in its infancy, having been founded only in 1923) was followed more than forty-five years later by a tribute to the pulp era generally:

Cheap only in being modestly priced, it [the pulp magazine] provided excitement for the youthful or the stay-at-home, instilling a morality as rigid as any Sunday School's. Despite stories of every kind, love or sport or war, so many featured mystery that we may consider this category on its own. Naive plots or not, perhaps something may be lacking in a day when fiction has become only an interlude between commercials. *Ave atque vale;* likewise, *eheu fugaces!*[2]

I have no doubt that Carr relished all the pulps of his youth; clearly he was pleased when one of his own supernatural tales, "The Door to Doom", appeared in *Horror Stories* for June 1935. But Carr read more literate horror also. The list of books in the Duc de Saligny's home in *Grand Guignol* (the list is changed somewhat in *It Walks by Night*) is impressive:

"Typewriter...What's this? Books. Open here; drawers are filled with them. The works of Edgar Allan Poe. Barbey D'Aurevilly, the *Diaboliques.* Odd fare for a sporting man....Baudelaire, Hoffmann; *La Vie de Gilles de Rais*—"[3]

M. R. James, the great ghost-story writer, comes in for frequent mention in Carr's detective tales. A lengthy passage in *The Three Coffins* (1935) cites James by name and paraphrases much of his brief preface to *More*

113

Ghost Stories of an Antiquary (1911)—we shall consider this passage a little later—while in *The Skeleton in the Clock* (1948) occurs another interesting mention, as a character considers a pair of field-glasses: "Martin's first idea, characteristically, was a recollection of that grisly ghost-story by M. R. James, in which such glasses contain a fluid brewed from dead men's bones" (12). The reference is to "A View from a Hill", from *A Warning to the Curious* (1925). A still more recondite mention of another author occurs in *My Late Wives* (1946):

There is somewhere a very fine ghost-story that describes the mounting terror of a man who dreams, year after year, the same nightmare, and then finds it taking form in real life. It sings to the evil refrain of, *"Jack will show you to your room; I have given you the room in the tower."* A similar terror shook the heart of Dennis Foster as he dropped their two valises on the floor. (10)

The story under discussion is "The Room in the Tower" (from the 1912 collection of that title) by E. F. Benson, another great ghost-story writer. Dr. Fell speaks intelligently of the Gothic romance in *Hag's Nook* (1933 [8]); Ambrose Bierce is cited very significantly (as we shall see later) as the epigraph to Part II of *The Crooked Hinge* (1938); Herman Pennik in *The Reader Is Warned* (1939) makes one character think of the ghostly Peter Quint in *The Turn of the Screw* (10); and Arthur Machen is quoted at length in *Below Suspicion* (1949 [13]), no doubt because Carr had reviewed his *Tales of Horror and the Supernatural* (1948) in a 1948 issue of the *New York Times Book Review*.

We must now return to the question of the function of the quasi-supernatural (for, of course, aside from one stupendous instance, the actual supernatural never comes into play in a detective novel) both in Carr's work and in his thought. The fact that the supernatural is ultimately resolved into the natural in Carr's novels (a trait that accidentally links him with such Gothic writers as Ann Radcliffe and Charles Brockden Brown) may possibly indicate Carr's belief in the rational order of the universe; a few passages seem to suggest this. In *It Walks by Night* (1930) Bencolin remarks of the case in general (not of any specifically supernatural-seeming manifestation): "There must be sanity to the play somewhere; if there is no meaning in any of these incidents, there is no meaning in all the world" (4). In *The Lost Gallows* (1931) a character states at one point: "It's not a murder case; it's a nightmare" (9). In *The Case of the Constant Suicides* (1941) Kathryn Campbell expresses relief at discovering the non-supernatural explanation of the apparent suicides in the tower room:

"At least, we do know it isn't—supernatural. When we were thinking about snakes and spiders and ghosts and whatnots, I tell you I was frightened out of my wits. And all the while it was nothing but a lump of dry ice!" (17)

Probably the clearest instance is in *He Who Whispers* (1946), although this novel will itself serve as a counter-example to this interpretation of the supernatural. Professor Rigaud speaks heatedly to Miles Hammond:

> "I say to you," Professor Rigaud's little eye gleamed in a sort of logical frenzy, "I say to you: 'Here are certain facts; please to explain them.' Facts, facts, facts! You reply to me that you cannot explain them, but that I must not—must not, must not!—talk such superstitious nonsense, because the thing I suggest upsets your universe and makes you afraid. You may be right in saying so. You may be wrong in saying so. But it is I who am practical and you who are superstitious." (9)

It is also true that witchcraft and Satanism are frequently alluded to in Carr's novels, only to be explained away. Fell lectures on the subject in *The Crooked Hinge:*

> "I believe that's the explanation," he told her, still with his attention on the window. "It's been argued, and I think reasonably, that in a great number of cases the 'witch' never left her own house or even her own room. She thought she had attended the Sabbath in the grove. She thought she had been conveyed by magic to the defiled altar and found a demon lover there. She thought so because the two chief ingredients of the ointment were aconite and belladonna. Do you know anything about the effects of poisons like that, rubbed into the skin externally?"
>
> "My father had a *Medical Jurisprudence* here," said Madeline. "I was wondering—"
>
> "Belladonna, absorbed through the pores of the skin—and under the quicks of the nails—would rapidly produce excitement, then violent hallucinations and delirium, and finally unconsciousness. Add to this the symptoms produced by aconite: mental confusion, dizziness, impaired movement, irregular heart-action, and an end in unconsciousness. A mind steeped in descriptions of Satanist revels (there was a book dealing with them on the table by Victoria Daly's bed) would do the rest. Yes, that's it. I think we know now how she 'attended the Sabbath' on Lammas Eve." (17)

We have already noted the lame attempt in *Below Suspicion* to supply a sociological account of witchcraft.

But in my view the dispelling of the supernatural manifestation into a natural—or, more specifically, a human—agency serves another function in Carr's work: it underscores the pervasiveness of human evil. When Dr. Fell asks quietly in *The House at Satan's Elbow* (1965), "Don't you believe in human evil?" (13), he expects an affirmative response. In *Death-Watch* (1935) Fell speaks grimly: "There's a real evil spirit here, who hates that girl with a patient, deadly, brilliant guile" (18). But this "evil spirit" is not a supernatural entity but a human being intent on framing the girl for murder. A later passage seems to suggest that Fell himself believes in the supernatural:

"If chance can play such tricks like that, then chance is not only frightful, but frightening. It savours not only of something supernatural, but something supernatural managed by the powers of darkness." (22)

But the fact is, as Fell goes on to say, that the chance or coincidence referred to here was not a coincidence but a carefully staged "accident". Throughout his work Carr's characters express horror at the depths to which human beings can sink, explicitly comparing this to apparently supernatural phenomena. *Poison in Jest* (1932) contains the earliest and one of the clearest examples:

"No ghost, nothing, is so bad as thinking one of the people you eat dinner with could get up in the middle of the night and keep on horribly, night after night— scaring your father..." (5)

Fell in *The Crooked Hinge* remarks bitterly: "Satanism itself is an honest and straightforward business compared to the intellectual pleasures a certain person has invented" (13)

What tends to deflate the supernatural as a reasonable explanation of events is its implausible admixture with the obviously human. Fell says briefly in *The Sleeping Sphinx* (1947): "Supernatural forces, presumably, do not concern themselves with poison bottles" (13). This idea was expressed more elaborately in an earlier radio play, "The Black Minute" (1940; in *The Dead Sleep Lightly*):

DR. FELL: Let me make it clearer. Suppose you tell me that the ghost of Julius Caesar appeared to Brutus before the Battle of Philippi and warned him of approaching death. All I can say is that I know nothing about it. But suppose you tell me that the ghost of Julius Caesar walked into the cutlery department at Selfridge's, bought a stainless-steel knife, paid for it with spectral banknotes, and then stabbed Brutus in the middle of Oxford Street. All I shall beg leave to murmur, gently, is: rubbish. You cannot mix the two worlds like that. (*More sternly*) This was a human crime, planned by a human being.

Throughout Carr's work, real horror is inspired not by the supposedly supernatural trappings of the case but by the grisliness of the murders and the appalling depths of human hate and evil they imply. Of a victim gored by a curious spherical knife in *The Plague Court Murders* (1934): it is said: "Funny. It—it looks like bayonet practice" (6). One of the most hideous descriptions in all Carr is the discovery of the strangled body on a wet tennis court in *The Problem of the Wire Cage* (1939): "At the other side of the net, far away from him, he thought he saw something like old clothes lying in the middle of the court" (5). This is vaguely similar to a loathsome description in M. R. James' famous story, "The Treasure of Abbot Thomas":

"The hole went some little way back, and also on the right and left of the entrance, and I could see some rounded light-coloured objects within which might be bags."[4]

Those "bags" turn out to be a noxious entity protecting the treasure of Abbot Thomas. But again, the description in James applies to something supernatural, in Carr to something natural caused by a human agency.

Three novels display human evil at its very height (or nadir). In *Castle Skull* (1931) we learn that the great magician Maleger has been kept a prisoner for seventeen years in the cellar of Castle Skull. The sight of him when he is resurrected, still alive, is perhaps the single most revolting passage in Carr:

The thing those policemen supported between them was, I suppose, a man. They had tried to clean it somewhat, and give it respectability. It wore a baggy salt-and-pepper suit, many sizes too large. A celluloid collar, also too large, was twisted halfway round on its scrawny neck. And it wore very new and very large shoes of a horrible bright yellow, which squeaked loudly in the silence as it shuffled toward us.

The red hair, thickly streaked with grey, had been trimmed a little round the neck. Its face was all heavy, dusty folds, collapsing at the chin, and it was drawn shiny over the cheek-bones. Only the nose jutted out, but even this seemed to droop above the lower lip. The eyes were sunken so far in the head they always seemed wriggling to emerge, like hideous shiny bugs—but you could tell that there was little sight in them. It blinked and blinked. The policemen supported its stumbling footfalls; its blind turns to the right and left, and the shaking palsy of its shoulders. . . .

The yellow shoes squeaked loudly across the luxurious carpet. The man was mumbling, turning his fallen jaw and his bleary eyes alternately at each policeman. Maleger the unconquerable. Maleger, the fallen Lord of Light. . . . (17)

Von Arnheim describes the captivity:

"He could keep Maleger chained like a dog to the wall. He could shut him into a windowless cell, lost and airless; give him dry bread and filthy straw; crush his body and darken his sight. But he could not banish the laughter, or trample down the defiance, which were as the laughter and defiance of the fallen Lord of Light. He could not, for the briefest instant, triumph over that titanic mirth.

"It is night. Lanterns move up the damp tower stairs and make cartwheels of light in a blue devilish gloom. The sliding panel in the door is partly open, for no cries can be heard beyond the thick walls there. Bauer, the watchman, leans against the wall and chuckles. Alison bends close to the sliding panel. A newspaper crackles, and his white lips move in the lantern-light. '. . .thrilled us with the power and passion of his portrayal. . .spellbound. . .surely one of the great actors of all time. . . .' Then, from within, first a rustle of straw, a clanking of fetters, a foul odor. And presently, struggling, the boom of laughter. 'Oh, go to hell,' whispers Maleger, 'you cheap barnstormer.' " (17)

Poison in Jest appears to involve a marble hand endowed with supernatural powers; but when the murderer is finally revealed to be the aged and half-insane Mrs. Quayle, our sense of horror is only augmented as Rossiter describes her increasingly frenzied actions as she tries to murder her husband:

"She was stark mad now, of course. She didn't care what happened. Her attempt at secrecy was all gone; she was opening the throttle wide and tearing straight for destruction. Before that, she had tried to shield herself with what she thought was great cunning, but why bother now? She got back to her room somehow, though she almost ran into the judge coming up the cellar stairs. The commotion roused the household, including the nurse. I rather fancy there was blood on her, too, and she hid it under the bedclothes. When she made her attempt on the judge, she just went into the bath between the two communicating rooms; locked one door, and went out the other. The nurse didn't see her slip downstairs. She must have drawn a wrapper over the blood on her nightgown...." ("Epilogue")

Finally, in *He Who Whispers* (1946) Gideon Fell describes one of the most sadistic murders ever to grace the pages of detective fiction:

"You creep up in the middle of the night. You gag your victim, before she can cry out, with some soft material that will leave no traces afterwards. You hold to her temple the cold muzzle of a pistol, an empty pistol. And for minutes, dragging terrible minutes in the small hours of the night, you whisper to her.

"You are going to kill her, you explain. Your whispering voice goes on, telling her all about it. She does not see a second pistol loaded with real bullets.

"At the proper time (so runs your own plan) you will fire a bullet close to her head, but not so close that the expansion of gases will leave powder-marks on her. You will then put the revolver into her own hand. After her death it will be believed that *she* fired at some imaginary burglar or intruder or ghost, and that no other person was there at all.

"So you keep on whispering, multiplying terrors in the dark. The time, you explain, is at hand now. Very slowly you squeeze the trigger of the empty gun, to draw back the hammer. She hears the oily noise of the hammer moving back...slowly, very slowly...the hammer creaking farther...the hammer at its peak before it strikes, and then..."

Whack!

Dr. Fell brought his hand down sharply on the table. It was only that, the noise of a hand striking wood; and yet all three of his listeners jumped as though they had seen the flash and heard the shot. (20)

Of course, the murderer does not actually shoot his victim; the victim is instead found dead of heart failure. Throughout the novel there has been talk of vampires and the occult, but before his explanation Fell dismisses all this with a contemptuous: "But what's occult about this?" (20). Once again a human agency is found to surpass any horrors inspired by the supernatural. As a result the quasi-supernatural in Carr is designed to emphasise not so much a metaphysical position (the rationality of the universe) as an ethical one (the persistence of human evil).

Two novels employ not the quasi-supernatural but quasi-science fiction. *The Crooked Hinge* features an automaton whose mechanism no one can seem to fathom. It is in this context that Carr's citation of Ambrose Bierce gains significance: at the beginning of Part II Bierce's tale "Moxon's Master" is quoted; this tale deals with an automaton that ultimately develops human emotions, and is regarded as an important forerunner of modern science fiction tales of this type. Of course, Carr's automaton is in the end explained without recourse to futuristic science; indeed, the solution is rather similar to Poe's article "Maelzel's Chess-Player". But the atmosphere of eeriness is enhanced by the presence of this ominous automaton lurking in the background; and at one point it comes close to ending Fell's career:

> And that was when the automaton moved.
> To this day Page swears that nobody pushed it. This may or may not be true....What they did see was the rotted dummy jerking forward with the stealthy suddenness of a motor-car slipping its brakes. What they did see was three-hundredweight of rattling iron darting out of reach and driving like a gun-carriage for the well of the stairs. What they heard was the screech of the wheels, the tap of Dr. Fell's stick on the stairs, and Elliot's scream:
> *"For God's sake, look out below!"*
> Then the crash as it went over.
> Page reached it. He had his fingers round the iron box, and he might just as well have tried to stop a runaway gun; but he kept it upright when it might have gone head-over-heels-side-to-side, sweeping the whole staircase in crazy descent and crushing everything in its way. The black weight kept to its wheels. Sprawling down the first steps, Page saw Dr. Fell peering upwards—half-way down. He saw the daylight from the open door at the foot of the stairs. He saw Dr. Fell, unable to move an inch in that enclosed space, throw up one hand as though to ward off a blow. He saw, out of an inferno of crashing, the black shape plunge past within a hair's clearance. (13)

Fell is, however, unhurt, and later it is ascertained that he was not even the target of the attack; but it is one of the most acutely frightening moments in all Carr's work.

   The Reader Is Warned comes closer to genuine science fiction. Pennik's apparent power of killing with thought is labelled "Teleforce" by the popular press; but Pennik is careful to specify the nature of his gift: "I certainly don't lay claim to supernatural powers" (7). This is correct because "Teleforce"—granting for the moment its reality—would not be a *contravention* of known natural law (as with ghosts or vampires) but an *extension* of it. So little is still known about the powers of the mind that someday the reality of "Teleforce" might conceivably be established by science. And yet, as in the best science fiction, this new power also inspires horror: "For some reason," Pennik notes with smug arrogance, "they [the guests] seem—all except the doctor here—to regard me with a kind of superstitious terror" (7). (Parenthetically, it is worth pausing to study the somewhat curious phrase "superstitious terror" or its variants, which Carr appears to use to designate a terror at the suspicion of the supernatural. The phrase is employed frequently, as in a passage in *The Man Who Could Not ̄Shudder* [6] when a character sees a gun literally jump from a wall, appear to hang in midair, and shoot its victim.) Pennik's claims, of course, are punctured at the end, and Merrivale gives a somewhat unfortunate lecture on the matter:

120   John Dickson Carr: A Critical Study

"And the next time alarmists go scurryin' from house to house, the next time they tell you about a super-bomb that'll drop from an enemy airplane and wipe out a whole county, the next time they picture London as one cloud of poison-gas from Hampstead to Lambeth, then you look at your back-garden and softly murmur, 'Teleforce' and be comforted." (20)

Six years later the atom bomb would be dropped.

It is worth examining how Carr lays the horrific groundwork in some of his more shuddersome detective stories. One of the most potent moments actually comes in the radio play "The Dead Sleep Lightly" (1943), where a man appears to speak in the telephone to his long-dead sweetheart:

VOICE: Yes? Who is it?
PENDLETON (*wildly*): There's been some mist...
VOICE (*with sudden eagerness*): George dear, is that you?
PENDLETON (*Alarmed*): Who is that? Who's speaking?
VOICE: It's Mary Ellen, dear. Don't you recognize my voice?
PENDLETON: No! No! No!
VOICE: I knew you'd call me sooner or later, dear. But I've waited *ever* so long.
PENDLETON: I...
VOICE (*eagerly*): And of course I'll come if you want me. I'll be there just as soon as I can.
PENDLETON: I tell you—!
VOICE: I'll be there by seven o'clock, truly I will. But you mustn't be frightened at how I look now.
PENDLETON: You're not Mary Ellen! This is a trick! *Mary Ellen is dead!*
VOICE: Yes, dear. But the dead sleep lightly. And they can be lonely too.
PENDLETON: Don't talk to me! You can't talk to me! I won't listen to you! I...
VOICE: I'll wear a veil, dear. Because I'm not very pretty now. But I won't hurt you, my darling. Truly I won't!

(The Dead Sleep Lightly)

This theme of the ghostly lover is the subject of several famous tales of supernatural horror, notably Oliver Onions' "The Beckoning Fair One" and Robert Hichens' "How Love Came to Professor Guildea". And although in Carr this conversation is ultimately explained away rather laboriously as a hocussing of the telephone, the sensation is real while it lasts.

Hag's Nook (1933) is perhaps the work where Carr prepared the most systematically weird backdrop for what eventually is a pure detective story. The first five chapters contain masterful strokes of horrific atmosphere. The Hag's Nook itself is, as Fell offhandedly informs Tad Rampole, "where they used to hang witches" (2). A prison was constructed in this unwholesome spot, and our first view of it is unnerving:

"There's the prison," said Dr. Fell.
...the American was staring at the promontory to the right. Incongruous in this place, crude and powerful as Stonehenge, the stone walls of Chatterham prison humped against the sky.

They were large enough, though they seemed much bigger in the distortion of moonlight. And "humped," Rampole thought, was the word; there was one place where they seemed to surge and buckle over the crest of a hill. Through rents in the masonry vines were crooking fingers against the moon. A teeth of spikes ran along the top, and you could see tumbled chimneys. The place *looked* damp and slime-painted, from occupation by lizards; it was as though the marshes had crept inside and turned stagnant. (2)

Chapter two ends on a somewhat hysterical and artificial note, but by now the atmosphere has got hold of us:

These old woman's tales might have influenced his outlook. But, just for a moment, he could have sworn that he had seen something looking over the wall of Chatterham prison. And he had a horrible impression that the something was *wet....*

Much attention is devoted to the history of the prison, which had been run by the Starberth family for much of its duration. Anthony Starberth, governor of the prison from 1797 to 1820, is portrayed as an embittered and slightly crazed individual, and when Rampole reads excerpts from his diary, there is further cause for unease:

They call me a "limping Herrick," do they? [he writes in 1812]. A "Dryden in falsetto." But I begin to think of a plan. I do heartily abhor and curse each of those to which I have the misfortune to be bound by ties of blood. There are things one can buy and things one can do to defeat them. *By which I am reminded that the rats are growing thicker lately.* They come into my room, and I can see them beyond the circle of my lamp as I write. (5)

All this horror may be laid on a trifle thick, but it is sufficiently interspersed with lighter moments (the vignette of Mrs. Fell, the budding romance of Rampole and Dorothy Starberth) that the atmosphere does not remain uniformly oppressive. Although many other detective writers have been attracted to the supernatural, I know of none who can handle it with such flair and vividness as Carr.

And now we come to *The Burning Court* (1937). It is almost a shame that I have to let the cat out of the bag and declare that this straightforward-seeming, "fair play" detective novel pulls the rug out from under our feet at the end and becomes a supernatural novel; for the experience of stumbling upon the "Epilogue"—after the murder has apparently been satisfactorily explained—where Marie Stevens is seen to be a two-hundred-year-old witch and actually responsible for the crimes is one of the most jarring moments in literature. I do not wish by any means to imply that this sudden reversal is artificial or contrived; indeed, in a sense it is Carr's most rigorous use of the "fair play" convention.

I wish now to return to Dr. Fell's lecture on ghost stories in *The Three Coffins*. There he says:

"The ghost should be malignant. It should never speak. It should never be transparent, but solid. It should never hold the stage for long, but appear in brief vivid flashes like the poking of a face round a corner. It should never appear in too much light. It should have an old, an academic or ecclesiastical background; a flavour of cloisters or Latin manuscripts. There is an unfortunate tendency nowadays to sneer at old libraries or ancient ruins; to say that the really horrible phantom would appear in a confectioner's shop or at a lemonade stand. This is what they call applying the 'modern test.' Very well; apply the test of real life. Now, people in real life honestly *have* been frightened out of their five wits in old ruins or churchyards. Nobody would deny that. But, until somebody in actual life really does scream out and faint at the sight of something at a lemonade stand (other, of course, than that beverage itself), then there is nothing to be said for this theory except that it is rubbish." (12)

What is interesting about this is that, when Carr came to write his lone full-length excursion into the genuinely supernatural a scant two years later, he abandoned the Gothicism of *Hag's Nook* and its congeners and set the tale precisely in the modern age so despised by Fell. *The Burning Court* takes place in 1929 in Pennsylvania, and at one point a character speculates on terror in the modern world:

"Suppose the powers of hell really could lay hold, suppose they could run on our smooth rails and get into our steam-heated lives past such a shower of banalities as Ingelford's Soothing Hour...then I tell you the powers of hell must be strong and terrible. We huddle together in cities, we make bonfires of a million lights, we can get a voice from across the ocean to sing to us so that we needn't feel lonely; it's a sort of charmed circle, with no heaths to walk at night in the wind. But suppose you, Ted, in your apartment in New York; or you, Part, in your flat in London; or John Smith in his house anywhere in the world—suppose you went home at night, and opened the ordinary door, and heard another kind of voice. Suppose you didn't want to look behind the umbrella-stand, or go down to attend to the furnace at night, because you might see something climbing up?" (7)

Fell is talking through his hat: Carr knew that a true supernatural tale, if it is not to be a mere excursion into playful nostalgia, cannot be a wooden imitation of the Gothic novels but must be set in our own day and be written in a vigorous modern idiom. What Carr is really doing in *The Burning Court* is playing tricks with genre: by this time he already had a reputation for writing "fair play" detective stories, where the supernatural atmosphere was used merely for colour. And as we read this novel also, we expect the accusations against the attractive Marie Stevens as a witch to fall by the wayside at the end—as, in fact, they seem to do when Lieutenant Brennan constructs an apparently sound and satisfying case against the nurse of old Miles Despard. But certain features remain naggingly disturbing. For one thing, the seemingly guilty party protests her innocence to the end, something that rarely happens in detective fiction:

"I didn't kill him. I did not. I never thought of it. I didn't want any money. All I wanted was Mark. He didn't run away because he did anything like that. He ran away because of that—that's his wife. You can't prove I killed the old man. You can't find the body, and you can't prove it. I don't care what you do to me. You can beat me till I die, but you won't get anything out of me. You know that. I can stand pain like an Indian. You'll never—"

She broke off, choking. She added, with sudden rather terrifying misery: "Doesn't anybody believe me?" (21)

And if Dr. Fell had been on the scene, he may have noticed certain "small details"—in particular, as regards Marie's actions—that are never properly explained. How, for example, did she know that, when Miles Despard's coffin in his sealed mausoleum is opened so that an autopsy can be performed, his body would be missing?

The "Epilogue" is a masterpiece of subtlety. Carr does not have Marie blurt out, "I am a witch", but records her thoughts obliquely so that the truth gradually and appallingly dawns on us:

It is well that I am beginning to remember. At first I could remember her only faintly, as I see my reflection in this glass now. Once, when the smoke lifted in the Mass at Guibourg, I thought I remembered—an eye there, a tip of the nose there, or ribs with a knife through them. I wonder, now, when I shall see Gaudin again. His was a crooked reflection; perhaps the headgear was different, but I knew him at once. At least I knew quite clearly that I must go to him for help. It is true that, this time, I was in no danger from their lawyers. But I did not want my husband to guess, not yet. I love him, I love him; he will be one of us presently, if I can transform him without pain. Or too much pain.

Her husband Ted, knowing nothing of this, has been desperately—and entirely sincerely—pleading her innocence and warding her off from suspicion; and the poignant thing is that she really cares for him. "I love him, I love him."

I do not know what metaphysical conclusions we are to draw from this work—probably none. Carr does not believe in witches. If anything the novel gives startling life to the hackneyed detective axiom, "Eliminate the impossible and whatever is left, however improbable, must be true." The fact is that *all* aspects of the case cannot be explained except by recourse to the supernatural; in this sense *The Burning Court* could be seen as a still greater triumph of logical reasoning than his other novels. It is even said at one point: "If you're talking of pure actual *evidence*, there's more evidence to show this thing was supernatural than it was natural" (8). Douglas G. Greene, remarking on what I believe is a mistaken view that Carr's ordinary detective tales "confirm the orderliness, rationality and fundamental justice of the universe",[5] goes on to say that *The Burning Court* appears not to fit this paradigm; but in fact precisely the reverse could be said. This novel expands the realm of logic to include the supernatural.

Whatever our final conclusions are about this enigmatic and disturbing novel, we can scarcely deny it a very high—perhaps the highest—place in Carr's *oeuvre*. In its quiet intensity, lack of histrionics, careful characterisation, vast ingenuity in producing a plausible natural explanation of the phenomena, and stunning climax, it is perhaps Carr's greatest novel. It is greater *as a novel* than something like *The Arabian Nights Murder* because of the philosophical ramifications it involves and its fundamental seriousness of intent. Over and above even the historical mysteries, *The Burning Court* is Carr's one true *tour de force*.

The supernatural (or quasi-supernatural) functions, in Carr's novels, as a sort of analogue to the locked room; it is really a variation of the "impossible" crime—i.e., the crime that is shown ultimately not to be impossible. A haunted tower room is reduced to dry ice; killing with thought is shown to be a myth and a hoax; a gun leaping from a wall and firing of its own accord is proved to be a feat of electrical trickery. In all this the prevailing metaphor used by Carr is *sleight-of-hand*. References to magic and sleight-of-hand appear with great frequency in his work; Part I of *The Crooked Hinge* cites a Professor Hoffmann's treatise on *Modern Magic*:

The first rule to be borne in mind by the aspirant is this: Never tell your audience beforehand what you are going to do. If you do so, you at once give their vigilance the direction which it is most necessary to avoid, and increase tenfold the chances of detection.

Both the supernatural and the "impossible" crime are products of sleight-of-hand in Carr: more than mere atmosphere, they function as devices to *distract* the reader's attention from the usually simple human means at work in the crime. And what we are left with when both the supernatural and the "impossible" crime are dispensed with is the brute facts of human greed, selfishness, cruelty, and evil. If this is Carr's ultimate philosophical message, it is a suitably grim one; even in the supernatural *Burning Court* we overhear a character say with crude honesty, "I ain't a-skeered of any dead people, and don't you be a-skeered of any dead people, either. It's these *livin'* sons-of-bitches you want to watch out for" (7).

Style and Characterisation

In a celebrated review of *The Mad Hatter Mystery* that did much to launch Carr's career, Dorothy L. Sayers wrote:

Mr. Carr can lead us away from the small, artificial, brightly-lit stage of the ordinary detective plot into the menace of outer darkness. He can create atmosphere with an adjective, make a picture from a wet iron railing, a dusty table, a gas-lamp blurred by the fog. He can alarm with an illusion or delight with a rollicking absurdity. He can invent a passage from a lost work of Edgar Allan Poe which sounds like the real thing. In short, he can write—not merely in the negative sense of observing the rules of syntax, but in the sense that every sentence gives a thrill of positive pleasure.[1]

Pretty as this sounds, it is largely exaggeration. The fact is that Carr is not distinguished purely as a prose stylist. Perhaps Sayers was simply astonished that a detective writer could write with energy, enthusiasm, and grammatical purity; Sayers' own style, her supporters' contentions notwithstanding, is not of especial interest either, and falls far short of her two disparate models, P. G. Wodehouse and Evelyn Waugh. If Carr also looked to Wodehouse in part, it was not so much in actual prose rhythm as in a tone and atmosphere of pure-hearted hilarity. It would also be a mistake to regard G. K. Chesterton as a model for Carr in prose: granted that Carr took much from him in the construction of paradoxical situations, nothing could be further from the calculatedly uncontrolled nature of Carr's early work than the stately, mincing, and whimsically philosophical tone of the Father Brown stories.

Carr can be studied as a prose stylist, but the subject is perhaps not as rewarding as one might imagine. If Carr's prose is generally grammatical (his only persistent mistake is to regard "gingerly" and "leisurely" as adverbs), this is a mere negative virtue. Moreover, the substance of Carr's style cannot be exhibited in small sections but cumulatively over the course of an entire work, the longer the better; this is why he is so much better a novelist than a short story writer. Carr's true virtues as a prose stylist are an unrelenting vigour that matches the bizarrerie of his plots (here he has made a genuine advance upon Chesterton) and, as Sayers rightly noted, an ability to change the atmosphere with startling suddenness. Both these qualities are somewhat difficult to display by analysis or even quotation, but we shall offer a few notes and suggestions.

Very early in his career Carr wrote an interesting description of a play written by a character in *It Walks by Night;* in many ways it could serve as a perfectly encapsulated account of Carr's own early style:

I do not know whether it was a good play; calmly considered, no doubt, the thing was clap-trap in the extreme. The characters spoke in a dialogue like nothing of heaven or earth, but behind it was an imperially purple imagination, the "tiger's blood and honey" of Barbey D'Aurevilly, and a kind of grotesque smiling detachment, like a gargoyle on a tower. (13)

The key words here are "calmly considered": Carr, throughout his career but especially in his early novels, aims at achieving so breathless a narrative pace that the reader is not given time to reflect either on the plausibility of the incidents or the frenetically overheated manner of their narration. The reference to "an imperially purple imagination" is very likely a nod to a work now almost totally forgotten but very famous in Carr's day, Edgar Saltus' *Imperial Purple* (1892), a series of cynical prose-poems on the Roman emperors. Carr grew up with the generation that was succeeding the *fin-de-siècle* Symbolists and Decadents in France; and when in the late twenties Carr stayed in Paris, it is likely that he absorbed the work of Jules Barbey D'Aurevilly, J. K. Huysmans, and other wielders of poetic prose. In the English-speaking world, Oscar Wilde was coming posthumously to be regarded as a master of chiselled prose, and James Branch Cabell was at the height of his renown; and in that field of supernatural fiction that Carr read so faithfully throughout his life, the richly textured prose of Arthur Machen, Lord Dunsany, and M. P. Shiel was held in high esteem. As a literary as well as political conservative, Carr was most attracted to this school, and not the plodding realism of Dreiser, Cather, or Hemingway or the modernism of Eliot and Joyce. The Bencolin and even the early Fell novels are experiments in purple prose, and very frequently they are successful.

But early on Carr began to harness his style, weeding out some of the more extreme overcolouring but still retaining the breathless pace that would compel the reader's attention. The principal way in which Carr exercised his faculties in prose was landscape description. Such description tends to wane in the novels of his middle period, only to revive in the historical mysteries, but in the early work Carr paints his landscapes with unfailing vividness, whether it be Paris, England, Pennsylvania, or elsewhere. There is scarcely a work, short or long, in a setting not known to Carr from personal observation. We have already quoted one such passage from *The Corpse in the Waxworks* (1932); another passage from the same work exhibits a rather engaging mannerism that might be called the "generic 'you' ":

Vast spaces are hidden from Paris. The gardens of the Faubourg St.-Germain come with the suddenness of an illusion when these tall old walls open their gates. You would swear that the avenues of trees stretch away for miles, that pools are enchanted and flower-beds spectral, and that no such spacious countryside can exist in the very center of Paris traffic. Here are stone houses, gabled and turreted, on phantom estates. In summer, when all the flower hues flame against green, and the trees sparkle with sunlight, these houses still seem proud and forlorn and ghostly. But in autumn their gables against a grey-white sky make you feel you have strayed into a countryside which is a thousand leagues from Paris or reality, and which exists only in time. A light in a window startles you. On these gravel walks at twilight you might meet an unlighted coach, with footmen and four white horses, and you would realize, in the wind and thunder of its passing, that the passengers had been dead two hundred years. (9)

The effect of the "you" is a sort of pseudo-colloquialism that breaks down a barier between narrator and reader that might arise from too high-flown or stately a description; the narrator is made to sound like an ordinary guy, although few guys could create a tableau so evocative and poignant. This passage is already less overcoloured than most in *It Walks by Night*, although even here we find such attributes of poetic prose as metaphor ("flower hues flame"), polysyndeton ("proud and forlorn and ghostly") and piquant zeugma ("Paris or reality"). Carr would prune away this sort of thing more and more with the passage of time; in a sense that is an improvement— perhaps Carr was increasingly sensitive to charges of overwriting—but we lose much in atmosphere and the pure sensual thrill of fine writing.

Lest it be thought that only Paris received flowery description in Carr, let us quote his description of Cagliostro Street in London in *The Three Coffins* (1935):

This eerie feeling of streets in hiding, or whole rows of houses created by illusory magic to trick you, had never deserted Rampole in his prowlings through London. It was like wondering whether, if you walked out your own front door, you might not find the whole street mysteriously changed overnight, and strange faces grinning out of houses you had never seen before. He stood with Hadley and Dr. Fell at the entrance, staring down. The overflow of shops stretched only a little way on either side. They were all shuttered, or had their windows covered with a folding steel fretwork, with an air of defying customers as a fort would defy attackers. Even the gilt signs had an air of defiance. The windows were at all stages of cleanliness, from the bright gloss of a jeweller's farthest down on the right, to the grey murkiness of a tobacconist's nearest on the right: a tobacconist's that seemed to have dried up worse than ancient tobacco, shrunk together, and hidden itself behind news placards headlining news you never remembered having heard of. Beyond there were two rows of flat three-story houses in dark red brick, with window-frames in white or yellow, and drawn curtains of which a few (on the ground floor) showed a sportive bit of lace. They had darkened to the same hue with soot; they looked like one house except where iron railings went to the front doors from the lone line of area rails; they sprouted with hopeful signs announcing furnished rooms. Over them the chimney-pots stood up dark against a heavy grey sky. The snow had melted to patches of grey slush, despite a sharp wind that was swooping through the entrance and chasing a discarded newspaper with flaps and rustlings round a lamp-post. (13)

This description starts out flowery, but ends in a fairly neutral manner; indeed, in subsequent novels Carr rarely included descriptions of this length at all. As a result, Carr's settings do not become impressed in the reader's mind in set passages like the above (this is essentially short story technique) but gradually over the course of the entire work. And yet, the settings are no less crisply or powerfully realised for all that.

In the historical mysteries Carr can once again lavish attention to the physical setting, since in many instances the topography has changed radically in two or three hundred years. (This is, curiously, also the case in a small way with *The Mad Hatter Mystery*, in that the Tower of London is no longer quite as Carr described it in 1933; in particular, the Crown Jewels are no longer in Wakefield Tower but have now been transferred a considerable distance away to the Waterloo Barracks.) Carr's reproduction of seventeenth-, eighteenth-, and nineteenth-century idioms in speech and writing is not only academically flawless but entirely lacking in self-consciousness or pomposity: Carr did much study in the idiomatic and colloquial speech of these periods, to the point that he must occasionally supply footnotes elucidating archaic slang terms.

Even the pure detective novels include a lacing of the archaic from time to time. We have noted the transcription of a diary written in the early nineteenth century in *Hag's Nook* (1933); in *The Plague Court Murders* (1934) we find reproduced a long letter purporting to date from 1710, and Carr captures the diction perfectly:

> If it had pleased GOD to avert this misfortune which is upon your Lordship, and indeed on all of us, I should never have been constrained to speak. For indeed I thought it was but a passing calamity, but now I know it was not; and it is a sore task which is laid upon me now, since GOD knows I feel the weight of my guilt. I must tell your Lordship more than you have asked, and of events during my father's stewardship during the Great Plague; but of that I shall speak hereinafter. (5)

What Carr has avoided here is *excessive archaism:* he knows well that the language of the eighteenth century is not entirely different from that of our own age. He therefore avoids the censure of H. P. Lovecraft, who remarked about certain pulp writers attempting to duplicate archaic language:

> ...what sort of insanity gets hold of some of these birds (W. H. Hodgson is the classic and memorable offender, and Seabury Quinn has likewise pulled some choice boners in this line) when they try to represent the diction of an age which after all is, historically speaking, essentially modern? Haven't they ever read Goldsmith and Fielding and Johnson and Gibbon and Sterne and Smollett and dozens of other prose writers of that fairly recent yesterday? What...causes them to drag down from the remoter reaches of antiquity a cobwebbed jargon more Chaucerian or Elizabethan than anything else, and serve it up as contemporary with Burke's speeches and the seditious Declaration of Independence?[2]

Carr never makes a mistake of this kind: he has read Goldsmith and Fielding and Johnson and the rest, and his language is entirely appropriate to its context. In *The Plague Court Murders* the eighteenth-century document adds a touch of hoary antiquity and brings in suggestions of the supernatural (can there be a centuries-old curse on the house in question?). This, added to the verbatim transcripts of witnesses' testimony, gives the novel a textural variety not often found in Carr's work.

We have already touched upon certain points of narrative style. The overwhelming predominance of a protagonist who functions as narrator and as the reader's eyes is to be remarked; even in later works this figure remains young, vigorous, and male. In the solitary instance of *Behind the Crimson Blind* (1952) we have a female protagonist; typically, she is treated with condescension by almost everyone, including Merrivale. Whether the protagonist is always supposed to be autobiographical—whether, in other words, he always embodies Carr's views and outlook—is a moot point: I suspect he is, but the question does not strike me as being of any especial importance as far as critical analysis is concerned. It is a question best left to Carr's biographer.

It is curious how unwilling Carr is to allow events to be seen from any other perspective but that of the protagonist. The result, as we have noted frequently, is that this figure must tag along somewhat uselessly with the investigators so that he can report all the developments in the case; it also means that he must be present at any important occurrence, whether with the detectives or with other characters. In the early novels the protagonist participates with great energy in the case; Jeff Marle is the prototypical example. Marle, indeed, is perhaps the most effective protagonist Carr ever created, as his perfect ingenuousness (just on this side of *naïveté*) is the perfect foil to the misanthropic and sardonic cynicism of Bencolin. Ken Blake is a scarcely less active figure, but his contrast to Merrivale is not nearly as pronounced.

Hag's Nook offers a very early example of the temporary interruption of the protagonist's narration. Here the entirety of chapter fifteen is devoted to following the actions of the butler Budge as he returns home from a night with friends; and although the whole chapter seems to poke somewhat malicious fun at Budge's bourgeois conventionality, the change in perspective is refreshing.

The Problem of the Wire Cage (1939) introduces another slight variant. Here, for the first time, the reader is given certain facts not known to the investigators. Shortly after they discover the body, Hugh Rowland and Brenda White concoct a lie that momentarily wards off suspicion from them; but not only do Fell and Hadley suspect a lie, but as a result of it an apparently innocent man, Arthur Chandler, is accused of the crime, and the lie is detected.

Narrative structure in Carr is an enormously complicated issue, as it is the principal distinguishing feature of Carr's work. It is not merely that he conceived incredibly elaborate plots, but that he unfolded them in so convoluted a fashion that we are occasionally distracted from the events of the tale to marvel instead at the author's structural virtuosity. *The Blind Barber* (1934) contains, at almost its exact centre, an "Interlude" titled "Observations of Dr. Fell": the narrative is interrupted, as Fell discusses

the case with the protagonist, who has come to consult him on it. Fell
then supplies "eight clues...eight suggestions, if you will", as follows:

The Clue of Suggestion.
The Clue of Opportunity.
The Clue of Fraternal Trust.
The Clue of Seven Razors.
The Clue of Seven Radiograms.
The Clue of Elimination.
The Clue of Terse Style.

It is the pinnacle of Fell's mystification. Of course, at the end Fell deals
with each of these clues point by point. *The Arabian Nights Murder* (1936)
is perhaps the single most complicated work in detective fiction, and at
its very opening Sir Herbert Armstrong remarks: "This damned case is a
kind of chrysalis, which opens layer by layer, with a successive explanation
on each layer, and under it the word 'Stung' " ("Prologue"). This is really
a description of the narrative structure; but more than mere elaborateness,
the greatness of this work stems from the fact that, as each successive layer
is uncovered, the tone becomes grimmer and grimmer as we finally come
face to face with the reality of murder. At the end all the hilarity of the
novel is a dim memory.

One mannerism of Carr's narrative structure that is immediately obvious
to any reader is the way in which each chapter of a work ends on a dramatic
revelation. Carr has to be careful not to make any of these revelations supersede
or overshadow the final revelation of the murderer (or, in some cases, the
method of murder, which frequently is the real culmination of the work),
and in general he succeeds in so doing. But he then leaves himself open
to the opposite charge of creating false or hollow climaxes. A typical example
can be culled from so early a work as *The Lost Gallows* (1931); here is
the conclusion to chapter three:

The long room was lighted only by the yellow firelight, which threw a broad
unsteady glare on the carvings of the farther wall. A shadow loomed up sharp and
gigantic and thin across this wall. It was the shadow of a gallows.
From the cross-beam dangled the figure of a man, swaying wry-necked on a
rope.

But at the very beginning of the next chapter Bencolin remarks airily, "No
need for alarm. It's only the toy gallows." To Carr's credit, even this climax
is not entirely false, as it has some bearing on the conclusion; but repeated
doses of these miniature climaxes can become wearisome. Many of these
climaxes consist of Carr's characters making some highly theatrical utterance,
or entering the scene precisely as they are being discussed by other characters.
I cannot make up my mind whether Carr's characters are histrionic in order
to supply climaxes or whether the climaxes were conceived in order to make

the characters histrionic; the sequence of cause and effect is not entirely clear, and perhaps does not matter.

The real secret to Carr's narrative structure—and, accordingly, to his intense readability—is his ability to explain parts of the puzzle throughout the course of the work, so that as the end approaches only the problem of who (or, more frequently and pertinently, how) remains to be answered. If Carr had saved the solution of the entire puzzle to the end, it is quite possible that nearly half the book would be devoted to the elucidation; as it is, even so sympathetic a reader as Dorothy L. Sayers, in her review of *The Mad Hatter Mystery*,[3] felt that that novel was marred by "a good deal of long-winded explanation at the end", something "that is a drawback to all plots of this type". In all respect to Sayers, even this mild criticism is, I think, not justified in the best of Carr's work: although he rarely departs from the formula of gathering all (or at least some) of the principals in the case and allowing the detective to explain the matter in lecture-room style, this section is customarily written with liveliness and flair; in any case, we are by this time so consumed with interest that we will put up with much to learn the truth.

We must, admittedly, give Carr great credit for this elaborate structure: I can think of no works in all detective fiction (or, indeed, in literature as a whole) that produce an analogous effect, or that dovetail so nicely at the end. I have no doubt that Carr spent much time working out the structure of his novels; Robert Lewis Taylor in fact supplies some hints as to Carr's working methods:

First, in the preparation of a new book, he draws up what he calls a "clue outline," marking points in the narrative at which he plans to plant the signposts to the guilt of whichever fiend he is building. Then, with elaborate pains, he makes working sketches of the characters, sometimes promoting minor players to star roles, and the reverse, as he goes, depending on how they respond to the call to creation. He jots down snatches of dialogue as he visualizes the characters and hears their speech in his mind. Plotting is easy for Carr—he habitually sees the entire network of human relations as a slough of intrigue—and the blocking out of the separate scenes is perhaps his favorite chore. He hates the actual writing, however, and does it in anguish, emerging from each long session hollow-eyed and spent. As one of his detective-writer friends has remarked, "This is a hell of a tough rap for a man who has to write four books a year to stay happy."[4]

All this may be literary skill of the second order—ingenuity, not genius—but, if so, it is ingenuity that Carr in his best work raised very close to real genius.

The issue of Carr's characterisation can be dealt with very simply: he could not draw character at all. There are exceptions—Fell (not Merrivale) lives as a true character, Hadley a little less so, and individuals like Judge Horace Ireton in *Death Turns the Tables* (1941)—but on the whole Carr's characters are stereotyped and mechanical. An unintentionally hilarious passage in *Dark of the Moon* (1967) gets to the heart of Carr's problem in this regard: "Sometimes I think everybody in this house needs a tranquillizer" (5). No truer word was ever said about Carr's characters as a whole.

Carr's female characters are a particularly sorry lot; there are few writers in all literature who treated their women with such studied and systematic condescension. Incredibly, Carr was actually proud of his characterisation of women. Robert Lewis Taylor waxes eloquent on the subject:

> Carr's women represent an important contribution to mystery literature. "I can't stand these anemic, dimensionless, overcivilized heroines," he says. "Women ought to be healthy and ripe." Perhaps because of his long residence abroad, he has a more candid attitude toward sex than most American mystery writers. Carr's women love life; their sweaters are full, their blood warm.

Well, this much is true, in any case. The fact is, however, that Carr cannot help regarding all women as overgrown children. In his work they cry with great frequency or else take to squealing *"Eeee!"* or *"Ooooh!"* Some characters—like Sheila Bitton in *The Mad Hatter Mystery* and Peggy Glenn in *The Blind Barber*—are made to appear entirely empty-headed; very few men are treated in this fashion.

Carr's young women are never *beautiful*—this would make them too unapproachable—but always wholesomely pretty. To be sure, they may be "healthy and ripe", and even feisty and quarrelsome, but always in a "cute" and unthreatening way; and in the end they always give in to their men. I want to quote several descriptions of women in Carr's work to show how pervasive and unchanging is this attitude:

Though she was not pretty in any conventional sense, health and vigor made her seem so. (*The Peacock Feather Murders* [1937 (6)])

Without being a striking beauty, Monica was nevertheless one of those pretty, hearty, fresh-complexioned girls who radiate innocence. (*And So to Murder* [1940 (1)])

In her late twenties, tall and well-shaped, Caroline was very attractive without being in the least pretty. Her brown eyes were straightforward, her fair hair naturally curly. If sometimes she appeared stolid in contrast to her mercurial fiancée, Caroline loved being dominated and obeyed Toby Saunders' every whim. (*The Dead Man's Knock* [1958 (2)])

Her age he estimated in the middle twenties; as he afterwards learned, she was twenty-seven. 'Beautiful' would have been too strong a word. But she was very pretty, with those healthy, fresh-complexioned good looks which seem to radiate innocence or even naïveté. (*The Ghosts' High Noon* [1969 (2)])

The quotations we have cited span a period of more than thirty years; and there is no difference from the first to the last. This sort of figure is obviously to Carr's liking; whether it is a description of his wife I have no idea, nor does it seem to matter much, since in any event this is how Carr wanted all women to be. Even in Carr's later novels, when he himself was advancing in years, he rarely features women (or men) in middle age. Of Judy Knox in *Panic in Box C* (1966) it is said: "She would be forty-four in November, even if she looked little more than half that" (3).

At this point we shall not make much of Carr's consistent use of "girl" for grown women. No doubt Carr would have been implacably hostile to women's liberation and therefore would have seen nothing wrong with referring, on the first page of *Dark of the Moon* (1968), to "a man and a girl"—the "girl" in question being twenty-seven years old. And yet, Carr was aware of this sort of condescension, as he refers to it in another stereotypical passage, this one from *In Spite of Thunder* (1960):

> Out of the lift stepped a gentle, modest, well-rounded girl, tall and slender, with black hair and a sympathetic manner. You thought 'girl' rather than 'woman,' though she must have been in her middle or later thirties. Though she was not exactly pretty, a clear complexion and large eyes made her seem so. And, except for her very fashionable clothes, she might have been the vicar's daughter on holiday. (3)

Carr seems to regard the word "girl" here as a compliment, since he fancies that all women are eternally striving to look as young as possible.

The pinnacle of Carr's bare-faced chauvinism occurs in an early work, *The Bowstring Murders* (1933):

> Tairlaine thought that she was even lovelier than last night. He liked fragility in women as much as he disliked strongmindedness; thus had been the tenor of whatever rusty bachelor dreams lay behind him. Looking at the pale beauty and wide eyes of this girl, he felt a warmth or protective kindness. It was unimportant that few thoughts would ever mar the serenity of that forehead; thoughts would only frighten her. (15)

Women must not be disturbed with thinking. All this is the more interesting because this character, Patricia Steyne, is clearly meant to stand in contrast to Lady Brayle, a "strongminded" and (what's worse) "modern" woman portrayed as follows:

> But Lady Rayle was neither funny nor in bad taste. The decorations glared about her like too much mascara on a beautiful face. She herself was beautiful; very pale red hair combed over her ears, heavy reddish eyebrows, and smoky yellow-green eyes in a square and pale face. Her neck was strong, like her strong and well-kept hands, and she was smiling faintly.
> "Good evening, gentlemen," she said.
> A fine, rather deep voice. You were conscious of at least two things: that she cordially detested her stepson, and that there was about her nothing of the quality called Nonsense. You suspected also that she had been a singer connected with musical comedy. (7)

Note that this woman is "beautiful". Even Sir Henry Merrivale gets into the act on one occasion. In *The Unicorn Murders* (1935) he says of Evelyn Cheyne: "She's a member of the Intelligence Department; oh, far from intelligent, I admit! Her purpose is merely to be charming" (16).

Carr's hostility to any sort of feminism was of very long standing. As early as "The Murder in Number Four" (1928) we have a very crude and malicious satire against a "militant feminist".[6] In *The Third Bullet* (1937) it is remarked of one character that "There's nothing hard-boiled or modern about her. She's fine"; the murder is then saddled upon the hardnosed Carolyn Mortlake, who is described as follows:

A woman came out between the bead curtains (which still exist) of an archway to the right. Carolyn Mortlake was one of those startling family contrasts (which, also, still exist). Where Ida was rather tall and soft, Carolyn was short, stocky, and hard. Where Ida was fair, Carolyn was dark. She had a square, very good-looking but very hard face; with black eyes of a snapping luminousness and a mouth painted dark red. They could see her jaw muscles.

This curious note about jaw muscles occurs again in *The Nine Wrong Answers* (1952): "Joy's jaw muscles were a trifle too firm, her dark-red lips too knowing" (6). Nothing could better encapsulate Carr's fear of strong and intelligent women than this single sentence.

But there are dim traces of a slightly healthier attitude. We have noted the remarkable transformation of Lady Pamela de Saxe from the prototypical airhead to a fiercely determined woman in *Patrick Butler for the Defence* (1956). In the historical novels appear some ambiguous examples. Lady Caroline Ross, in *The Bride of Newgate* (1950), expresses heated objections to the marriage conventions of her time:

"In marriage, it's understood, the husband has a certain 'right.' I will not grant *that* right to any man." She rapped her knuckles on the table, breathing quickly. "Do you understand me, sir?"

"Perfectly."

"That aspect," said Caroline, "I have always considered rather ridiculous and faintly revolting. But, under your precious law, the husband has still another right. Everything I own becomes his property, even to the house we stand in at this moment. And what, pray, do I get in exchange?

"I receive a boorish lout who will stamp home smelling of the stables, rattle out his oaths, and be hopelessly drunk by three o'clock in the afternoon. Or an empty-pated dandy (praise heaven the breed is passing!) who pays fabulous compliments, has a sour temper, and gambles away every farthing at Watier's or White's. If one lives à la mode, that's a husband.

"And for *this*," Caroline went on, with bitter disdain, "we're taught to simper, and swoon, and tap coquettishly with a fan, and cry, 'Fie!' at some mildly bawdy jest. For what purpose? To 'catch,' dear me, a husband who is not worth the trouble to catch!" (1)

It is not certain, however, how we are to interpret this statement at this point: later in the novel Caroline becomes warm and loving; but here it seems that these sentiments are put into her mouth so as to make the reader think of her as a frigid bitch. In *Papa Là-bas* (1968) one ante-bellum Southerner admits grudgingly, "I have always thought...that we keep our women too swathed in cotton-wool" (7); but later in the novel another character takes his fiancée over his knee and spanks her, then remarks: "Walloping a woman's behind...is only fair, proper, and righteous; it's what she ought to expect" (11). To be sure, there is humour here, but it is humour directed not at the man but at the woman who objected to being treated in this fashion.

The curious thing is why Carr populated his novels with so many brainless and pretty women; inevitably they fall in love with some male character (usually the protagonist or narrator), and occasionally there are a pair of such lovers, who all end up happily married at the conclusion. It is this mechanical element of romance that is one of the major drawbacks to Carr's work: there is rarely any variation in the conduct or outcome of these romances; we know all too well that they will end quite satisfactorily to all parties. The few exceptions where this is not the case—*Death in Five Boxes* and *Below Suspicion* come to mind—become the more refreshing as a result. The major problem with these romances, of course, is that they take place in the midst of one or more murders; and Carr, in an unintentionally hilarious passage in *Dark of the Moon* (1967), makes reference to one character's malapropos romantic feelings, as he and his lover overhear a conversation by the detectives:

Constantly, as they stood so close together and listened, he had been tempted to press her still closer, lift her head, and kiss her at some length. Now, with screams piercing up at that dead hour of the morning, he knew it would have been the wrong moment. (11)

It is indeed a trifle awkward to kiss someone while screams are reverberating through the house. But fear not: once the murder is cleared up, the path to true love lies open.

What is odd about all this is that Carr knew it was unnecessary. In discussing John Buchan's *The Thirty-nine Steps*, he makes explicit and praiseworthy mention of the fact that "there is no heroine in the story".[7] In fact, Carr's early novels are the more commendable in this regard. We have noted how, in *The Corpse in the Waxworks* (1932), Jeff Marle is fleetingly attracted to the alluring Marie Augustin, in spite of the fact that he is engaged (to Sharon Grey, presumably, although she is never mentioned by name). Although Carr bungled in trying to develop the Marle-Grey romance over the course of several novels (as he did the romance of Ted Rampole and Dorothy Sterberth in the early Fell novels), the sentiments Marle feels toward Marie are at least more true to life: very largely they are sexual, with an increment of furtive curiosity at her peculiar role in maintaining the private

136   John Dickson Carr: A Critical Study

Club of the Silver Key. This is the sort of thing any of us may feel from
time to time, and in the overwhelming number of cases it amounts, as here,
to nothing. But in later novels it seems that Carr's fanaticism for tying
up all loose ends of the puzzle also extended to human emotions, which
are much less amenable to neat solutions.

If there is one character type that Carr excelled in portraying, it is the
odiously pompous, self-important, and pretentious figure, mostly male.
Edouard Vautrelle in *It Walks by Night* (1930) already conforms to this
type, but the first great example is Maurice Bohum in *The White Priory
Murders* (1934):

> Bennett's dislike of Maurice Bohun was growing with every word he uttered.
> It might have been his intolerable assumption of rightness in everything, especially
> when he happened to be right; and his old-maidish way of expressing it. Bennett
> began even more fiercely to sympathize with Katharine. He noticed, too, that Masters
> had been feeling the discomfort. Masters, in whose big face there was a suppressed
> anger, folded up his own napkin and said a surprising thing.
> "Do you never get tired, sir," said the stolid practical Masters, "of playing God?"
> (8)

It is inevitable that Bohun would reply "Never." In the detective novels
Carr has the restraint rarely to make these hateful characters the actual
culprits—that would have been too easy. In the historical mysteries such
characters flourish in abundance; the best is perhaps the arrogant dandy
Jack Buckstone in *The Bride of Newgate,* who encounters Richard Darwent
in his cell at Newgate:

> Standing near the door, he still held up the lantern to inspect Darwent against
> the opposite wall. Buckstone's boots and breeches were dust-stained. He had ridden
> hard from Oatlands, country home of His Royal Highness the Duke of York, in
> response to a fast messenger from Caroline. From his right wrist hung a riding crop,
> with a short thong like a whip.
> "But, damme," he insisted, "what does ail the fellow?"
> "Jack! If you please!"
> "Went to see Bedlam once," Buckstone explained. "Watched all the madmen
> dance and howl. Damme, that was sport! This ain't. Is the demnition convict a deaf-
> mute? Why don't he speak? Or can't he?"
> This time there was a reply.
> "I can speak, sir," Darwent informed him, so that Caroline started involuntarily.
> "If only to remark that your manners are almost as bad as your grammar."
> "My dear fellow!" the Rev. Horace cried out in expostulation.
> Buckstone, with a perplexed look, pushed his buff-colored hat to the back of
> his head.
> "Impudent, ain't he?" Buckstone inquired of Caroline.
> Buckstone was not angry. He was only puzzled, as though a peaceful-seeming
> mongrel dog had shown teeth at him. He shifted the lantern to his left hand, and
> strolled forward. Without rancor, but with a heavily muscled arm, Buckstone lifted
> the riding crop and slashed it viciously across Darwent's face. (4)

Passages like this can make our blood boil; but in these novels Carr is too predictably fond of giving such figures their comeuppance—sure enough, Buckstone is later bested in a duel by Darwent. Here again, like Carr's romances, this tit-for-tat vengeance lends an air of the hackneyed and formulaic to novels that might otherwise be rich in substance and sensitive character portrayal.

It is in style and characterisation that we can most clearly trace Carr's gradual decline as a novelist. The novels of the sixties and seventies find Carr lapsing into conventionalised stylistic usages (as it is, throughout his career he was excessively wedded to certain turns of phrase, such as "Steady!" or "There was a silence"—this last phrase being found in nearly every single novel), as characterisation descends to stereotype and dialogue becomes trite and mechanical. And yet, it is still remarkable how late this decline really sets in. The first novel that seems genuinely padded is *Panic in Box C* (1966); and the last four historical novels—*Papa Là-bas*, *The Ghosts' High Noon*, *Deadly Hall*, and *The Hungry Goblin*—are quite lifeless and dull. Carr's dialogue in general has come under criticism for being unrealistic, but I am not sure the charge is sound: we have already maintained that his work should not be judged by conventional standards of realism, and the extreme theatricality of his dialogue actually suits the frenetic and hyperbolic nature of the plots. Aside from the slightly irritating phenomenon that few characters ever finish their utterances—they are too frequently interrupted by other characters—Carr's dialogue, if not distinguished in itself, serves the purpose for which it is designed.

We have already seen that characterisation in itself was neither a goal Carr set for himself nor a high requirement for the type of work he chose to write. To be sure, less stereotyped characters would have made his work both more interesting and more literarily substantial, but Carr evidently made a conscious decision to direct his attention elsewhere—principally to the puzzle and to plot construction. That this really was a conscious decision and not an intrinsic failing on Carr's part is evident from the several characters—aside from his detectives—who stand out in our minds long after the puzzle and its convolutions have been forgotten. The historical mysteries on the whole have somewhat better characterisation than the detective stories, although they were mostly written at a time when Carr's native vigour was running down, so that his figures were less crazily hyperactive than in his earlier work. Still, no one would read Carr for his characters; and his failure in this regard may ultimately point to more significant failures in his work generally—lack of observation, lack of true novelistic technique, or, most serious of all, a fundamental lack of interest in people.

Conclusion

John Dickson Carr had very pronounced views on the nature and purpose of literature. They are, admittedly, not especially profound or even interesting views, but Carr adhered to them throughout his career. In so early a work as a round-robin tale written during his college years, Carr wrote: "I sometimes wish to God that story-tellers would get a bit more old-fashioned. They'd be more entertaining."[1] What this means is that story-tellers really should be *story tellers*—that the narrative impulse should be supreme in fiction. This leads not only to the exaltation of the story line as the supreme quality in a novel but to the condemnation of the many modern writers who, according to Carr, do not or have forgotten how to observe this rule. In the "Notes for the Curious" to *The Devil in Velvet* (1951) Carr writes: "The first duty of any novelist, a duty so often forgotten nowadays, is to tell a story." But is this the novelist's only duty? Carr—if not explicitly, then at least by example—appears to think so. The most exhaustive enunciation of this view occurs in *Night at the Mocking Widow* (1950), as Merrivale attempts to revise a young girl's literary tastes (forced upon her by her mother and a psychiatrist) by hurling some books out the window:

> There was a whirr of leaves and then three separate thuds as Dostoevski, Tolstoy, and Chekhov flew out of the open window and struck the bole of an oak tree.
> "The idea is," explained H.M., "I want you to read some fellers named Dumas and Mark Twain and Stevenson and Chesterton and Conan Doyle. They're dead, yes; but they can still whack the britches off anybody at tellin' a story." (15)

Carr's hostility to Russian literature seems to have increased with age; consider this passage from *Deadly Hall* (1971), where he handily conjoins his political and literary conservatism:

> "Then you don't approve," Serena asked, "of Russia's beautiful new communistic experiment or its various five-year plans?"
> "I loathe their communistic experiment and everything it stands for. There's more than that; I don't like Russians. I can't like Russians since I tried to read their novels, which highbrows rave about but which to me seem mere humorless hogwash, as pretentious as clumsily inept." (10)

This sort of remark will not incline anyone to rank Carr with F. R. Leavis or Harold Bloom; in fact, it is quite obvious that Carr has made no effort to understand the writers he attacks so wildly. An assault on Henry James in *Death in Five Boxes* (1938) is equally fatuous: "What between the atropine and Haye's Henry-Jamesian tendency never to say a straight thing straight out without some underlying pun or joke or double-meaning, the result was confused" (15)

This very narrow and limiting theory of literature—if it can be called that—carries with it a hostility to subtlety, delicate nuances of character analysis, and a slow accumulation of emotional intensity; and it is no surprise that Carr's writing uniformly lacks all these qualities. Where there is emotional intensity, it is produced—even at its best, as in *The Emperor's Snuff-Box* (1942)—through blunt and sensationalist means. As it is, the best criticism of the sort of fast-paced action story Carr both wrote and approved of is a remark by Gerard Manley Hopkins on Stevenson:

His doctrine, if I apprehend him, is something like this. The essence of Romance is incident and that only, the type of pure Romance the *Arabian Nights:* those stories have no moral, no character-drawing, they turn altogether on interesting incident. The incidents must of course have a connection, but it need be nothing more than that they happen to the same person, are aggravations and so on. As history consists essentially of events likely or unlikely, consequences of causes chronicled before or what may be called chance, just retributions or nothing of the sort, so Romance, which is fictitious history, consists of event, of incident. His own stories are written on this principle; they are very good and he has all the gifts a writer of fiction should have, and at first you notice no more than an ordinary well told story, but on looking back in the light of this doctrine you see that the persons illustrate the incident or strains of incident, the plot, *the story*, not the story and incidents the persons.[2]

This is the real reason why even such writers as Stevenson or Conan Doyle are deservedly of the second rank in literature: if one does not have anything to say, it makes no difference how cleverly or entertainingly one says it. Carr, fundamentally, had nothing to say. This brutal truth—that Carr had no significant or profound view of the world or of human relations to convey through his work—is what will rank him even lower than such figures in detective fiction as Margery Allingham or Rex Stout, who cannot approach Carr's pure narrative skill. We have seen how Carr frequently avoids any philosophical discussions in his work, and resolutely refuses to regard his novels and tales as anything but entertainment. Even the nonfictional *Murder of Sir Edmund Godfrey* (1936) is placed in this category when Carr writes that "the intent is only to amuse" ("Preface"). No one's view of life will be changed by reading Carr.

Given this view of literature, Carr is immediately faced with a criticism he no doubt actually received in reviews: the fact that his stories lack depth or profundity. Carr more often than not evades this subject than faces it forthrightly. In *The Dead Man's Knock* (1958) he says that detective stories are "the noblest form of relaxation from academic work" (20). This implies a very humble place for the detective story, and elsewhere Carr makes basically the same point with a certain bitterness:

"Depth" and "profundity" are relative terms, too often used for the merely pretentious or phony. Since giants like Mark Twain and G. K. Chesterton always revelled in blood and thunder, any condescending attitude belongs with the snows of yesteryear. A good story needs no justification; let's make our own appraisal.[3]

The logical fallacy in this argument is very apparent: since Mark Twain (a genuinely first-rate writer) revelled in blood and thunder, any writer can do so without incurring charges of superficiality; but Carr overlooks that it is not blood and thunder that makes Twain a great writer. The tone of the above remark betrays, I think, a real insecurity—the insecurity of one who finds himself aligned against a literary and critical establishment that does *not* find a good story its own justification. Carr may feel vindicated by sophistically passing off such an attitude as "pretentious or phony", but the nagging question remains: what does this "good story" really amount to? How is the "entertainment" provided by literature different from that provided by a crossword puzzle or a football game? Carr cannot answer these questions, or perhaps does not realise that they need answering.

But if Carr has by his own admission relegated himself to the level of an entertainer, a supplier of "relaxation", let us admit that in this humble domain he has acquitted himself admirably. Instead of lamenting the lack of depth in Carr's work, let us focus on his real strengths as a writer.

His foremost strength is narrative drive. This quality he possessed perhaps even in excess of any of his idols—Conan Doyle, Chesterton, even Stevenson and Twain. No writer can keep one reading more than John Dickson Carr. Even if some of his narrative devices are merely tricks—the trick of ending each chapter or section on a startling revelation; the trick of having characters make dramatic entrances like actors in a melodrama— they all work to produce a consuming interest in the puzzle and its attendant circumstances that is not satisfied until the final resolution and explanation. Save in his late works, Carr never wastes a word; his language is always tight and compact, his style almost exhilarating in its forward energy and unceasing flow.

It might be said that Carr was trying to achieve—and almost always did achieve—the effects of a group of writers he always held in high regard: narrative historians. When, in *The Murder of Sir Edmund Godfrey*, he wrote that "To write good history is the noblest work of man" ("Preface"), he was referring to the great historians of the past, especially Macaulay, Froude, and J. R. Green. These writers transformed an enormous mass of raw data into a fluid and seamless narrative; similarly, Carr had the skill to take a stupendously complex plot and marshal all its details and ramifications into a narrative that may be *baffling* but never *confusing*. In his historical mysteries Carr joined even more intimately his dual role as historian and detective writer; from this perspective these novels may well occupy a central place in his work. At the very least, it was inevitable that he would come to write these works, and a few of them are equal to the very best of his detective stories.

The most noticeable feature of Carr's detective novels is their combination of intricate plot, supernatural chills, and boisterous humour. *The Eight of Swords* (1934) encapsulates this hybridism when it is remarked: "The whole thing was at once baffling, ludicrous, and terrible" (11). Again, although much of the humour is slapstick and some of the shudders are artificial (as in *Castle Skull*), this picturesque union is on the whole quite effective. The Bencolin novels produce the most harmonious joining of these disparate qualities, as the humour tends to be markedly sardonic and hence appropriate to the grotesque horror of the background and central events. In other works humour and horror alternate, sometimes in a blindingly quick fashion. The clowning of Sir Henry Merrivale usually subsides after the actual murder, and occasionally novels that begin with the frothy hilarity of a Wodehouse end with the grimness of Bierce. On still other occasions Carr can create an atmosphere of sustained sombreness, lightened by almost no humour, that ironically is not nearly as far from that of his hated Russian novelists as he would like to believe. *Poison in Jest* (1932) is the earliest and perhaps the best example.

What all this means is that Carr is a master of tone, mood, and atmosphere. In saying this we approach the true greatness and the true distinguishing feature of his work. To be sure, he concocted more elaborate puzzles than anyone in detective fiction; he created three of the most engaging detectives in the field; he wrote one magnificent supernatural novel and his unique historical mysteries; but the fact is that Carr is not a mere logician devising plots like a literary computer wizard. Carr did not, as we have seen, consider detective stories—or at least his type of detective stories—as belonging to the realm of realism, but rather to the realm of fantasy. The truth is, therefore, that Carr is a great fantaisiste. He could have written some of the finest supernatural fiction of the century if he had been so inclined. In spite of the obvious care he takes in the exact dovetailing of a complicated plot, he is interested not so much in this as in creating a series of images that shock, baffle, and horrify. It is for this end, and this end only, that Carr sets in motion all the narrative and structural skills he has at his disposal: the stage must be carefully set for that arresting tableau which, fleeting as it may be, is the real heart of the work. A man found decapitated as if bending down to the guillotine; a dead woman lying in a waxen satyr's arms; a gun that seems to leap from a wall, hang in midair, and shoot its victim—these are the scenes we remember long after the contrived puzzle is forgotten, and it is they that make John Dickson Carr the supreme colourist in detective fiction.

Notes

Part I
Introduction

[1] Robert Lewis Taylor, "Two Authors in an Attic" (Part I), *New Yorker*, 8 September 1951, p. 43.

[2] We even know who the upstart undergraduate was. On the last page of the second instalment of the story in the December 1926 issue is the note: "This tale is told. And the person who guessed the truth was Edward G. Taulane, Haverford, '30" (p. 92).

[3] Taylor, p. 44.

[4] "Introduction" to *Hag's Nook* (New York: Har/Row Books, 1971), p. 5.

[5] James Sandoe reports in *The Art of the Mystery Story*, ed. Howard Haycraft (New York: Simon & Schuster, 1946), that "Lillian de la Torre argues warmly for *The Murder of Sir Edmund Godfrey*" as Carr's best work (p. 499).

[6] BBC, May 22, 1944.

Chapter I

[1] *The Door to Doom and Other Detections* (1980), p. 58.

[2] Ibid.

[3] "The Murder in Number Four" (1928), in *The Door to Doom*, p. 105.

[4] *Grand Guignol*, serialised in *The Haverfordian*, March 1929 (pp. 202-54) and April 1929 (pp. 259-81). Subsequent references to this work will occur by page number in the text.

[5] *The Door to Doom*, p. 106.

[6] Ibid., pp. 109-10.

[7] Ibid., p. 110.

[8] Ibid.

[9] Carr has Fell express his distaste for excessive violence (something that offended him in the hard-boiled novels of Hammett and Chandler) in *The Blind Barber* (1934): "If a man's required to turn around every second and pick up a new person who has been knocked out by somebody, he isn't apt to have much time for cool reflection" (20).

[10] Carr himself laid down, as one of his few rules for detective writing, that "The criminal shall never turn out to be the detective" ("The Grandest Game in the World", *The Door to Doom*, p. 323). No doubt this would apply only to the principal detective, and strictly speaking we would have no right to feel cheated if any other figure, however closely associated with the detective, proves to be the criminal.

[11] Dorothy L. Sayers, review of *The Mad Hatter Mystery*, *Sunday Times* (London), 24 March 1933, p. 7.

Chapter II

[1]Robert Lewis Taylor, "Two Authors in an Attic" (Part II), *New Yorker*, 15 September 1951, p. 37. A minor character in Carr's early humorous tale "The Deficiency Expert" (*The Haverfordian*, May 1927, p. 358) may have been a prototype for Fell: "He was expansive, red-faced, and white-whiskered, rather like Santa Claus."

[2]It is reproduced in Aidan Reynolds and William Charlton, *Arthur Machen: A Short Account of His Life and Work* (London: Richards Press, 1963; rpt. Oxford: Caermaen Books, 1988), facing page 124.

[3]James E. Keirans directs me to a delightful play on Holmes' penchant for using a magnifying glass; in *He Who Whispers* Fell remarks: "Candidly speaking, I'm not sure it would be much good to me. But it makes an impressive picture, and gives the user a magnificent sense of self-importance" (9).

[4]In *Mortal Consequences* (New York: Harper & Row, 1972) Symons thanks Edmund Crispin for correcting "at least one howler": "I had forgotten that John Dickson Carr's Dr. Fell at one time had a wife" (p. 16).

Chapter III

[1]This is pronounced "AR-khans", and refers to the leading magistrates of the Athenian democracy, principally in the fifth and fourth centuries B.C.

[2]"Best Mysteries of the Month", *Ellery Queen's Mystery Magazine*, February 1969, p. 150.

[3]As *The Maze* (1932) in England. In a sense, however, Macdonald's intent is close to Carr's in that he too wishes a strict fair play battle between reader and writer. In an introduction Macdonald states: "You, the reader, and he, the detective, are upon an equal footing. You know just as much as and no more than he knows. He knows just as much as and no more than you. He finds out: could you have found out without his help?...In this book I have striven to be absolutely fair to the reader. There is *nothing*—nothing at all—for the detective that the reader has not had. More, the reader has had his information in exactly the same form as the detective—that is, the verbatim report of evidence and question."

[4]Robert Lewis Taylor, "Two Authors in an Attic" (Part II), *New Yorker*, 15 September 1951, p. 37.

Chapter IV

[1]There is, curiously, a character named Patrick Butler in a Father Brown story of G. K. Chesterton ("The Man in the Passage", in *The Wisdom of Father Brown* [1914]), but I am not convinced that this is anything but a coincidence. In Chesterton he is described as follows: "The prisoner was defended by Mr. Patrick Butler, K.C., who was mistaken for a mere *flâneur* by those who misunderstood the Irish character—and those who had not been examined by him."

Chapter V

[1]Douglas G. Greene, "A Bibliography of the Works of John Dickson Carr" in *The Door to Doom and Other Detections* (1980), p. 334.

[2]*National Review* No. 499 (September 1924) 138-45.

[3]*The Popish Plot* (London: William Heinemann, 1972), p. 264n.

[4]*The Killing of Justice Godfrey* (London: Granada, 1984), p. 200.

[5]"The Red Heels", *The Haverfordian*, April 1926, p. 296.

Chapter VI

[1]Aside from the college stories, there is only one legitimate uncollected Carr story: "Detective's Day Off" (1957). See Bibliography, Section A.6.

[2]In all fairness to Derleth (whose Solar Pons pastiches I confess to finding genuinely entertaining), he was a substantial and powerfully original writer in his principal chosen field of regional and historical fiction, in particular such works as *Place of Hawks* (1935) and *Evening in Spring* (1941); but as a detective or horror or science fiction writer (he wrote prolifically in all these fields), he had absolutely nothing to say, and his works are to be judged solely by the degree to which they duplicate the effects of his favourite writers, principally Conan Doyle and H. P. Lovecraft.

[3]Still later Carr used the basic scenario as his contribution to the round-robin tale "Crime on the Coast" (1954).

Part II

Chapter I

[1]"The Jury Box", *Ellery Queen's Mystery Magazine*, June 1971, p. 73.

[2]*The Door to Doom and Other Detections* (1980), p. 32.

[3]Ibid., p. 77.

[4]Ibid., p. 88.

[5]Ibid., p. 93.

[6]Ibid., p. 105.

[7]"Twenty Rules for Writing Detective Stories" (1928), in *The Art of the Mystery Story*, ed. Howard Haycraft (New York: Simon & Schuster, 1946), p. 191.

[8]In "The Grandest Game in the World" (written 1946) Carr writes: "The criminal shall not turn out to be the detective, or any servant, or any character whose thoughts we have been allowed to share." *The Door to Doom*, pp. 323-24.

[9]James E. Keirans tells me that, from the month and days given in the novel, it must date to August 1935.

[10]"Introduction" to *The Door to Doom*, p. 24.

[11]Ibid., p. 22.

Chapter II

[1]"The Jury Box", *Ellery Queen's Mystery Magazine*, April 1973, p. 112.

[2]"Notes on the Writing of Weird Fiction" (c. 1932), *Marginalia* (Sauk City, WI: Arkham House, 1944), pp. 138-39.

[3]"The Simple Art of Murder" (1944; rev. 1946), cited in Howard Haycraft, ed., *The Art of the Mystery Story* (New York: Simon & Schuster, 1946), p. 222.

[4]"With Colt and Luger", *New York Times Book Review*, 24 September 1950, p. 36.

[5]*The Art of the Mystery Story*, p. 232.

[6]*The Door to Doom and Other Detections* (1980), p. 310.

[7]"The Jury Box", *Ellery Queen's Mystery Magazine*, January 1971, p. 82.

[8]"The Jury Box", *Ellery Queen's Mystery Magazine*, June 1975, p. 110.

[9]"Story Development", *The Mystery Writer's Handbook*, ed. Herbert Brean (New York: Harper & Brothers, 1956), p. 169.

[10]"The Jury Box," *Ellery Queen's Mystery Magazine*, July 1972, p. 88.

[11]"The Grandest Game in the World", *The Door to Doom*, p. 323.
[12]Ibid., p. 324.
[13]*Tales and Sketches 1831-1842 (Collected Works of Edgar Allan Poe,* Volume II), ed. T. O. Mabbott et al. (Cambridge, MA: Harvard University Press, 1978), pp. 547-48.
[14]*Grand Guignol, The Haverfordian*, March 1929, pp. 206-7.
[15]*The Haverfordian*, April 1929, p. 276.

Chapter III
[1]*The Havefordian*, May 1927, p. 355.
[2]"The Jury Box", *Ellery Queen's Mystery Magazine*, February 1973, p. 82.
[3]*The Haverfordian*, March 1929, p. 244.
[4]*The Collected Ghost Stories of M. R. James* (London: Edward Arnold, 1931), p. 175.
[5]*The Door to Doom and Other Detections* (1980), p. 271.

Chapter IV
[1]*Sunday Times* (London), 24 March 1933, p. 7.
[2]H. P. Lovecraft, Letter to James F. Morton, March [?] 1937; *Selected Letters 1934-1937,* ed. August Derleth and James Turner (Sauk City, WI: Arkham House, 1976), pp. 430-31.
[3]See note 1.
[4]Robert Lewis Taylor, "Two Authors in an Attic" (Part II), *New Yorker*, 15 September 1951, p. 40.
[5]Ibid., p. 37.
[6]*The Door to Doom and Other Detections* (1980), p. 95.
[7]"The Jury Box", *Ellery Queen's Mystery Magazine*, February 1971, p. 101.

Conclusion
[1]"The New Canterbury Tales", *The Haverfordian*, March 1927, p. 230.
[2]Gerard Manley Hopkins, Letter to R. W. Dixon, 15 August 1883; *The Correspondence of Gerard Manley Hopkins and Richard Watson Dixon,* ed. Claude Colleer Abbott (London: Oxford University Press, 1935), p. 114.
[3]"The Jury Box", *Ellery Queen's Mystery Magazine*, May 1974, p. 106.

Bibliography

This bibliography is broadly divided into primary works (by Carr) and secondary works (about Carr). Of the primary works, editions of Carr's book-length writings are divided into novels (those published under his various bylines—John Dickson Carr, Carter Dickson, and Roger Fairbairn—not distinguished but uniformly listed in exact sequence of publication, as far as is ascertainable), short story collections, nonfiction, omnibuses, and works edited. I claim here to have listed every edition of Carr's work but not the many different printings within those editions; reset editions by the same publisher are also not listed. I also have listed as many translations of Carr's book-length works as I have been able to find. I confess that I have actually not personally examined a single foreign translation, but have had to rely exclusively on citations found in the various national bibliographies of the countries in question. It is conceivable that some of this information is inadequate or inaccurate; indeed, I have included at the very end of the bibliography a list of unidentified translations, and would be grateful if any reader can supply additional information on these titles.

After the book-length works I list Carr's shorter writings—short stories, poems, articles and reviews, introductions to works by others, and stage plays. (It is interesting to note that a fourth byline—"John Dixon Carr"— is found on two of Carr's pulp stories of the 1930s.) I have decided not to list Carr's radio plays, as I could not add anything to the comprehensive lists already prepared by Francis M. Nevins, Jr., and Douglas G. Greene. For all these works I have tried to provide full bibliographical information on the first appearance and then to list any collections in which these works appear. Douglas G. Greene's bibliography is to be consulted for the many other appearances of the short stories.

The secondary works are divided into bibliographies, articles in books and magazines (obituaries are listed at the end of this section), and reviews. I have listed only the more significant of the many entries on Carr appearing in reference works on detective fiction; I have also supplied a (no doubt incomplete) listing of some foreign criticism on Carr, usually from general works on the detective story. Readers of the text of my work may feel that I have been a little uncharitable in so rarely citing previous work on Carr; but, to be frank, aside from Robert Lewis Taylor's biographical article and the work of Douglas G. Greene, I have found very little of this material of especial use. The list of reviews is no doubt vastly incomplete; certainly, Carr's later novels were reviewed in many newspapers around the country,

Bibliography 147

and it would be a monumental task to trace all these items. I have generally supplied only those reviews that appeared in important nationally distributed magazines or important newspapers.

I trust that this bibliography—itself founded upon the work of others— may provide the impetus for a full-scale descriptive bibliography of Carr. It may be a hopeless task to track down the seemingly countless foreign translations of his work, but a mere awareness of their number should strongly suggest how popular Carr has been and remains throughout the world.

I wish to make special mention of the assistance of James E. Keirans in the compilation of this bibliography.

A. *Works by John Dickson Carr*

1. Novels
Grand Guignol. The Haverfordian, March 1929 (pp. 202-54) and April 1929 (pp. 259-81).
It Walks by Night. New York: Harper & Brothers, 1930. London: Harper & Brothers, 1930. New York: Grosset & Dunlap, 1932. Harmondsworth: Penguin, 1938. New York: Pocket Books, 1941. New York: Avon, 1955. New York: Zebra, 1986.
Translations:
German: *Geheimnis um Saligny*, tr. Otto Zeltin (Leipzig: Oldemburg, 1931). *Elf Uhr Dreissig*, tr. Hanna Ricker (Zurich: Albert Müller, 1941).
Swedish: *Steg i natten*, tr. Johan Severin (Stockholm: Fredborgs, 1946), *Någon går darute*, tr, Maj Frisch (Stockholm: Rabén & Sjogren, 1966).
Spanish: *Anda de noche*, tr. Fernando Santos (Madrid: Saturnino Calleja, 1949).
Turkish: *Karanlikta ayak sesleri*, tr. Gönül Suveren (Istanbul: Akba Yayinevi, 1963).
Greek: *Vgainei tē nychta*, tr. Dēmētrē Giagtzoglou (Athens: Angyra, 1971).
French: *La Marie perd la tête*, tr. Jean-André and Claudine Rey (Paris: Champs-Elysées, 1985).
The Lost Gallows. New York: Harper & Brothers, 1931. London: Hamish Hamilton, 1931. New York: P. F. Collier, 1931. New York: Pocket Books, 1947. New York: Berkeley, 1960. New York: Carroll & Graf, 1986.
Translations:
German: *Die Strasse des Schreckens*, tr. Ursula von Wiese (Zurich: Albert Müller, 1952; rpt. Gütersloh: Mohn, 1961).
Turkish: *Kayip darağaci*, tr. Gönül Suveren (Istanbul: Altin Kitaplar Yayinevi, 1964).
Swedish: *Den försvunna galgen*, tr. Nils Pontén-Möller (Stockholm: Tiden, 1967).
French: *Le Secret du gibet*, tr. ? (Paris: Clancier-Guénaud, 1984).
Castle Skull. New York: Harper & Brothers, 1931. New York: Pocket Books, 1947. New York: Berkley, 1960. London: Severn House, 1976. New York: Zebra, 1987.
Translations:
Spanish: *El castillo de la calavera*, tr. ? (Mexico City, 1953). *La calavera del castillo*, tr. Heriberto F. Morek (Mexico City: Diana, 1957 [=preceding?]).
German: *Tod in Flammentanz*, tr. Margrit Körner (Zurich: Albert Müller, 1967).
The Corpse in the Waxworks. New York: Harper & Brothers, 1932. London: Hamish Hamilton, 1932 (as *The Waxworks Murder*). New York: Grosset & Dunlap, 1934. Harmondsworth: Penguin, 1938 (as *The Waxworks Murder*). New York: Avon, 1943. New York: Dell, 1954. New York: Berkley, 1958. New York: Collier, 1965.

148   John Dickson Carr: A Critical Study

Translations:
German: *Der Klub der bunten Masken,* tr. Rudolf Hochglend (Zurich: Albert Müller, 1941). *Der Club der Masken,* tr. Luise Däbritz (Munich: Desch, 1962; rpt. Munich: Heyne, 1977).
Spanish: *El crimen de las figuras de cera,* tr. Estela Canto (Buenos Aires: Emecé, 1951 [3rd ed.]; rpt. Madrid: Alianza, 1974).
Italian: *L'Ultima carta,* tr. Bruno Scurto (Milan: Mondadori, 1955).
Serbo-Croatian: *Ubistvo kraj voštanih figura,* tr. Branko Golović (Sarajevo: Džepna Knjiga, 1959).
Turkish: *Ölümün gölgesi,* tr. Gönül Suveren (Istanbul: Akba Yayinevi, 1962).
Swedish: *Mordet i vaxkabinettet,* tr. Maj Frisch (Stockholm: Rabén & Sjögren, 1967).
Poison in Jest. New York: Harper & Brothers, 1932. London: Hamish Hamilton, 1932. Harmondsworth: Penguin, 1940. n.p.: Lothian, 1945. New York: Popular Library, 1951. New York: Berkley, 1957. New York: Collier, 1965. Leicester: Ulverscroft, 1970.
Translations:
French: *La Main de marbre,* tr. Jean George (Paris: Champs-Elysées, 1939).
Spanish: *Veneno en broma,* tr. Léonidas Labanca (Buenos Aires: Lautaro, 1948 [2nd ed.]).
Italian: *Piazza pulita,* tr. Iti/Dussich/Knowles (Milan: Mondadori, 1953).
Turkish: *Zehirli şaka,* tr. Gülten Suveren (Istanbul: Ceylân Yayinlari Muessesesi, 1963).
Swedish: *Döden driver gäck,* tr. Roland Adlerberth (Stockholm: Prisma, 1965).
Polish: *Trucizna?,* tr. Tadeusz Evert (Warsaw: Iskry, 1966).
Greek: *To marmarino cheri,* tr. L. Tsoukala (Athens: Anghyra, 1971).
Hag's Nook. New York: Harper & Brothers, 1933. London: Hamish Hamilton, 1933. New York: Grosset & Dunlap, 1935. Harmondsworth: Penguin, 1940. Baltimore: Penguin, 1943. New York: Dell, 1951. New York: Berkley, 1958. New York: Collier, 1963. New York: Har/Row, 1971. New York: International Polygonics, 1985.
Translations:
Spanish: *Nido de brujas,* tr. Valerio Ferreyra (Buenos Aires: Lautaro, 1948). *El rincón de la bruja,* tr. Giménez Sales (Barcelona: Molino, 1967).
Swedish: *Häxstupet,* tr. Gösta Dahlman (Stockholm: Bonnier, 1948). *Häxgropen,* tr. Hans Granqvist (Stockholm: Rabén & Sjögren, 1966).
German: *Das Zeichen im Brunnen,* tr. Ursula von Wiese (Zurich: Albert Müller, 1952; rpt. Gütersloh: Mohn, 1961). *Tod im Hexenwinkel,* tr. Andreas Graf (Cologne: DuMont, 1986).
Italian: *In cantuccio della strega,* tr. Bruno del Bianco (Milan: Mondadori, 1955).
The Mad Hatter Mystery. New York: Harper & Brothers, 1933. London: Hamish Hamilton, 1933. New York: Grosset & Dunlap, 1935. New York: Popular Library, 1945. Harmondsworth: Penguin, 1947. New York: Dell, 1953. New York: Berkley, 1958. New York: Collier, 1965. Leicester: Ulverscroft, 1968.
Translation:
Swedish: *Hattmysteriet,* tr. Gunvor Blomqvist (Stockholm: Tiden, 1965; rpt. Stockholm: Prisma, 1970).
The Bowstring Murders (as by Carr Dickson [1st ed.] and Carter Dickson [subsequent eds.]). New York: William Morrow, 1933. London: William Heinemann, 1934. New York: Grosset & Dunlap, 1935. New York: Triangle, 1938. New York: Pocket, 1940. London: British Publishers Guild, 1944. London: Pan, 1960. New York: Berkley, 1959. New York: Belmont Tower, 1974.

Translations:
Dutch: *Het geheim van de wapenzaal,* tr. W.A. Gotjé and R. Renquin (Laren: A.G. Schoonderbeek, 1939).
French: *La Flèche peinte,* tr. Jeanne Fournier-Pargoire (Paris: Editions des Loisirs, 1941).
Danish: *D∮den i Vaabensalen,* tr. Asta Heiberg (Copenhagen: Athenaeum, 1942; rpt. Copenhagen: Lademann, 1979).
Finnish: *Rautahansikasmurhaaja,* tr. K. J. Kaasaleinen (Helsingissa: Pellervo Seura, 1948).
Turkish: *Bir saat durdu,* tr. Enver Günsel (Istanbul: Hüsnütabiat Matbaasi, 1966).
German: *Die Uhr steht still,* tr. Renate Hertenstein (Bern: Scherz, 1949; rpt. Frankfurt am Main: Ullstein, 1970).
The Eight of Swords. New York: Harper & Brothers, 1934. London: Hamish Hamilton, 1934. New York: Grosset & Dunlap, 1935. New York: Berkley, 1957. London: Pan, 1961. New York: Collier, 1962. New York: Har/Row, 1971. New York: Zebra, 1986.
Translations:
German: *Schatten der Vergangenheit,* tr. Ursula von Wiese (Zurich: Albert Müller, 1946; rpt. Frankfurt am Main: Ullstein, 1965).
Spanish: *El ocho de espadas,* tr. Susana Uriburu (Buenos Aires: Emecé, 1949).
Italian: *Otto di spade,* tr. Silvia Albini Boninsegna (Milan: Mondadori, 1955).
Danish: *D∮dskortet,* tr. Lone Lowry (Copenhagen: Martin, 1965).
Swedish: *Åtten i svärd,* tr. Margareta Nylander (Stockholm: Rabén & Sjögren, 1966).
Dutch: *Het geheim van de acht zwaarden,* tr. Jos. G. Heilker (Utrecht: Het Spectrum, 1968 [2nd ed.]).
Greek: *To oktō spathi,* tr. Ath. Skopélitis (Athens: Lychnari, 1968).
The Plague Court Murders (as by Carter Dickson). New York: William Morrow, 1934. London: William Heinemann, 1935. New York: Grosset & Dunlap, 1936. New York: Triangle, 1938. New York: Avon, 1941. Harmondsworth: Penguin, 1951. New York: Berkley, 1959. New York: Belmont Tower, 1974. London: Remploy, 1979.
Translations:
Italian: *La casa stregata,* tr. Giorgio Monicelli (Milan: Alpe, 1939).
French: *La Maison de la peste,* tr. Jacqueline Halmos (Paris: Hachette, 1949).
Danish: *Boddelen går igen,* tr. Grete Juel Jorgensen (Copenhagen: Hirschsprung, 1957). *Boddelen går igen,* Mogens Cohrt (Copenhagen: Skrifola, 1966).
Swedish: *Klockam klämtar för mord,* tr. Gerald De Geer (Stockholm: Geber, 1960 [with a novel by Harry Olesker]).
Norwegian: *B∮ddenlen går igjen,* tr. Finn B. Larsen (Sj∮holt: Norild, 1978).
The Blind Barber. New York: Harper & Brothers, 1934. London: Hamish Hamilton, 1934. New York: Grosset & Dunlap, 1936. Baltimore: Penguin, 1943. Harmondsworth: Penguin, 1952. New York: Berkley, 1957. New York: Collier, 1962. Bath: Lythway Press, 1976.
Translations:
German: *Der blinde Barbier,* tr. Ursula von Wiese (Zurich: Albert Müller, 1953; rpt. Frankfurt am Main: Ullstein, 1965).
Dutch: *De moord met het scheermes,* tr. C. E. van der Heijden (Utrecht: Het Spectrum, 1959).
Swedish: *Den blinde barberaren,* tr. Christina Strandberg (Stockholm: Prisma, 1965; rpt. Stockholm: Tiden, 1977).

150   John Dickson Carr: A Critical Study

The White Priory Murders (as by Carter Dickson). New York: William Morrow, 1934.
London: William Heinemann, 1935. New York: Grosset & Dunlap, 1936. New
York: Pocket, 1942. New York: Books, Inc., 1944. Harmondsworth: Penguin,
1951. New York: Berkley, 1963. New York: Belmont Tower, 1973. New York:
Bantam, 1982.
Translations:
Dutch: *De mord op Marcia Tait,* tr. H. S. Lansen (Laren: A.G. Schoonderbeek, 1938).
French: *S.M. intervint,* tr. Armène Répond (Geneva: Editions Ditis, 1945).
Norwegian: *Døden i speilet,* tr. Finn B. Larsen (Sjøholt: Norild, 1980).
Devil Kinsmere (as by Roger Fairbairn). New York: Harper & Brothers, 1934. London:
Hamish Hamilton, 1934.
Death-Watch. New York: Harper & Brothers, 1935. London: Hamish Hamilton, 1935.
New York: Grosset & Dunlap, 1937. New York: Dell, 1952. Harmondsworth:
Penguin, 1953. New York: Berkley, 1958. New York: Collier, 1963.
Translations:
Spanish: *El reloj de la muerte,* tr. Clara de la Rosa (Buenos Aires, 1957; rpt. Madrid:
Alianza, 1975).
Portuguese: *O relógio da morte,* tr. Béni Homan (Lisbon: Empresa Nacional de
Publicidade, 1959?).
German: *Der vergoldete Uhrzeiger,* tr. Bernhard Kempner (Bern: Scherz, 1960).
Greek: *To roloi tou thanatou,* tr. Petrou Délatollas (Athens: Viper, 1971).
Hungarian: *A gyilkos óra,* tr. Falvay Milhály (Budapest: Magvetö, 1976).
The Red Widow Murders (as by Carter Dickson). New York: William Morrow, 1935.
London: William Heinemann, 1935. New York: Grosset & Dunlap, 1936. New
York: Pocket, 1940. Cleveland: World Publishing Co., 1942. Harmondsworth:
Penguin, 1951. New York: Berkley, 1963. New York: International Polygonics,
1988.
Translations:
French: *La Maison du bourreau,* tr. Perrine Vernay (Paris: Nouvelle Revue Critique,
1936; rpt. Paris: Champs-Elysées, 1986).
Dutch: *De kamer der roode weduwe,* tr. A. D. Baert (Laren: A. D. Schoonderbeek,
1939).
Spanish: *Los crimenes de la viuda roja,* tr. Alfredo de León (Buenos Aires: Libreria
Hachette, 1944).
Italian: *Le vedova rossa,* tr. Dora Favilli (Milan: Alpe, 1945).
Portuguese: *Os crimes da viuva vermelha,* tr. Baptista Carvalho (Lisbon: Rádio
Renascença, 1949).
German: *Das Zimmer der roten Witwe,* tr. Alexandra Brun (Bern: Scherz, 1951; rpt.
Klagenfurt: Kaiser, 1965 [with novels by Agatha Christie and Frances Crane];
rpt. Frankfurt am Main: Ullstein, 1970).
Danish: *Vaerelset der myrder,* tr. Lilian Plon (Copenhagen: Hirschsprung, 1957).
Turkish: *Kizil dul,* tr. Gönül Suveren (Istanbul: Akba Yayinevi, 1963).
The Three Coffins. New York: Harper & Brothers, 1935. London: Hamish Hamilton,
1935. New York: Popular Library, 1949. Harmondsworth: Penguin, 1951. New
York: Dell, 1960. New York: Award, 1974. New York: Buccaneer, 1976. London:
Remploy, 1977. Boston: Gregg Press, 1979. New York: International Polygonics,
1986. (All British editions use the title *The Hollow Man.*)
Translations:
Spanish: *El hombre hueco,* tr. Aida Aisenson (Buenos Aires: Emecé, 1951).

Dutch: *De onzichtbare moordenaar,* tr. Ben Rahman (Amsterdam: De Bezige Bij, 1957). *De holle man,* tr. Dolf Koning (Amsterdam: De Arbeiderspers, 1973).

Swedish: *Den ihålige mannen,* tr. Claës Gripenberg (Stockholm: Bonnier, 1964).

Turkish: *Uç tabut,* tr. Gönül Suveren (Istanbul: Altin Kitaplar Yayinevi, 1964).

German: *Der Unsichtbare,* tr. Alexandra Brun (Bern: Scherz, 1953; rpt. Frankfurt am Main: Ullstein, 1966).

Norwegian: *Den hule mannen,* tr. Bjørn Carling (Oslo: Gyldendal, 1973).

Italian: *Le tre bare,* tr. Maria Luisa Bocchino (Milan: Club degli Editori, 1979).

The Unicorn Murders (as by Carter Dickson). New York: William Morrow, 1935. London: William Heinemann, 1936. New York: Dell, 1943. Cleveland: World Publishing Co., 1945. New York: Berkley, 1964. London: Tom Stacey, 1972.

Translations:

Dutch: *In geheimen dienst,* tr. ? (Helmond: Drukkerij Helmond, 1936).

Portuguese: *Os crimes do unicórnio,* tr. Pedro Faria (Lisbon: Empresa Nacional de Publicidade, 1950).

Danish: *Enhjørningen draeber,* tr. Grete Juel Jørgensen (Copenhagen: Hirschsprung, 1959).

Spanish: *Los crimenes del unicornio,* tr. Leonardo A. Wadel (Buenos Aires: Peuser, 1963?).

Norwegian: *Enhjørningen,* tr. Kjell Midttun (Oslo: Elingard, 1973).

The Arabian Nights Murder. New York: Harper & Brothers, 1936. London: Hamish Hamilton, 1936. New York: Grosset & Dunlap, 1938. New York: Hillman, 1943. New York: Collier, 1965.

Translations:

Swedish: *Tusen-och-en-natt-mysteriet,* tr. Greta Åkerhielm (Stockholm: Skoglund, 1936; rpt. Stockholm: Geber, 1964).

Italian: *Notti arabe,* tr. Maria Colombi (Milan: Alpe, 1945). *Delitti da mille e una notte,* tr. Maria Luisa Bocchino (Milan: Club degli Editori, 1980).

Portuguese: *O crime das mil e uma noites,* tr. A. J. Barreto (Lisbon: Editorial Minerva, 1956).

The Punch and Judy Murders (as by Carter Dickson). London: William Heinemann, 1936 (as *The Magic-Lantern Murders*). New York: William Morrow, 1937. New York: Grosset & Dunlap, 1938. New York: Pocket, 1943. New York: Berkley, 1964. New York: International Polygonics, 1988.

Translations:

Dutch: *Op bevel van den chef,* tr. H. Koerts (Helmond: Drukkerij Helmond, 1938).

German: *Der umgekehrte Blumentopf,* tr. Renate Welling (Zurich: Albert Müller, 1947).

French: *Arsenic et boutons de manchettes,* tr. Benoit-Fleury (Paris: Hachette, 1950).

Swedish: *Morden på Kasperteatern,* tr. Jan Samuelson (Stockholm: Tiden, 1966).

The Burning Court. New York: Harper & Brothers, 1937. London: Hamish Hamilton, 1937. New York: Popular Library, 1944. London: British Publishers Guild, 1952. New York: Bantam, 1954. New York: Award, 1969. London: Tandem, 1970. New York: International Polygonics, 1985.

Translations:

German: *Die Schnur mit neun Knoten,* tr. Rosemarie von Jankó (Vienna: Ibach, 1938). *Die Doppelgängerin,* tr. Kurt Wagenseil (Bern: Scherz, 1956; rpt. Frankfurt am Main: Ullstein, 1965).

Swedish: *Svart sabbat,* tr. Rolf Wiesler (Stockholm: Bonnier, 1939; rpt. Stockholm: Aldus/Bonnier, 1963).

Norwegian: *Sort messe*, tr. Niels Christian Brøgger (Oslo: Aschehoug, 1941; rpt. Oslo: Fredhøi, 1966; rpt. Stabekk: Bokklubben, 1977).

Italian: *La magia nell'amore*, tr. ? (Naples: Società Editrice Partenopea, 1946).

Spanish: *La cámera ardiente*, tr. María Romero (Santiago, Chile: Zig-Zag, 1951). *La cámera ardiente*, tr. Juan José Mira (Barcelona: Planeta, 1953; rpt. Barcelona: Gerplá, 1957).

French: *La Chambre ardente*, tr. Maurice-Bernard Endrèbe (Paris: Club du Livre Policier, 1958; rpt. Paris: Livre de Poche, 1962; rpt. Paris: Néo-Nouvelles Editions Oswald, 1983).

Dutch: *Het lijk in de crypt*, tr. C. Verlinden-Bakx (Utrecht: Het Spectrum, 1960; rpt. Kalmthout, Belgium: W. Beckers, 1970).

Portuguese: *O enigma de cripta*, tr. Baptista de Carvalho (Lisbon: Editorial Minerva, 1960?).

Turkish: *Dokuz düğumlü ip*, tr. Meral Gaspirali (Istanbul: Tifdruk Matbaacilik Sanayii, 1963).

The Peacock Feather Murders (as by Carter Dickson). New York: William Morrow, 1937. London: William Heinemann, 1937. Leipzig: Tauchnitz, 1938. New York: Grosset & Dunlap, 1939. New York: Pocket, 1942. Harmondsworth: Penguin, 1951. New York: Berkley, 1963. London: Tom Stacey, 1971. London: Severn House, 1975. New York: International Polygonics, 1987. (All British editions use the title *The Ten Teacups*.)

Translations:

Dutch: *De noodlottige pauwenveeren*, tr. J. D. A. van Gumster (Laren: A. G. Schoonderbeek, 1938).

French: *La Police est invitée*, tr. S. Lechevrel (Paris: Nouvelle Revue Critique, 1938).

German: *Zehn Teetassen*, tr. Heinz Zürchner (Zurich: Albert Müller, 1941).

Finnish: *Kymmenen teekuppia*, tr. Eero Ahmavaara (Helsinki: Söderström, 1953).

Swedish: *De tio tekopparna*, tr. Nils Jacobson (Stockholm: Almqvist & Wiksell/Geber, 1958).

Spanish: *La policía está invitada*, tr. Alfredo de León (Buenos Aires: Peuser, 1963).

Turkish: *On çay fincani*, tr. Gönül Suveren (Istanbul: Altin Kitaplan Yayinevi, 1966).

The Four False Weapons. New York: Harper & Brothers, 1937. London: Hamish Hamilton, 1938. New York: Popular Library, 1950. New York: Berkley, 1957. London: Pan, 1961. New York: Collier, 1962. London: Tom Stacey, 1973. Feltham: Hamlyn, 1982.

Translation:

German *Zweimal ermordet?*, Karl Hellwig (Bern: Scherz, 1957).

The Third Bullet (as by Carter Dickson). London: Hodder & Stoughton, 1937.

To Wake the Dead. London: Hamish Hamilton, 1937. New York: Harper & Brothers, 1938. Leipzig: Tauchnitz, 1938. New York: Grosset & Dunlap, 1940. New York: Popular Library, 1943. New York: Books, Inc., 1944. London: Pan, 1948. New York: Dell, 1952. New York: Berkley, 1956. New York: Collier, 1965. London: Severn House, 1975.

Translations:

Swedish: *Väck ej de döda!*, tr. Ingalisa Munck (Stockholm: Bonnier, 1940).

Spanish: *El brazelete romano*, tr. Pablo Antoñana (Barcelona: Luis de Caralt, 1961).

German: *Der magische Stein*, tr. Maria Meinert (Bern: Scherz, 1962).

The Judas Window (as by Carter Dickson). New York: William Morrow, 1938. London: William Heinemann, 1938. New York: Grosset & Dunlap, 1940. New York: Pocket, 1943. Harmondsworth: Penguin, 1951. New York: Berkley, 1964 (as

Bibliography   153

The Crossbow Murder). London: Tom Stacey, 1971. New York: International Polygonics, 1987.

Translations:

Dutch: *Het Judasventer,* tr. J. D. A. van Gumster (Laren: A. G. Schoonderbeek, 1939). *Het Judasoog,* tr. E. Kuiper-de Boer (Utrecht: Het Spectrum, 1962).

Swedish: *Det slutna rummet,* tr. Torsten Ehrenmark (Stockholm: Geber, 1953). *Det slutna rummet,* tr. Karl Olof Hedström (Stockholm: B. Wahlström, 1960).

Finnish: *Juudaksen ikkuna,* tr. Eero Ahmavaara (Helsinki: Söderström, 1954).

German: *Der dritte Pfeil,* tr. Renate Hertenstein (Bern: Scherz, 1955).

Danish: *Døden i Judasvinduet,* tr. Grete Juel Jørgensen (Copenhagen: Hirschsprung, 1958).

Norwegian: *Judasøyet,* tr. Bjorn Carling (Oslo: Gyldendal, 1976; rpt. Sjøholt: Norild, 1985).

Italian: *L'occhio de Guida,* tr. A. Sole (Milan: Mondadori, 1985).

Death in Five Boxes (as by Carter Dickson). New York: William Morrow, 1938. London: William Heinemann, 1938. New York: Grosset & Dunlap, 1940. New York: Dell, 1946. Harmondsworth: Penguin, 1951. New York: Berkley, 1964. New York: Belmont Tower, 1973. New York: Bantam, 1982.

Translations:

Dutch: *Het geheim der verzegelde doozen,* tr. J. D. A. van Gumster (Laren: A. G. Schoonderbeek, 1939).

German: *Der vierte Gast,* tr. Heinz Zürchner (Zurich: Albert Müller, 1940; rpt. Frankfurt am Main: Ullstein, 1958).

Italian: *Le cinque scatole,* tr. Stanislal La Bruna (Milan: Alpe, 1941).

Turkish: *Dördüncü misafir,* tr. Sedar Elman (Istanbul: Turkiye Yayinevi, 1944).

French: *Ils étaient quatre à table,* tr. Jean-Pierre Dubois (Geneva: Editions Ditis, 1945; rpt. Paris: Néo-Nouvelles Editions Oswald, 1983).

Serbo-Croatian: *Usodnih pet škatel,* tr. Majda Stanovnik (Llubljana: Državna Založba Slovenije, 1962; 2 vols.)

Spanish: *Muerte en cinco cajas,* tr. Marta M. Sánchez Albornoz (Madrid: Alianza, 1976).

The Crooked Hinge. New York: Harper & Brothers, 1938. London: Hamish Hamilton, 1938. New York: Popular Library, 1943. New York: Dell, 1955. London: Pan, 1957. New York: Berkley, 1958. New York: Collier, 1964. San Diego: University Extension, University of California, San Diego, 1976.

Translations:

French: *Le naufragé du "Titanic",* tr. Paul Jean Hughes (Paris: Nouvelle Revue Critique, 1939; rpt. Paris: Champs-Elysées, 1987).

Swedish: *Det krökta gångjärnet,* tr. Erik Lindegren (Stockholm: Bonnier, 1940).

Italian: *Il segreto dell'automa,* tr. Ilde Fima (Milan: Alpe, 1941). *L'Automa,* tr. Fluffy Mazzucato (Milan: Mondadori, 1948).

Norwegian: *Det hvite hengslet,* tr. Hans Heiberg (Oslo: Aschehoug, 1941; rpt. Oslo: Fredhøi, 1966).

German: *Gesucht: Ein Motiv,* tr. U. Müller-Kuhle (Bern: Scherz, 1959).

Danish: *Doden og dukken,* tr. Erik Haugmark (Copenhagen: Skrifola, 1959; rpt. Glostrup: Winther, 1970).

Fatal Descent (as by John Rhode [pseud. of C. J. C. Street] and Carter Dickson). New York: Dodd, Mead, 1939. London: William Heinemann, 1939 (as *Drop to His Death*). New York: Popular Library, 1947. New York: Dover, 1987.

Translations:

Dutch: *Moord of vergelding?*, tr. A. D. Baert (Laren: A. G. Schoonderbeek, 1940).
German: *Endstation Tod*, tr. Maria Meinert (Bern: Scherz, 1958).
The Problem of the Green Capsule. New York: Harper & Brothers, 1939. London:
Hamish Hamilton, 1939. New York: Grosset & Dunlap, 1941. New York: Books,
Inc., 1944. New York: Bantam, 1947. London: Pan, 1947. London: New English
Library, 1965. New York: Berkley, 1970. New York: Award, 1976. New York:
International Polygonics, 1986. (All British editions use the title *The Black
Spectacles.*)
Translations:
Dutch: *Het mysterie van de groene capsule*, tr. Dicky Wafelbakker (Amsterdam: Ned.
Keurboekerij, 1940). *Blinde ooggetuigen*, tr. G. van Bergen van der Grijp-Matla
(Utrecht: Het Spectrum, 1960).
Italian: *Occhiali neri*, tr. Alfredo Pitta (Milan: Sonzogno, 1941). *Occhiali neri*, tr.
Bruno Segre (Milan, 1953).
Danish: *Den grønne Kapsel*, tr. Asta Heiberg (Copehnagen: Athenaeum, 1942).
Spanish: *Los anteojos negros*, tr. ? (Buenos Aires: Emecé, 1951). *Los anteojos negros*,
tr. Marta Acosta van Praet (Barcelona: EDHASA, 1956; rpt. Havana: Instituto
del Libro, 1969 [as *Los espejuelos oscuros*]; rpt. Buenos Aires: Alianza Emecé,
1973 [as *Las gafas negros*]).
German: *Die grüne Kapsel*, tr. Carla Signorell (Bern: Scherz, 1954; rpt. Frankfurt
am Main: Ullstein, 1966).
Portuguese: *A problema da cápsula verde*, tr. Berta Mendes (Lisbon: Editorial Século,
1957?).
Serbo-Croatian: *Tajna zelene Kapsle*, tr. Branko Golović (Sarajevo: Svjetlost, 1964).
French: *Les Yeux en bandoulière*, tr. Jane Fillion (Paris: J'ai Lu, 1968; rpt. Paris:
Champs-Elysées, 1986).
The Reader Is Warned (as by Carter Dickson). New York: William Morrow, 1939.
London: William Heinemann, 1939. New York: Grosset & Dunlap, 1941. New
York: Pocket, 1945. Harmondsworth: Penguin, 1951. New York: Berkley, 1964.
Translations:
French: *Le Lecteur est prévenu*, tr. Henri Thies (Paris: Nouvelle Revue Critique,
1940).
Danish: *Vi advarer Dem*, tr. Vicky Merlin (Copenhagen: Hirschsprung, 1956; rpt.
Copenhagen: Aschehoug, 1964).
Swedish: *Lasaren varnas*, tr. Thomas Bennett (Stockholm: Almqvist & Wiksell/Geber,
1957).
Portuguese: *Desafio ao leitor*, tr. Almeida Campos (Lisbon: Editorial Minerva, 1960).
Polish: *Ostrzegam czytelnika*, tr. Krystyna Tomorowicz (Warsaw: Czytelnik, 1972).
Norwegian: *Hvis tanker kan drepe*, tr. Truls Huff (Oslo: Gyldendal, 1979).
The Problem of the Wire Cage. New York: Harper & Brothers, 1939. London: Hamish
Hamilton, 1940. New York: Grosset & Dunlap, 1942. New York: Books, Inc.,
1944. New York: Bantam, 1948. London: Pan, 1949. New York: Berkley, 1970.
London: Corgi, 1970. London: Severn House, 1977. New York: Zebra, 1986.
Translations:
German: *Mord am Netz*, tr. Rudolf Hochglend (Zurich: Albert Müller, 1941; rpt.
Frankfurt am Main: Ullstein, 1969). *Tennisspieler und Sielakrobaten*, tr. Karl
Hellwig (Bern: Scherz, 1962).
French: *Meurtre après la pluie*, tr. Gabrielle Ferraris (Geneva: Editions Ditis, 1947).
Spanish: *La jaula mortal*, tr. Julio Vacareyza (Buenos Aires: Acmé, 1951).

Dutch: *Moord op de tennisbaan*, tr. L. Oudendijk-Grossouw (Utrecht: Het Spectrum, 1961).
Turkish: *Ayak izleri*, tr. Azize Bergin (Istanbul: Tifdruk Matbaacilik Sanayii, 1963).
Greek: [Title unknown], tr. Évanguélos Kochlatzis (Athens: Viper, 1976).
Swedish: *Som av en osynlig hand*, tr. Gunilla Berglund (Höganäs: Läsabra, 1982).
Norwegian: *Den usynlige hånden*, tr. Finn B. Larsen (Sjøholt: Norild, 1984).
And So to Murder (as by Carter Dickson). New York: William Morrow, 1941. London: William Heinemann, 1941. New York: Grosset & Dunlap, 1942. New York: Dell, 1947. Harmondsworth: Penguin, 1951. New York: Berkley, 1965. Bath: Chivers, 1987. New York: Zebra, 1988.
Translations:
German: *Der Tod dreht einen Film*, tr. Rudolf Hochglend (Zurich: Albert Müller, 1941). *Vitriol und Belladonna*, tr. Walter Baumann (Bern: Scherz. 1963).
Turkish: *Ölüm film çeviriyor*, tr. Sedat Elman (Istanbul: Turkiye Yayinevi, 1945).
Danish: *Der blaendes op for mord*, tr. Grete Juel Jørgensen (Copenhagen: Hirschsprung, 1956; rpt. Copenhagen: Aschehoug, 1964).
The Man Who Could Not Shudder. New York: Harper & Brothers, 1940. London: Hamish Hamilton, 1940. New York: Grosset & Dunlap, 1942. New York: Books, Inc., 1944. New York: Collier, 1946. New York: Bantam, 1949. New York: Berkley, 1971. London: Severn House, 1977. New York: Zebra, 1986.
Translations:
German: *Der verhexte Haus*, tr. Ursula von Wiese (Zurich: Albert Müller, 1943; rpt. Frankfurt am Main: Ullstein, 1965).
Dutch: *De man die niet bang was*, tr. A. J. Richel (Utrecht: Het Spectrum, 1966 [with novels by Ellery Queen, Patrick Quentin, Ngaio Marsh, and Edgar Wallace]; rpt. Utrecht: Het Spectrum, 1969 [Carr novel only]).
Italian: *Fantasma party*, tr. A. M. Francavilla (Milan: Mondadori, 1983).
Nine—and Death Makes Ten (as by Carter Dickson). New York: William Morrow, 1940. London: William Heinemann, 1940 (as *Murder in the Submarine Zone*). New York: Grosset & Dunlap, 1943. New York: Pocket Books, 1945. London: World Distributors, 1959 (as *Murder in the Atlantic*). New York: Berkley, 1966. New York: International Polygonics, 1987.
Translations:
German: *Mörder an Bord*, tr. Ursula von Wiese (Zurich: Albert Müller, 1944).
Swedish: *Nio och döden blir tio*, tr. K. Stubbendorff (Stockholm: Tiden, 1945; rpt. Stockholm: Prisma, 1965). *Mord i ubåtszonen*, tr. Gunnar Unger (Höganäs: Bra Bocker, 1973).
Spanish: *Nueve e la muerte son diez*, tr. J. Dalino (Madrid: Ediciones Albatros, 1948).
Turkish: *Ölüm gemisi*, tr. Nihal Karamağali (Istanbul: Tifdruk Matbaacilik Sanayii, 1963).
Danish: *Mord ombord*, tr. Ib Christiansen (Copenhagen: Lademann, 1976).
Norwegian: *Ni pluss døden blir ti*, tr. Thor Christian Borch (Oslo: Aschehoug, 1980).
Italian: *Fantasma in mare*, tr. Bruno Just Lazzari (Mondadori, 1983).
The Case of the Constant Suicides. New York: Harper & Brothers, 1941. London: Hamish Hamilton, 1941. New York: Grosset & Dunlap, 1943. New York: Dell, 1945. New York: Books, Inc. 1946. Bern: Scherz Phoenix, 1947. Harmondsworth: Penguin, 1953. New York: Berkley, 1957. New York: Collier, 1963. Hornchurch: Ian Henry, 1982.
Translations:

Danish: *Selvmord igen?*, tr. Asta Heiberg (Copenhagen: Athenaeum, 1942; rpt. Copenhagen: Skrifola, 1959 [as *Doden spiller på soekkepibe*]; rpt. Copenhagen: Winther, 1969).

German: *Verwirrung auf Schloss Shira*, tr. Ursula von Wiese (Zurich: Albert Müller, 1944; rpt. Gütersloh: Signum, 1962).

French: *Suicides à l'Ecossaise*, tr. Adrienne Perroy (Geneva: Editions Ditis, 1946; rpt. Paris: Champs-Elysées, 1984).

Swedish: *Dörren låst inifrån*, tr. Gosta Dahlman (Stockholm: Bonnier, 1950).

Spanish: *Los suicidios constantes*, tr. Lucrecia Moreno de Sáenz (Buenos Aires: Emecé, 1952).

Portuguese: *O casio dos suicidíos*, tr. Béni Homan (Lisbon: Empresa Nacional de Publicidade, 1960?).

Dutch: *Den moordenaar was een Schot*, tr. Iet Houwer (Utrecht: Het Spectrum, 1965; rpt. Eindhoven: Grootdruk-Uitgeverij, 1982).

Hungarian: *A sorozatos öngyilkosságok esete*, tr. Bart István (Budapest: Alföldi, 1971).

Norwegian: *Dodstårnet*, tr. Nils Nordberg (Oslo: Gyldendal, 1972).

Seeing Is Believing (as by Carter Dickson). New York: William Morrow, 1941. London: William Heinemann, 1942. New York: Grosset & Dunlap, 1943. Cleveland: World Publishing Co., 1945. New York: Pocket, 1946. London: World Distributors, 1959 (as *Cross of Murder*). New York: Berkley, 1966.

Translations:

German: *Mit Dolch und Strychnin*, tr. Ursula von Wiese (Zurich: Albert Müller, 1943).

French: *On n'en croix pas ses yeux*, tr. Gabrielle Ferraris (Geneva: Editions Ditis, 1946; rpt. Paris: J'ai Lu, 1964; rpt. Paris: Champs-Elysées, 1985).

Danish: *Øjet kan bedrage*, tr. Nils Andersen (Copenhagen: Hirschsprung, 1956; rpt. Copenhagen: Aschehoug, 1964).

Norwegian: *Øyet kan bedra*, tr. Finn B. Larsen (Sjøholt: Norild, 1977).

Death Turns the Tables. New York: Harper & Brothers, 1941. London: Hamish Hamilton, 1941. Bern: Scherz, 1943. New York: Grosset & Dunlap, 1944. New York: Pocket, 1945. New York: Books, Inc., 1946. New York: Collier, 194-. New York: Berkley, 1959. London: Pan, 1960. London: New English Library, 1965. New York: International Polygonics, 1985. (All British editions and the Bern edition use the title *The Seat of the Scornful.*)

Translations:

French: *Le Juge Ireton est accusé*, tr. Estelle Lauber-Mercier (Geneva: Editions Ditis, 1945; rpt. Paris: Champs-Elysées, 1985).

Swedish: *Mördaren skipar rättvisa*, tr. Gösta Dahlman (Stockholm: Bonnier, 1945).

Portuguese: *O mistério de areia vermelha*, tr. José de Natividade Gaspar (Lisbon: Sociedade Nacional de Tipografia, 1946).

Norwegian: *Anklaget*, tr. Arnljot Thuve (Oslo: Ekko, 1947). *Katt og mus*, tr. Per Christian Karlsen (Oslo: For Alle, 1979).

Italian: *Il guidice è accusato*, tr. ? (Milan: Mondadori, 1947).

Spanish: *La sede de la soberbia*, tr. Elvira Martín (Buenos Aires: Emecé, 1947).

Dutch: *Het laatste schaakspel*, tr. J. de Groot (Utrecht: Het Spectrum, 1960).

German: *Auf dass ihr nicht gerichtet werdet*, tr. Marlen Scherm (Frankfurt am Main: Ullstein, 1964).

The Gilded Man (as by Carter Dickson). New York: William Morrow, 1942. London: William Heinemann, 1942. New York: Grosset & Dunlap, 1944. New York:

Pocket, 1947 (as *Death and the Gilded Man*). London: Pan, 1951. New York: Berkley, 1966. New York: International Polygonics, 1988.

Translations:

French: *L'Homme en or*, tr. Jean Loriot (Paris: Hachette, 1947).

Spanish: *Hombre de oro*, tr. Armando Lazaro Ros (Madrid: Saturnino Calleja, 1948).

Dutch: *Het gemaskerde huis*, tr. André E. Steentjes ('s-Gravenh: Servire, 1952).

German: *Das Haus der Masken*, tr. Hans M. Tilgen (Bern: Scherz, 1957).

The Emperor's Snuff-Box. New York: Harper & Brothers, 1942. London: Hamish Hamilton, 1943. New York: Grosset & Dunlap, 1944. New York: Pocket, 1946. New York: Books, Inc., 1946. Bern: Scherz, 194-. Harmondsworth: Penguin, 1953. New York: Berkley, 1959. Hornchurch: Ian Henry, 1982. New York: Carroll & Graf, 1986. New York: Critics Choice, 1986.

Translations:

French: *Un Coup sur la tabatière*, tr. Madeleine Répond (Geneva: Editions Ditis, 1945; rpt. Paris: Néo-Nouvelles Editions Oswald, 1983). *Un Coup sur la tabatière*, tr. André Maury (Paris: J'ai Lu, 1964).

Italian: *La tabacchiera dell'imperatore*, tr. Alberto Tedeschi (Milan: Mondadori, 1946; rpt. Milan: Mondadori, 1975).

Portuguese: *A caixa de rape*, tr. Humberto Santos (Lisbon: Empresa Nacional de Publicidade, 1961?).

German: *Des Kaisers Schupftabakdose*, tr. Max Bertschinger (Zurich: Albert Müller, 1947; rpt. Frankfurt am Main: Ullstein, 1964).

Norwegian: *Keiserans snusdåse*, tr. Gunvor Havrevold (Oslo: Aschehoug, 1947).

Spanish: *La tabaquera del emperador*, tr. T. G. Esparza (Barcelona: Luis de Caralt, 1953). *La tabaquera del emperador*, tr. L. M. (Barcelona: G. P. Hermanos, 1958).

Serbo-Croatian: *Careva Burmutica*, tr. Andelija Ninčić (Belgrade: Kosmos, 1955).

Polish: *Tabakierka cesarza*, tr. Krystyna Tomorowicz (Warsaw: Czytelnik, 1968).

Dutch: *De snuifdoos van de Keizer*, tr. A. B. H. van Bommel-van Terwisga (Utrecht: Het Spectrum, 1974).

She Died a Lady (as by Carter Dickson). New York: William Morrow, 1943. London: William Heinemann, 1943. New York: Grosset & Dunlap, 1944. New York: Pocket, 1948. Milan: Mondadori, 1948. Stockholm: Zephyr, 1948. Harmondsworth: Penguin, 1951. New York: Berkley, 1966. London: Tom Stacey, 1972. New York: Zebra, 1987.

Translations:

French: *Je préfère mourir*, tr. Gabrielle Ferraris (Geneva: Editions Ditis, 1946; rpt. Paris: Champs-Elysées, 1987).

German: *Spuren am Klippenrand*, tr. Margaret Boesch (Zurich: Albert Müller, 1946; rpt. Gütersloh: Signum, 1962).

Swedish: *Hon dog som en dam*, tr. Sonja Bergvall (Stockholm: Bonnier, 1946; rpt. Stockholm: Aldus/Bonnier, 1960).

Spanish: *Murió como una dama*, tr. Eva Iribarne (Buenos Aires: Espasa-Calpe Argentina, 1947; rpt. Madrid: Espasa-Calpe, 1967).

Dutch: *Zij stierf als dame*, tr. M. M. Janzen-Marquard (Utrecht: Het Spectrum, 1965; rpt. Amsterdam: Amsterdam Boek, 1973).

He Wouldn't Kill Patience (as by Carter Dickson). New York: Hampton Publishing Co./William Morrow, 1944. London: William Heinemann, 1944. New York: Dell, 1950. Harmondsworth: Penguin, 1951. New York: Berkley, 1966. New York: International Polygonics, 1988.

158   John Dickson Carr: A Critical Study

Translations:
French: *Il n'aurait pas tué Patience*, tr. Guite Barbet Massin (Paris: La Jeune Parque, 1946; rpt. Paris: Néo-Nouvelles Editions Oswald, 1983).
Norwegian: *Det forseglede rommet*, tr. Nils Brantzeg (Oslo: Amsterdam, 1952; rpt. Sjøholt: Norild, 1982).
German: *Der versiegelte Zimmer*, tr. Hans M. Tilgen (Bern: Scherz, 1956).
Swedish: *Listig som en orm*, tr. Roland Adlerberth (Halmstad: Spektra, 1974).
Italian: *Perché uccidere Patience?*, tr. A. M. Francavilla (Milan: Mondadori, 1985).
Till Death Do Us Part. New York: Harper & Brothers, 1944. London: Hamish Hamilton, 1944. New York: Walter J. Black (Detective Book Club), 1944? Bern: Scherz, 1946. New York: Grosset & Dunlap, 1946. New York: Collier, 194-. India: Thacker & Co., 194-. New York: Bantam, 1950. Harmondsworth: Penguin, 1953. New York: Berkley, 1971. New York: International Polygonics, 1985.
Translations:
Spanish: *Hasta que la muerte nos separe*, tr. Alberto Horowitz (Buenos Aires: El Ateneo, 1947; rpt. Buenos Aires: Emecé, 1951; rpt. Barcelona: EDHASA, 1956; rpt. Madrid: Alianza, 1975).
German: *Der Wahrsager und die Wahrheit*, tr. Ilse Leisi-Gugler (Zurich: Albert Müller, 1948; rpt. Gütersloh: Mohn, 1961).
Swedish: *Tills döden skiljer oss at*, tr. Gosta Dahlman (Stockholm: Bonnier, 1949).
Italian: *Fino alla morte*, tr. ? (Milan: Mondadori, 1951).
Norwegian: *Till døden skiller oss åt*, tr. Ragnvald Skredo (Oslo: Aschehoug, 1953).
Portuguese: *O mistério do cofre secreto*, tr. Maria Isabel de Savedra Aboim Inglês (Lisbon: Editorial Século, 1958).
Danish: *Til døden os skiller*, tr. Knud Müller (Copenhagen: Skrifola, 1959; rpt. Copenhagen: Winther, 1969).
Greek: *To teleutaio enklēma*, tr. Giannē Pissē (Athens: Viper, 1973).
The Curse of the Bronze Lamp (as by Carter Dickson). New York: William Morrow, 1945. London: William Heinemann, 1946 (as *Lord of the Sorcerers*). New York: Editions for the Armed Services, 1946. New York: Grosset & Dunlap, 1947. New York: Pocket, 1949. New York: Pan, 1956. New York: Berkley, 1967. New York: Carroll & Graf, 1984. London: Hogarth, 1987.
Translations:
French: *L'Habit fait le moine*, tr. Gabrielle Ferraris (Geneva: Editions Ditis, 1947; rpt. Paris: Néo-Nouvelles Editions Oswald, 1983).
German: *Der Hexenmeister*, tr. Ursula von Wiese (Zurich: Albert Müller, 1947).
Italian: *La lampada di bronzo*, tr. ? (Milan: Mondadori, 1950).
Swedish: *Bronslampan*, tr. Margareta Ångström (Stockholm: Almqvist & Wiksell/ Geber, 1955; rpt. Stockholm: Prisma, 1965).
Spanish: *La lámpara de bronce*, tr. A. Rivero (Barcelona: G.P. Hermanos, 1958).
Norwegian: *Bronselampens forbannelse*, tr. Truls Hoff (Oslo: Gyldendal, 1980).
He Who Whispers. New York: Harper & Brothers, 1946. London: Hamish Hamilton, 1946. New York: Walter J. Black (Detective Book Club), 1946? New York: Bantam, 1951. Harmondsworth: Penguin, 1953. New York: Award, 1976. Bath: Lythway Press, 1977. New York: International Polygonics, 1986.
Translations:
German: *Der Flüsterer*, tr. ? (Bern: Scherz, 1947; rpt. Frankfurt am Main: Ullstein, 1966).
Norwegian: *Stemmen som hvisket*, tr. Jacob R. Sverdrup (Oslo: Aschehoug, 1950).
Italian: *Il terrore che mormora*, tr. ? (Milan: Mondadori, 1951).

Danish: *Kun dǿden taler sagte*, tr. Knud E. Andersen (Copenhagen: Skrifola, 1960).
Portuguese: *A bengala-de-estoque*, tr. Béni Homan (Lisbon: Empresa Nacional de Publicidade, 1960?).
Dutch: *De fluisterende moordenaar*, tr. G. van Bergen van der Grijp-Matla (Utrecht: Het Spectrum, 1964).
French: *Celui qui murmure*, tr. Elisabeth Gille (Paris: J'ai Lu, 1969; rpt. Paris: Néo-Nouvelles Editions Oswald, 1982).
My Late Wives (as by Carter Dickson). New York: William Morrow, 1946. New York: Editions for the Armed Services, 1946. London: William Heinemann, 1947. New York: Grosset & Dunlap, 1948. New York: Pocket, 1949. London: Pan, 1953. London: World Distributors, 1960. New York: Berkley, 1967. New York: Zebra, 1988.
Translations:
German: *Die verschundenen Gattinen*, tr. ? (Bern: Scherz, 1947; rpt. Klagenfurt: Kaiser, 1965 [with novels by Agatha Christie and Mignon G. Eberhart]; rpt. Munich: Goldmann, 1974).
French: *La Maison de la terreur*, tr. Léo Delval (Paris: Hachette, 1948).
Swedish: *Mina framlidna fruar*, tr. Nils Jacobsson (Stockholm: Almqvist & Wiksell/ Geber, 1954; rpt. Stockholm: B. Wahlstrom, 1961).
Danish: *Mine ekskoner*, tr. Th. Behrens (Copenhagen: Hirschsprung, 1956; rpt. Copenhagen: Aschehoug, 1964).
Norwegian: *Mine ekskoner*, tr. Finn B. Larsen (Sjǿholt: Norild, 1979).
The Sleeping Sphinx. New York: Harper & Brothers, 1947. London: Hamish Hamilton, 1947. New York: Editions for the Armed Services, 1947. New York: Walter J. Black (Detective Book Club), 1947. New York: Bantam, 1952. London: Pan, 1962. New York: Berkley, 1971. London: Severn House, 1976. New York: International Polygonics, 1985.
Translations:
German: *Die schlafende Sphinx*, tr. Renate Hertenstein (Bern: Scherz, 1948).
Italian: *La sfinge dormiente*, tr. ? (Milan: Mondadori, 1949).
French: *Le Sphinx endormi*, tr. Maurice-Bernard Endrèbe (Geneva: Editions Ditis, 1948; rpt. Paris: Christian Bourgois, 1971; rpt. Paris: Livre de Poche, 1978; rpt. Paris: Champs-Elysées, 1985).
Norwegian: *Den sovende sfinksen*, tr. Otto Carlmar (Oslo: Aschehoug, 1949).
Spanish: *La esfinge durmiente*, tr. ? (Buenos Aires: Acmé, 1952).
Serbo-Croatian: *Speča sfinga*, tr. Vinko Kopač (Llubljana: Državna Založba Slovenije, 1962).
Danish: *Den sovende sfinks*, tr. Mogens Cohrt (Copenhagen: Skrifola, 1965).
The Skeleton in the Clock (as by Carter Dickson). New York: William Morrow, 1948. London: William Heinemann, 1949. New York: Dell, 1951. London: Pan, 1958. New York: Berkley, 1967. New York: Belmont Tower, 1973. New York: Bantam, 1982.
Translations:
Turkish: *Saatteki iskelet*, tr. Leylâ Yazicioǧli (Istanbul: Türkiye Yayinevi, 1953).
Swedish: *Släkten är värst*, tr. Astrid Borger (Stockholm: B. Walhström, 1958).
Danish: *Morderen i spejlet*, tr. Grete Juel Jǿrgensen (Copenhagen: Hirschsprung, 1959)
German: *Das Skelett*, tr. Bodo Baumann (Bern: Scherz, 1965).

160   John Dickson Carr: A Critical Study

Below Suspicion. New York: Harper & Brothers, 1949. London: Hamish Hamilton, 1950. New York: Bantam, 1953. Harmondsworth: Penguin, 1956. London: Corgi, 1971. London: Tom Stacey, 1972. New York: Award, 1976. New York: International Polygonics, 1986.

Translations:

Norwegian: *Heksesabbat,* tr. Leo Strøm (Oslo: Aschehoug, 1951). *Mistanken,* tr. Åke Immer (Oslo: For Alle, 1976).

German: *Das umgekehrte Kreuz,* tr. Renate Hertenstein (Bern: Scherz, 1952; rpt. Klagenfurt: Kaiser, 1966 [with novels by Erle Stanley Gardner and Ursula Curtiss]; rpt. Frankfurt am Main: Ullstein, 1973).

Spanish: *Oscura sospecha,* tr. Juan José Mira (Barcelona: Planeta, 1952; rpt. Barcelona: G.P. Hermanos, 1956; rpt. Barcelona: Edisven, 1968).

Portuguese: *Sob suspeita,* tr. Fernando Carmo Quirino (Lisbon: Editorial Século, 1956?).

Danish: *Giften i vandet,* tr. Mogens Cohrt (Copenhagen: Lademann, 1975).

French: *Satan vaut bien une messe,* tr. Jane Fillion (Paris: J'ai Lu, 1968; rpt. Paris: Champs-Elysées, 1986).

A Graveyard to Let (as by Carter Dickson). New York: William Morrow, 1949. London: William Heinemann, 1950. New York: Dell, 1951. London: Pan, 1955. London: World Distributors, 1960. New York: Berkley, 1968. New York: Belmont Tower, 1973. New York: Zebra, 1988.

Translations:

Dutch: *Een kerkhof te huur,* tr. P. Honeij ('s-Gravenh: Servire, 1954).

French: *Passe-passe,* tr. Marie-Claude Morel (Paris: Champs-Elysées, 1961).

The Bride of Newgate. New York: Harper & Brothers, 1950. London: Hamish Hamilton, 1950. New York: Avon, 1952. London: Corgi, 1956. New York: Curtis, 1972. New York: Carroll & Graf, 1986.

Translations:

Turkish: *Hapishane gelini,* tr. Seniha Sami (Istanbul: A. Halit Yasaroğlu, 1951).

Danish: *Galgebruden,* tr. Arne Stevns (Copenhagen: Hasselbalch, 1953).

Spanish: *La desposada de Newgate,* tr. Carlos Paytuvi de Sierra (Barcelona: Luis de Caralt, 1955; rpt. Barcelona: G.P. Hermanos, 1957).

Portuguese: *O caso do coche fantasma,* tr. A. J. Cruz Barreto (Lisbon: Editorial Minerva, 1957?).

Swedish: *Bruden i Newgate,* tr. Roland Adlerberth (Stockholm: Prisma, 1962).

Italian: *La sposa di Newgate,* tr. A. M. Francavilla (Milan: Mondadori, 1984).

Night at the Mocking Widow (as by Carter Dickson). New York: William Morrow, 1950. London: William Heinemann, 1951. New York: Dell, 1953. London: Pan, 1959. New York: Berkley, 1969. New York: Zebra, 1988.

Translations:

Swedish: *Den gäckande änkan,* tr. Bertil Lagerstrom (Stockholm: B. Wahlström, 1962).

Spanish: *La noche de la viuda burlona,* tr. Clara de la Rosa (Madrid: Alianza; Buenos Aires: Emecé, 1977; rpt. Barcelona: Bruguera, 1983).

Norwegian: *Enkens onde øye,* tr. Truls Hoff (Oslo: Gyldendal, 1980).

The Devil in Velvet. New York: Harper & Brothers, 1951. London: Hamish Hamilton, 1951. New York: Bantam, 1952. Harmondsworth: Penguin, 1957. New York: Carroll & Graf, 1987.

Translations:

German: *Einen Namen für den Mörder,* tr. Maria Meinert (Bern: Scherz, 1965).

Swedish: *Djävulen i sammet,* tr. Roland Adlerberth (Stockholm: Prisma, 1969).

Behind the Crimson Blind (as by Carter Dickson). New York: William Morrow, 1952. London: William Heinemann, 1952. New York: Dell, 1953. London: Pan, 1960. London: Thriller Book Club, n.d.

Translation:

German: *Treffpunkt Tangier*, tr. Renate Hertenstein (Bern: Scherz, 1954; rpt. Klagenfurt: Kaiser, 1965 [with novels by Ellery Queen and Frances Crane]).

The Nine Wrong Answers. New York: Harper & Brothers, 1952. London: Hamish Hamilton, 1952. New York: Bantam, 1955. London: Corgi, 1956. New York: Carroll & Graf, 1986. (All paperback editions abridged.)

Translations:

French: *Les Neuf Mauvaises Réponses*, tr. Mounette Lewis (Paris: Editeurs Francais Réunis, 1964; rpt. Paris: Néo-Nouvelles Editions Oswald, 1983).

German: *Die schuldige Antwort*, tr. Marianne Kalow (Bern: Scherz, 1964).

The Cavalier's Cup (as by Carter Dickson). New York: William Morrow, 1953. London: William Heinemann, 1954. London: Pan, 1960. New York: Zebra, 1987.

Translation:

Swedish: *Inta så illa menat*, tr. Holger Norelius (Stockholm: B. Wahlström, 1956).

Captain Cut-Throat. New York: Harper & Brothers, 1955. London: Hamish Hamilton, 1955. New York: Bantam, 1956. Harmondsworth: Penguin, 1960. New York: Award, 1976. New York: Carroll & Graf, 1988.

Translations:

German: *Ihr ergebener Halsabschneider*, tr. Bernhard Kempner (Bern: Scherz, 1961).

Dutch: *De Franse spionne*, tr. O. de Marez Oyens-Schilt (Utrecht: Het Spectrum, 1965).

Fear Is the Same (as by Carter Dickson). New York: William Morrow, 1956. London: William Heinemann, 1956. New York: Bantam, 1959. London: World Distributors, 1959.

Patrick Butler for the Defence. New York: Harper & Brothers, 1956. London: Hamish Hamilton, 1956. New York: Bantam, 1957. Harmondsworth: Penguin, 1959.

Translations:

German: *Der Zauberer*, tr. Hans M. Tilgen (Bern: Scherz, 1958; rpt. Klagenfurt: Buchgemeinde Alpenland, 1964 [with novels by Agatha Christie and Erle Stanley Gardner]; rpt. Hamburg: Xenos-Verlagsgesellschaft, 1976 [as *Der Tod des Zauberers*]).

Danish: *De blodige handsker*, tr. Rita Damm (Copenhagen: Skrifola, 1960; rpt. Copenhagen: Winther, 1969).

Swedish: *Handsken är kastad*, tr. Torsten Blomkvist (Stockholm: Bonnier, 1960).

Dutch: *Moord zonder moordenaar*, tr. H. S. Lanson (Utrecht: Het Spectrum, 1967).

Fire, Burn! New York: Harper & Brothers, 1957. London: Hamish Hamilton, 1957. New York: Bantam, 1959. Harmondsworth: Penguin, 1961. New York: Award, 1975. New York: Carroll & Graf, 1987.

Translations:

Swedish: *Korn åt små fåglar*, tr. Sven Bergström (Stockholm: Bonnier, 1959).

French: *Hier, vous tuerez*, tr. Elisabeth Gille (Paris: J'ai Lu, 1969; rpt. Paris: Clancier-Guénaud, 1984).

Italian: *La fiamma e la morte*, tr. A. M. Francavilla (Milan: Mondadori, 1987).

The Dead Man's Knock. New York: Harper & Brothers, 1958. London: Hamish Hamilton, 1958. New York: Bantam, 1960. Harmondsworth: Penguin, 1961. New York: Zebra, 1987.

Translations:
German: *Die verschlossene Tür,* tr. Karl Hellwig (Bern: Scherz, 1959).
Portuguese: *O sinal do morto,* tr. Lima da Costa (Lisbon: Livros do Brasil, 1960?).
French: *Le Mort frappe à la porte,* tr. ? (Paris: Clancier-Guénaud, 1983).
Scandal at High Chimneys. New York: Harper & Brothers, 1959. London: Hamish
    Hamilton, 1959. Roslyn, NY: Walter J. Black (Detective . Book Club), 1959.
    New York: Bantam, 1960. London: Pan, 1962. London: Corgi, 1970. New York:
    Carroll & Graf, 1988.
Translations:
German: *Spuk im Giebelhaus,* tr. Margaret Haas (Bern: Scherz, 1958; rpt. Klagenfurt:
    Buchgemeinde Alpenland, 1964 [with novels by Agatha Christie and Rex Stout]).
Swedish: *Skandal på High Chimneys,* tr. Sven Bergström (Stockholm: Bonnier, 1961).
Hungarian: *A kastély titka,* tr. Árokszállásy Zoltan (Budapest: Európa, 1979).
In Spite of Thunder. New York: Harper & Brothers, 1960. London: Hamish Hamilton,
    1960. New York: Bantam, 1961. Harmondsworth: Penguin, 1966. Leicester:
    Ulverscroft, 1972. New York: Carroll & Graf, 1987.
Translations:
German: *Hinter den Kulissen,* tr. Lola Humm-Sernau (Bern: Scherz, 1961).
Spanish: *Pese al trueno,* tr. Elena Torres Galare (Buenos Aires: Emecé, 1962).
The Witch of the Low-Tide. New York: Harper & Brothers, 1961. London: Hamish
    Hamilton, 1961. New York: Bantam, 1963. Harmondsworth: Penguin, 1964.
Translations:
German: *Das Gespenst der Gezeiten,* tr. Margaret Haas (Bern: Scherz, 1962).
Swedish: *Häxkonster vid lågvatten,* tr. Sven Bergström (Stockholm: Bonnier, 1962).
The Demoniacs. New York: Harper & Row, 1962. London: Hamish Hamilton, 1962.
    New York: Bantam, 1964. Harmondsworth: Penguin, 1965.
Translations:
German: *Die schmutzige Stadt,* tr. Margaret Haas (Bern: Scherz, 1964).
Hungarian: *A London Bridge rejtelye,* tr. Takács Ferenc (Budapest: Albatrosz Konyvek,
    1976).
French: *Les Démoniaques,* tr. Joëlle Ginsberg (Paris: PAC-Editions, 1978).
Most Secret. New York: Harper & Row, 1964. London: Hamish Hamilton, 1964.
    New York: Berkley, 1969.
Translations:
Swedish: *Strängt hemligt,* tr. Ingmar Forsström (Stockholm: Bonnier, 1966).
Dutch: *De twee ringen,* tr. J. Emous (Utrecht: Het Spectrum, 1968).
The House at Satan's Elbow. New York: Harper & Row, 1965. London: Hamish
    Hamilton, 1965. New York: Signet, 1967. London: Pan, 1969. Leicester:
    Ulverscroft, 1971. New York: Award, 1974. New York: International Polygonics,
    1987.
Translations:
Swedish: *Huset på Djävulshornet,* tr. Astrid Borger (Stockholm: Bonnier, 1967).
Spanish: *El codo de Satanás,* tr. Lila de Mora y Araujo (Buenos Aires: Emecé, 1968;
    rpt. Madrid: Alianza, 1977 [as *La casa en el codo de Satán*]).
Panic in Box C. New York: Harper & Row, 1966. London: Hamish Hamilton, 1966.
    New York: Berkley, 1968. London: Pan, 1970. New York: Carroll & Graf, 1987.
Translations:
German: *Vorhang auf für den Mörder,* tr. Astrid Alexa Strange (Bern: Scherz, 1969).
Danish: *Panik in loge C,* tr. Leif Tronholm (Copenhagen: Lademann, 1970).

Bibliography 163

Spanish: *La muerte acude al teatro*, tr. Miguel Saurina (Barcelona: Bruguera, 1981; rpt. Barcelona: Planeta, 1986).

Dark of the Moon. New York: Harper & Row, 1967. London: Hamish Hamilton, 1968. New York: Berkley, 1969. London: Corgi, 1970. New York: Carroll & Graf, 1987.

Translations:

Spanish: *Oscuridad en la luna*, tr. María Cristina Cochella (Buenos Aires, 1970).

Dutch: *Moordenaar voor de bijl*, tr. J. P. D. Baas-van Dijk (Utrecht: Het Spectrum, 1970).

German: *Roulett der Rächer*, tr. Eva Tabory (Bern: Scherz, 1971).

Danish: *Mork måne*, tr. Henning Ipsen (Copenhagen: Lademann, 1978).

French: *Lune sombre*, tr. Joëlle Ginsberg (Paris: PAC-Editions, 1978).

Papa Là-bas. New York: Harper & Row, 1968. London: Hamish Hamilton, 1969.

Translations:

German: *Die Voodoo-Königin*, tr. Hermann Baer (Frankfurt am Main: Ullstein, 1970).

Swedish: *Papa La-bas*, tr. Roland Adlerberth (Bromma: Delta, 1975)

Italian: *I fantasmi della casa maledetta*, tr. A. M. Francavilla (Milan: Mondadori-De Agostini, 1984).

The Ghosts' High Noon. New York: Harper & Row, 1969. London: Hamish Hamilton, 1970.

Translations:

Spanish: *Mediodía de espectros*, tr. Manuel Barberá (Buenos Aires: Compañía Impresora Argentina, 1971).

Swedish: *Rösten*, tr. Gösta Dahl (Stockholm: Tiden, 1971).

Deadly Hall. New York: Harper & Row, 1971. London: Hamish Hamilton, 1971.

Translations:

Spanish: *Mansión de la muerte*, tr. Andrés Osvaldo Bottaro (Buenos Aires: Compañía Impresora Argentina, 1971; rpt. Buenos Aires: Emecé, 1975; rpt. Madrid: Alianza, 1975).

German: *Die schwarzen Lilien van Delys Hall*, tr. Mechtild Sandberg (Frankfurt am Main: Ullstein, 1972).

The Hungry Goblin. New York: Harper & Row, 1972. London: Hamish Hamilton, 1972.

2. Collections of Short Stories and Radio Plays

The Department of Queer Complaints (as by Carter Dickson). New York: William Morrow, 1940. London: William Heinemann, 1940. New York: Editions for the Armed Services, 1946? London: Pan, 1963. Boston: Gregg Press, 1981.

Dr. Fell, Detective, and Other Stories. Ed. Ellery Queen. New York: American Mercury, 1947.

The Exploits of Sherlock Holmes (with Adrian Conan Doyle). New York: Random House, 1954. London: John Murray, 1954. New York: Ace, 1956. Freeport, NY: Books for Libraries Press, 1971. New York: Pocket, 1976. London: Sphere, 1978.

Translations:

Spanish: *Las hazañas de Sherlock Holmes*, tr. Vicente de Artadi (Barcelona: Exito, 1955).

Portuguese: *Novas aventuras de Sherlock Holmes*, tr. José de Natividade Gaspar (Lisbon: Editorial Minerva, 1958).

Danish: *Sherlock Holmes' bedrifter*, tr. Georg Brandt (Copenhagen: Martin, 1966).

German: *Sherlock Holmes' Nachlass*, tr. Arno Dohm et al. (Hamburg: Mosaik, 1967 [in Sir Arthur Conan Doyle, *Gesammelte Werke*, Volume 17]).

French: *Exploits de Sherlock Holmes*, tr. Gilles Vaulthier (Paris: Livre de Poche, 1968; rpt. Paris: Lafont, 1975).

Swedish: *Sherlock Holmes bedrifter*, tr. Lars Gustav Hellström (Höganäs: Läsabra, 1981).

Italian: *Le nuove imprese di Sherlock Holmes*, tr. Oreste del Bruno (Milan: Mondadori, 1983).

The Third Bullet and Other Stories. New York: Harper & Brothers, 1954. London: Hamish Hamilton, 1954. New York: Walter J. Black (Detective Book Club), 1954. New York: Bantam, 1956. Leicester: Ulverscroft, 1965.

The Men Who Explained Miracles. New York: Harper & Row, 1963. London: Hamish Hamilton, 1964. New York: Pyramid, 1964. Harmondsworth: Penguin, 1966.

Translations:

Dutch: *Detective verhalen*, tr. J. de Beij (Utrecht: Het Spectrum, 1966).

Spanish: *El hombre que explicaba milagros*, tr. Ramón Margalef Llambrich (Barcelona: Molino, 1966).

The Door to Doom and Other Detections. Ed. Douglas G. Greene. New York: Harper & Row, 1980. New York: Ellery Queen Mystery Club/Walter J. Black, 1980. London: Hamish Hamilton, 1981.

Translation:

Italian: *La porta sull'abisso*, tr. A. M. Francavilla (Milan: Mondadori, 1986).

The Dead Sleep Lightly. Ed. Douglas G. Greene. Garden City, NY: Doubleday, 1983.

3. Nonfiction

The Murder of Sir Edmund Godfrey. New York: Harper & Brothers, 1936. London: Hamish Hamilton, 1936. Garden City, NY: Doubleday (Dolphin), 1962. Westport, CT: Hyperion Press, 1975. New York: International Polygonics, 1989.

Translation:

Swedish: *Brottsligt förflutet samt novellen; Okända personer eller varelser*, tr. Roland Adlerberth (Halmstad: Spectra, 1977).

The Life of Sir Arthur Conan Doyle. New York: Harper & Brothers, 1949. London: John Murray, 1949. London: Pan, 1953. Garden City, NY: Doubleday (Dolphin), 1960. New York: Vintage, 1975. New York: Carroll & Graf, 1987.

Translations:

Swedish: *Conan Doyle*, tr. Nils Holmberg (Stockholm: Bonnier, 1950).

Spanish: *La vida de Sir Arthur Conan Doyle*, tr. José Donosa Yañez (Santiago: Zig-Zag, 1951).

Italian: *La vita di Sir Arthur Conan Doyle, il creatore di Sherlock Holmes*, tr. Maria Gallone (Milan: Rizzoli, 1956).

French: *La Vie de Sir Arthur Conan Doyle*, tr. André Algarron (Paris: Lafont, 1958; rpt. Kappellen, Belgium: Beckers, 1966 [as *La Vie fantastique de Sir Arthur Conan Doyle*]).

4. Omnibuses

A John Dickson Carr Trio. New York: Harper & Brothers, 1957. [Contains: *The Three Coffins, The Crooked Hinge, The Case of the Constant Suicides*.]

A Dr. Fell Omnibus. London: Hamish Hamilton, 1959. [Contains: *The Mad Matter Mystery, Death-Watch, The Problem of the Green Capsule* (as *The Black Spectacles*), *Death Turns the Tables* (as *The Seat of the Scornful*).]

Three Detective Novels. New York: Harper & Brothers, 1959. [Contains: *The Arabian Nights Murder, The Burning Court, The Problem of the Wire Cage.*]

Novelas escogidas. Tr. Jose Frexas, Julio Vacarez, Alfredo de Leon, et al. Madrid: Aguilar, 1961. [Contains: *Con guantes de acero* (?), *Sangre en el espejo de la reina* (?), *Los crimenes de la viuda roja (The Red Widow Murders), La policia esta invitada (The Peacock Feather Murders).*]

Das Haus der Masken (The Gilded Man); Die Doppelgangerin (The Burning Court); Gesucht: Ein Motiv (The Crooked Hinge). Tr. ?. Klagenfurt: Buchgemeinde Alpenland, 1964.

Gideon Fell: Il delitto perfetto non esiste. Tr. Marco Polillo. Milan: Mondadori, 1976. [Contains: *Occhiali neri (The Problem of the Green Capsule), Il colpo di fucile (Till Death Do Us Part), Il terrore che mormora (He Who Whispers), La sfinge dormiente (The Sleeping Sphinx).*]

Il giudice è accusato (Death Turns the Tables); L'Automa (The Crooked Hinge); Una croce era il segnale (Below Suspicion). Trs. F. Mazzucato and R. De Michele. Milan: Club degli Editori, 1976.

Un colpo di fucile (Till Death Do Us Part); La sfinge dormiente (The Sleeping Sphinx). Tr. ?. Milan: Club degli Editori, 1981.

John Dickson Carr Omnibus. Tr. ?. Utrecht: Het Spectrum, 1984. [Contains: *Moord op de tennisbaan (The Problem of the Wire Cage), De Franse spionne (Captain Cut-Throat), Zij stierf als dame (She Died a Lady).*]

Cinque delitti impossibili per Gideon Fell. Tr. Marco Polillo. Milan: Mondadori, 1984. [Contents not known.]

Het laatste schaakspel (Death Turns the Tables); De fluisterende moordenaar (He Who Whispers). Tr. ?. Utrecht: Het Spectrum, 1985.

L'esimio Gideon Fell. Tr. Marco Polillo. Milan: Mondadori, 1988. [Contains: *Il cappellaio matto (The Mad Hatter Mystery); L'Automa (The Crooked Hinge); Gideon Fell e il caso dei suicidi (The Case of the Constant Suicides).*]

Four Complete Dr. Fell Mysteries. New York: Avenel Books, 1988. [Contains: *To Wake the Dead; The Blind Barber; The Crooked Hinge; The Case of the Constant Suicides.*]

5. Works Edited

Doyle, Sir Arthur Conan. *Great Stories.* New York: London House & Maxwell, 1959. London: John Murray, 1959.

6. Short Stories

" 'As Drink the Dead...' " *The Haverfordian,* March 1926. In *The Door to Doom and Other Detections* (1980).

"The Red Heels." *The Haverfordian,* April 1926, pp. 285-307.

"The Dim Queen." *The Haverfordian,* May 1926, pp. 326-41.

"The Blue Garden." *The Haverfordian,* November 1926, pp. 65-75.

"The Shadow of the Goat." *The Haverfordian,* November and December 1926. In *The Door to Doom and Other Detections* (1980).

"The Devil-Gun." *The Haverfordian,* December 1926, pp. 93-105.

"The Fourth Suspect." *The Haverfordian,* January 1927. In *The Door to Doom and Other Detections* (1980).

"The New Canterbury Tales." *The Haverfordian,* March 1927, pp. 226-73. (Round-robin tale; one chapter and the interludes—featuring Bencolin—by Carr.)

"The Inn of the Seven Swords." *The Haverfordian,* April 1927, pp. 298-317.

166   John Dickson Carr: A Critical Study

"The Ends of Justice." *The Haverfordian*, May 1927. In *The Door to Doom and Other Detections* (1980).

"The Deficiency Expert." *The Haverfordian*, May 1927, pp. 350-69.

"The Dark Banner." *The Haverfordian*, January 1928, pp. 147-53.

"The Murder in Number Four." *The Haverfordian*, June 1928. In *The Door to Doom and Other Detections* (1980).

"The Man Who Was Dead." *Dime Mystery* 8, No. 2 (May 1935) (as by "John Dixon Carr"). In *The Door to Doom and Other Detections* (1980).

"The Door to Doom." *Horror Stories* 1, No. 4 (June 1935): 86-98 (as by "John Dixon Carr"). In *The Door to Doom and Other Detections* (1980).

"Terror's Dark Tower." *Detective Tales* 1, No. 3 (October 1935). In *The Door to Doom and Other Detections* (1980).

"The Other Hangman." In *A Century of Detective Stories*, ed. anon. (introduction by G.K. Chesterton) (London: Hutchinson, 1935), pp. 931-46. In *The Department of Queer Complaints* (1940).

"Blind Man's Hood." *The Sketch*, Christmas Number, 1937, pp. 45-48, 53-54, xviii. In *The Department of Queer Complaints* (1940).

"The Proverbial Murder." First publication unknown but before 1941. In *Dr. Fell, Detective* (1947). In *The Third Bullet and Other Stories* (1954).

"The New Invisible Man." *The Strand Magazine* 94, No. 6 (April 1938): 666-75 (as by "Carter Dickson"). In *The Department of Queer Complaints* (1940).

"The Crime in Nobody's Room." *The Strand Magazine* 95, No. 2 (June 1938): 127-37 (as by "Carter Dickson"). In *The Department of Queer Complaints* (1940).

"Error at Daybreak." *The Strand Magazine* 95, No. 3 (July 1938): 278-88. In *The Department of Queer Complaints* (1940).

"Persons or Things Unknown." *The Sketch*, Christmas Number, 1938, pp. 17-18, 47-50. In *The Department of Queer Complaints* (1940).

"The Wrong Problem." In *Fifty Famous Detectives of Fiction*, ed. anon. (London: Oldhams Press, 1938), pp. 535-47. In *Dr. Fell, Detective* (1947). In *The Third Bullet and Other Stories* (1954).

"The Hiding Place." *The Strand Magazine* 96, No. 4 (February 1939): 452-59 (as by "Carter Dickson"). In *The Department of Queer Complaints* (1940; as "Hot Money").

"Death in the Dressing-Room." *The Strand Magazine* 96, No. 5 (March 1939): 525-33 (as by "Carter Dickson"). In *The Department of Queer Complaints* (1940).

"The Empty Flat." *The Strand Magazine* 97, No. 1 (May 1939): 83-91 (as by "Carter Dickson"). In *The Men Who Explained Miracles* (1963).

"The Silver Curtain." *The Strand Magazine* 97, No. 4 (August 1939): 367-76 (as by "Carter Dickson"). In *The Department of Queer Complaints* (1940).

"Strictly Diplomatic." *The Strand Magazine* 98, No. 2 (December 1939): 136-44 (as by "Carter Dickson"). In *Dr. Fell, Detective* (1947). In *The Men Who Explained Miracles* (1963).

"New Murders for Old." *The Illustrated London News*, Christmas Number, 1939, pp. 21-22, 31-33. In *The Department of Queer Complaints* (1940).

"Clue in the Snow." *The Strand Magazine* 98, No. 3 (January 1940): 262-71 (as by "Carter Dickson"). In *The Department of Queer Complaints* (1940; as "The Footprint in the Sky").

"The Locked Room." *The Strand Magazine* 99, No. 3 (July 1940): 213-21. In *Dr. Fell, Detective* (1947). In *The Third Bullet and Other Stories* (1954).

"A Guest in the House." *The Strand Magazine* 99, No. 6 (October 1940): 436-43. In *Dr. Fell, Detective* (1947). In *The Men Who Explained Miracles* (1963; as "The Incautious Burglar").

"The Clue of the Red Wig." *The Strand Magazine* 100, No. 2 (December 1940): 134-45. In *The Third Bullet and Other Stories* (1954).

"William Wilson's Racket." *The Strand Magazine* 100, No. 4 (February 1941): 254-60 (as by "Carter Dickson"). In *The Men Who Explained Miracles* (1963).

"The House in Goblin Wood." *Strand* 114, No. 2 (November 1947): 43-54, 104-8. *Ellery Queen's Mystery Magazine* 10, No. 5 (November 1947): 4-20. In *The Third Bullet and Other Stories* (1954).

"The Gentleman from Paris." *Ellery Queen's Mystery Magazine* 15, No. 4 (April 1950): 9-29. In *The Third Bullet and Other Stories* (1954).

"The Black Cabinet." *In Twenty Great Tales of Murder* (Mystery Writers of America), ed. Helen McCloy and Brett Halliday (New York: Random House, 1951), pp. 3-22. In *The Men Who Explained Miracles* (1963).

"The Adventure of the Seven Clocks" (with Adrian Conan Doyle). *Life* 33, No. 26 (29 December 1952): 51-61. In *The Exploits of Sherlock Holmes* (1954).

"The Adventure of the Black Baronet" (with Adrian Conan Doyle). *Collier's* 131, No. 21 (23 May 1953): 19-21, 54-59. In *The Exploits of Sherlock Holmes* (1954).

"The Adventure of the Gold Hunter" (with Adrian Conan Doyle). *Collier's* 131, No. 22 (30 May 1953): 26-33. In *The Exploits of Sherlock Holmes* (1954).

"The Adventure of the Highgate Miracle" (with Adrian Conan Doyle). *Collier's* 131, No. 23 (6 June 1953): 54-61. In *The Exploits of Sherlock Holmes* (1954).

"The Adventure of the Sealed Room" (with Adrian Conan Doyle). *Collier's* 131, No. 24 (13 June 1953): 60-65. In *The Exploits of Sherlock Holmes* (1954).

"The Adventure of the Wax Gamblers" (with Adrian Conan Doyle). *Collier's* 131, No. 25 (20 June 1953): 46-53. In *The Exploits of Sherlock Holmes* (1954).

"Crime on the Coast" (with Valerie White, Laurence Meynell, Joan Fleming, Michael Cronin, and Elizabeth Ferrars). *London News Chronicle*, 3-17 August 1954. London: Gollancz, 1984; New York: Berkley, 1987 (with "No Flowers by Request").

"Ministry of Miracles." *Housewife*, 1955. In *The Men Who Explained Miracles* (1963; as "All in a Maze").

"King Arthur's Chair." *Lilliput*, August 1957. In *The Men Who Explained Miracles* (1963; as "Invisible Hands").

"Detective's Day Off." *Weekend*, 25/29 December 1957.

[For a complete list of radio plays, see Douglas G. Greene's bibliography in *The Door to Doom and Other Detections* (1980), pp. 345-50.]

7. Poetry

"The Old Romance." *The Haverfordian*, December 1926, pp. 106-7.

"Last Lullaby." *The Haverfordian*, February 1927, p. 194.

8. Articles and Reviews

"Magicians' Progress." *Radio Times*, 14 July 1944, p. 3.

"Hammock Companions" (review of *Tales of Horror and the Supernatural* by Arthur Machen). *New York Times Book Review*, 1 August 1948, p. 10.

"When Conan Doyle Was Sherlock Holmes." *Harper's* 198, No. 1 (January 1949): 31-40. *Strand* 116, No. 4 (January 1949): 40-51 (as "Conan Doyle, Detective").

"With Colt and Luger" (review of *The Simple Art of Murder* by Raymond Chandler). *New York Times Book Review*, 24 September 1950, p. 36.

"Holmes Wouldn't Recognize It." *New York Times Magazine*, 21 February 1954, pp. 10, 35-37.

"Story Development." In *The Mystery Writer's Handbook* (Mystery Writers of America), ed. Herbert Brean (New York: Harper & Brothers, 1956), pp. 168-71.

"Another Glass, Watson," In *The Sherlock Holmes* (exhibition catalogue). London: Whitbread, 1957, pp. 5-10.

"The Sherlock Holmes." *House of Whitbread*, Spring 1958.

"The Grandest Game in the World." *Ellery Queen's Mystery Magazine* 41, No. 3 (March 1963): 49-68. In *The Door to Doom and Other Detections* (1980).

"Murder-Fancier Recommends." *Harper's* 229, No. 1 (July 1964): 104-6; 231, No. 1 (July 1965): 104, 106-8; 233, No. 1 (July 1966): 84, 86, 88; 235, No. 1 (July 1967): 90-92.

"Hail, Holmes!" *New York Times*, 14 February 1965, Section 2, pp. 1, 5.

[Speech at the University of North Carolina.] *The Bookmark* (Friends of the University of North Carolina Library) No. 38 (September 1968): 9-17.

"Best Mysteries of the Month." *Ellery Queen's Mystery Magazine* 53, No. 1 (January 1969): 151-52; 53, No. 2 (February 1969): 150-51; 53, No. 3 (March 1969): 110-11; 53, No. 4 (April 1969): 65-66; 53, No. 5 (May 1969): 103-4; 53, No. 6 (June 1969): 57-58; 54, No. 1 (July 1959): 52-53; 54, No. 2 (August 1969): 52-53; 54, No. 3 (September 1969): 65-66; 54, No. 4 (October 1969): 65-66; 54, No. 5 (November 1969): 103-4; 54, No. 6 (December 1969): 111-12; 55, No. 1 (January 1970): 117-18; 55, No. 2 (February 1970): 129-30; 55, No. 3 (March 1970): 114-15; 55, No. 4 (April 1970): 101-2.

"The Jury Box." *Ellery Queen's Mystery Magazine* 55, No. 5 (May 1970): 93-96; 55, No. 6 (June 1970): 114-16; 56, No. 1 (July 1970): 111-13; 56, No. 2 (August 1970): 65-67; 56, No. 3 (September 1970): 98-100; 56, No. 4 (October 1970): 126-28; 56, No. 5 (November 1970): 126-28; 56, No. 6 (December 1970): 101-3; 57, No. 1 (January 1971): 80-82; 57, No. 2 (February 1971): 99-101; [no book review in March 1971 issue]; 57, No. 4 (April 1971): 62-63; 57, No. 5 (May 1971): 76-77; 57, No. 6 (June 1971): 72-73; 58, No. 1 (July 1971): 95-96; 58, No. 2 (August 1971): 75-76; 58, No. 3 (September 1971): 73-74; 58, No. 4 (October 1971): 112-13; 58, No. 5 (November 1971): 93-94; 58, No. 6 (December 1971): 65-66; 59, No. 1 (January 1972): 109-10; 59, No. 2 (February 1972): 107-8; 59, No. 3 (March 1972): 91-92; 59, No. 4 (April 1972): 82-83; 59, No. 5 (May 1972): 70-71; 59, No. 6 (June 1972): 79-80; 60, No. 1 (July 1972): 87-88; 60, No. 2 (August 1972): 98-99; 60, No. 3 (September 1972): 105-6; 60, No. 4 (October 1972): 113-14; 60, No. 5 (November 1972): 83-84; 60, No. 6 (December 1972): 96-97; 61, No. 1 (January 1973): 112-13; 61, No. 2 (February 1973): 81-82; 61, No. 3 (March 1973): 86-87; 61, No. 4 (April 1973): 111-12; 61, No. 5 (May 1973): 116-17; 61, No. 6 (June 1973): 83-84; 62, No. 1 (July 1973): 122-23; 62, No. 2 (August 1973): 116-17; 62, No. 3 (September 1973): 103-4; 62, No. 4 (October 1973): 90-91; 62, No. 5 (November 1973): 125-26; 62, No. 6 (December 1973): 87-88; 63, No. 1 (January 1974): 119-20; 63, No. 2 (February 1974): 69-70; 63, No. 3 (March 1974): 111-12; 63, No. 4 (April 1974): 97-98; 63, No. 5 (May 1974): 105-6; 63, No. 6 (June 1974): 91-92; 64, No. 1 (July 1974): 93-94; 64, No. 2 (August 1974): 71-72; 64, No. 3 (September 1974): 64-65; 64, No. 4 (October 1974): 85-86; 64, No. 5 (November 1974): 101-2; 64, No. 6 (December 1974):

137-38; 65, No. 1 (January 1975): 103-4; 65, No. 2 (February 1975): 119-20; 65, No. 3 (March 1975): 89-90; 65, No. 4 (April 1975): 123-24; 65, No. 5 (May 1975): 110-11; 65, No. 6 (June 1975): 110-11; 66, No. 1 (July 1975): 74-75; 66, No. 2 (August 1975): 107-8; 66, No. 3 (September 1975): 93-94; 66, No. 4 (October 1975): 98-99; 66, No. 5 (November 1975): 94-95; 66, No. 6 (December 1975): 121-22; 67, No. 1 (January 1976): 138-39; 67, No. 2 (February 1976): 120-21; 67, No. 3 (March 1976): 119-20; 67, No. 4 (April 1976): 129-30; 67, No. 5 (May 1976): 102-4; [no reviews in issues for June 1976 and July 1976]; 68, No. 2 (August 1976): 131-32; 68, No. 3 (September 1976): 80-82; 68, No. 4 (October 1976): 124-26.

"Stand and Deliver!" *Ellery Queen's Mystery Magazine* 61, No. 3 (March 1973): 54-62; 61, No. 4 (April 1973): 113-20. In *The Door to Doom and Other Detections* (1980).

9. Introductions to Books by Others

Torquemada. *112 Best Crossword Puzzles.* London: Pushkin Press, 1942.

Doyle, Sir Arthur Conan. *The Valley of Fear.* New York: Bantam, 1950.

Mystery Writers of America. *Maiden Murders.* New York: Harper & Brothers, 1952, pp. ix-xiv.

Doyle, Sir Arthur Conan. *The Complete Sherlock Holmes.* Garden City, NY: Doubleday (Limited Edition), 1953.

Williams, John. *Suddenly at the Priory.* London: William Heinemann, 1957, pp. ix-x.

Doyle, Sir Arthur Conan. *The Lost World and The Poison Belt.* London: Eyre & Spottiswoode, 1958.

———— *Great Stories.* London: John Murray, 1959, pp. 5-7.

———— *The Poison Belt.* New York: Macmillan, 1964, pp. 9-17 (as "The Many-Sided Conan Doyle").

———— *The Maracot Deep.* New York: W. W. Norton, 1968.

10. Stage Plays

"Inspector Silence Takes the Air." Unpublished.

"The Adventure of the Conk-Singleton Papers." *Unicorn Mystery Book Club News* 1, No. 9 [1949]. In *The Door to Doom and Other Detections* (1980).

"The Adventure of the Paradol Chamber." *Unicorn Mystery Book Club News* 2, No. 3 [1949]. In *The Door to Doom and Other Detections* (1980).

B. *Works about John Dickson Carr*

1. Bibliographies

Briney, Robert E. "The Books of John Dickson Carr/Carter Dickson: A Checklist." In *The Crooked Hinge.* San Diego: University Extension, University of California, San Diego, 1976, pp. 277-83.

Busch, Lloyd. "A Checklist of the Paperback Editions of John Dickson Carr." *Collecting Paperbacks?* 2, No. 2 (May 1980): 9-18.

Greene, Douglas G. "A Bibliography of the Works of John Dickson Carr." In *The Door to Doom and Other Detections.* New York: Harper & Row, 1980, pp. 327-51.

———— "John Dickson Carr on British Radio." *Armchair Detective* 12, No. 1 (Winter 1979): 69-71.

170   John Dickson Carr: A Critical Study

Sneary, Rick. "A John Dickson Carr Checklist." *Mystery Readers/Lovers Newsletter* 3, No. 4 (April 1970): 13-15; 4, No. 1 (October 1970): 13-15.

2. Books and Articles

Adey, R. C. S. "My Favorite Detectives: Sir Henry Merrivale." *Mystery Readers/Lovers Newsletter* 3, No. 2 (December 1969): 11-14.
Bleiler, E. F. "Some Thoughts on Peacock Feet." *Mystery FANcier* 6, No. 3 (May-June 1982): 14-21.
Boucher, Anthony. "Introduction" to *The Blind Barber*. New York: Collier, 1962, pp. 5-6. Rpt. in Boucher's *Multiplying Villainies: Selected Mystery Criticism 1942-1968*, edited by Robert E. Briney and Francis M. Nevins, Jr. Boston: Bouchercon, 1973, pp. 118-20.
_____. "Introduction" to *Hag's Nook*. New York: Collier, 1963, pp. 5-7. New York: Har/Row Books, 1971, pp. 5-7.
Brean, Herbert. "How Holmes Was Reborn." *Life* 33, No. 26 (29 December 1952): 62-66.
Briney, R. E. "Carr, John Dickson." In *Twentieth-Century Crime and Mystery Writers*, ed. John M. Reilly. New York: St. Martin's Press, 1980, pp. 267-72 (with bibliography).
_____. "Introduction: The Art of the Magician." In *The Crooked Hinge*. San Diego: University Extension, University of California, San Diego, 1976, pp. v-xvi.
Champigny, Robert. *What Will Have Happened*. Bloomington: Indiana University Press, 1977, passim.
Diaz, Cesar E. *La novela policiaca*. Barcelona: Ediciones Acervo, 1973, pp. 95-98.
Dueren, Fred. "Henri Bencolin." *Armchair Detective* 8, No. 2 (February 1975): 98, 123.
French, Larry L. "The Baker Street-Carrian Connection: The Influence of Sherlock Holmes on John Dickson Carr." *Baker Street Journal* 29, No. 1 (March 1979): 6-10.
_____, ed. *Notes for the Curious: A John Dickson Carr Memorial Journal*. n.p.: Carrian Press, 1978. 32 pp. [Contains: "John Dickson Carr" by R. E. Briney (from *Armchair Detective*, April 1977), pp. 1-2; "The Man Who Was John Dickson Carr" by Larry L. French, pp. 3-7; "The Man Who Read (and Published) John Dickson Carr/Carter Dickson" by Larry L. French, pp. 8-11; "Commentaries for the Curious" (remarks by Otto Penzler, Chris Steinbrunner, Marvin Lachman, Charlie Shibuk, John L. Breen, Francis Nevins, Jon Lellenberg, Robert Lewis Taylor, Roger Herzel, Michael Harrison, Roy Winsor, Allen J. Hubin, John Kahn, R. E. Briney), pp. 11-20; "Carrian Canon for the Curious" by Larry L. French, pp. 20-26; "Epilogue: Culprit Confesses" by Larry L. French, pp. 27-28; "The Carr Chronology" by Larry L. French, pp. 29-30; "The Murder Club" by Larry L. French, p. 30; "Afterword" by Larry L. French, p. 32.]
Greene, Douglas G. "Adolf Hitler and John Dickson Carr's Least-Known Locked Room" *Armchair Detective* 14, No. 4 (Autumn 1981): 295-96.
_____. "Dr. Gideon Fell, Detective." In *Hag's Nook*. New York: International Polygonics, 1985, pp. 5-9.
_____. "Introduction" to *The Judas Window*. New York: International Polygonics, 1987, pp. 1-4.

_____ "Introduction—John Dickson Carr: The Man Who Created Miracles." In *The Door to Doom and Other Detections.* New York: Harper & Row, 1980, pp. 9-26.

_____ "Introduction: John Dickson Carr and the Radio Play." In *The Dead Sleep Lightly.* Garden City, NY: Doubleday, 1983, pp. 1-11.

_____ "John Dickson Carr, Alias Roger Fairbairn, and the Historical Novel." *Armchair Detective* 11, No. 4 (October 1978): 339-41.

_____ "A Mastery of Miracles: G. K. Chesterton and John Dickson Carr." *Chesterton Review* 10, No. 3 (August 1984): 307-15.

Haycraft, Howard. *Murder for Pleasure: The Life and Times of the Detective Story.* New York: D. Appleton-Century, 1941, pp. 199-204.

_____ ed. *The Art of the Mystery Story.* New York: Simon & Schuster, 1946, passim. (2nd ed., 1947, contains index.)

Herzel, Roger. "John Dickson Carr." In *Minor American Novelists,* ed. Charles Alva Hoyt. Carbondale: Southern Illinois University Press, 1970, pp. 67-80.

Holman, C. Hugh. "John Dickson Carr." *Bookmark* No. 38 (September 1968): 7-8.

Kahn, Joan. "Introduction" to *The Three Coffins.* Boston: Gregg Press, 1980, pp. v-vii.

Kingman, James. "John Dickson Carr and the Aura of Genius." *Armchair Detective* 14, No. 2 (Spring 1981): 166-67.

Lachman, Marvin. "The Life and Times of Gideon Fell." *Mystery FANcier* 2, No. 3 (May 1978): 3-18.

Levinson, Richard, and William Link. "Introduction" to *The Department of Queer Complaints.* Boston: Gregg Press, 1981.

Lithner, Klas. "Bravo, John Dickson Carr." *Dast* 14, No. 2 (1981): 53-54.

Lundin, Bo. "Den gamle masteren." *Jury* 1, Nos. 3/4 (1972): 16-18.

Medeiros e Alburquerque, Paulo. "Dr. Gideon Fell e Sir Henry Merrivale, dois grandes detetives de um mesmo autor." In *Os maiores detetives de todos os tempos.* Rio de Janeiro: Editora Civilizacao Brasileira, 1973, pp. 79-85.

Miller, Edmund. "Stanislaw Lem and John Dickson Carr: Critics of the Scientific World—View." *Armchair Detective* 14, No. 4 (Autumn 1981): 341-43.

Murch, A. E. *The Development of the Detective Novel.* Philadelphia: University of Pennsylvania Press, 1958, pp. 233-35.

Narcejac, Thomas. "John Dickson Carr." In *Une Machine à lire: Le Roman policier.* Paris: Denoël-Gonthier, 1975, pp. 127-42.

Nevins, Francis M., Jr. "The Sound of Suspense: John Dickson Carr as Radio Writer." *Armchair Detective* 11, No. 4 (October 1978): 335-38.

Nusser, Peter. *Der Kriminalroman.* Stuttgart: J. B. Metzlersche, 1980, passim.

Panek, LeRoy. "John Dickson Carr." In *Watteau's Shepards: The Detective Novel in Britain 1914-1940.* Bowling Green, OH: Bowling Green University Popular Press, 1979, pp. 145-84.

Symons, Julian. *The Detective Story in Britain.* London: Longmans, Green, 1962, pp. 23-24.

_____ *Mortal Consequences: A History—from the Detective Story to the Crime Novel.* New York: Harper & Row, 1972, pp. 119-21; New York: Viking Penguin, 1985 (as *Bloody Murder*), pp. 109-10.

Taylor, Robert Lewis. "Two Authors in an Attic." *New Yorker,* 8 September 1951, pp. 39-44, 46, 48; 15 September 1951, pp. 36-40, 42, 44, 46, 48, 51.

Unsigned. "John Dickson Carr." *Cronet* 39, No. 4 (February 1956): 109.

[Obituaries.] *Times* (London), 2 March 1977, p. 18; *Newsweek*, 14 March 1977, p. 39; *Time*, 14 March 1977, p. 70; *Publishers' Weekly*, 21 March 1977, p. 31; R. E. Briney, *Armchair Detective* 10, No. 2 (April 1977): 137.

3. Reviews

It Walks by Night (1930).

_____ *Saturday Review*, 22 February 1930, p. 761.

_____ *New York Times Book Review*, 23 February 1930, p. 28.

_____ *Outlook and Independent*, 26 February 1930, pp. 350-31 (Walter R. Brooks).

_____ *Bookman* 71 (March 1930): xxxi.

_____ *New York Herald Tribune Books*, 2 March 1930, p. 14 (Will Cuppy).

_____ *Spectator*, 5 April 1930, p. 582.

_____ *Times Literary Supplement*, 24 April 1930, p. 354.

_____ *New Statesman*, 10 May 1930, p. 162.

_____ *Saturday Review* (London), 17 May 1930, p. 634.

_____ *Spectator*, 28 June 1930, p. 1058 (Margaret Cole).

The Lost Gallows (1931).

_____ *New York Herald Tribune Books*, 29 March 1931, p. 13 (Will Cuppy).

_____ *Springfield Republican*, 5 April 1931, p. 7e.

_____ *Boston Transcript*, 29 April 1931, p. 3.

_____ *New York Times Book Review*, 31 May 1931, p. 24 (Bruce Rae).

_____ *Bookman* 73 (June 1931): xv.

_____ *Times Literary Supplement*, 1 October 1931, p. 757.

Castle Skull (1931).

_____ *New York Times Book Review*, 4 October 1931, p. 23 (Bruce Rae).

_____ *Outlook and Independent*, 14 October 1931, p. 218 (Walter R. Brooks).

_____ *Boston Transcript*, 31 October 1931, p. 1.

_____ *New York Herald Tribune Books*, 8 November 1931, p. 16 (Will Cuppy).

_____ *Springfield Republican*, 10 January 1932, p 73.

The Corpse in the Waxworks (1932).

_____ *Bookman* 75 (April 1932): xiv.

_____ *New York Herald Tribune Books*, 3 April 1932, p. 14 (Will Cuppy).

_____ *New York Times Book Review*, 3 April 1932, p. 23 (Isaac Anderson).

_____ *Boston Transcript*, 9 April 1932, p. 3.

_____ *Times Literary Supplement*, 28 April 1932, p. 313.

_____ *Wilson Library Bulletin* 28 (May 1932): 163.

_____ *Social Science* 7 (July 1932): 317.

_____ *Book World*, 19 August 1984, p. 13.

Poison in Jest (1932).

_____ *New York Evening Post*, 17 September 1932, p. 7 (Rumana McManis).

_____ *Boston Transcript*, 5 October 1932, p. 2.

_____ *New York Times Book Review*, 16 October 1932, p. 21 (Issaac Anderson).

_____ *New York Herald Tribune Books*, 1 January 1933, p. 10 (Will Cuppy).

Hag's Nook (1933).

_____ *New York Herald Tribune Books*, 9 April 1933, p. 17 (Will Cuppy).

_____ *Saturday Review*, 15 April 1933, p. 542.
_____ *New York Times Book Review*, 16 April 1933, p. 12 (Issac Anderson).
_____ *Boston Transcript*, 19 April 1933, p. 2.
_____ *Times Literary Supplement* 4 May 1933, p. 314.

The Mad Hatter Mystery (1933).
_____ *New York Evening Post*, 5 August 1933, p. 7 (Norman Klein).
_____ *Saturday Review*, 5 August 1933, p. 34.
_____ *New York Times Book Review*, 6 August 1933, p. 10 (Issac Anderson).
_____ *New York Herald Tribune Books*, 13 August 1933, p. 12 (Will Cuppy).
_____ *Boston Transcript*, 16 August 1933, p. 3.
_____ *Sunday Times* (London), 24 September 1933, p. 7 (Dorothy L. Sayers).
_____ *Times Literary Supplement*, 28 September 1933, p. 654.
_____ *Booklist* 30 (December 1933): 122.

The Bowstring Murders (1933).
_____ *Saturday Review*, 9 December 1933, p. 338.
_____ *New York Herald Tribune Books*, 10 December 1933, p. 17 (Will Cuppy).
_____ *New York Times Book Review*, 10 December 1933, p. 23 (Isaac Anderson).
_____ *Sunday Times* (London), 19 August 1934, p. 7 (Dorothy Sayers).

The Eight of Swords (1934).
_____ *New York Herald Tribune Books*, 18 February 1934, p. 16 (Will Cuppy).
_____ *New York Times Book Review*, 25 February 1934, p. 12 (Isaac Anderson).
_____ *Wilson Library Bulletin* 30 (March 1934): 92.
_____ *Chicago Daily Tribune*, 10 March 1934, p. 14 (Mortimer Quick).
_____ *Saturday Review*, 10 March 1934, p. 547.
_____ *Sunday Times* (London), 25 March 1934, p. 9 (Dorothy L. Sayers).
_____ *Boston Transcript*, 31 March 1934, p. 2.
_____ *Spectator*, 13 April 1934, p. 598 (Sylva Norman).
_____ *Times Literary Supplement*, 19 April 1934, p. 284.
_____ *Armchair Detective* 7, No. 4 (August 1974): 285 (Marvin Lachman).

The Plague Court Murders (1934).
_____ *Saturday Review*, 2 June 1934, p. 732.
_____ *New York Herald Tribune Books*, 3 June 1934, p. 12 (Will Cuppy).
_____ *New York Times Book Review*, 3 June 1934, p. 15 (Isaac Anderson).
_____ *Sunday Times* (London), 17 March 1935, p. 9 (Dorothy L. Sayers).

The Blind Barber (1934).
_____ *Saturday Review*, 27 October 1934, p. 251.
_____ *New York Herald Tribune Books*, 28 October 1934, p. 17 (Will Cuppy).
_____ *New York Times Book Review*, 4 November 1934, p. 20.
_____ *Sunday Times* (London), 11 November 1934, p. 9 (Dorothy L. Sayers).
_____ *Boston Transcript*, 1 December 1934, p. 2.
_____ *Times Literary Supplement*, 27 December 1934, p. 922.

The White Priory Murders (1934).
_____ *Saturday Review*, 8 December 1934, p. 362.
_____ *New York Times Book Review*, 2 December 1934, p. 33 (Issac Anderson).

_____ *New York Herald Tribune Books*, 9 December 1934 (Will Cuppy).
_____ *Sunday Times* (London), 28 July 1935, p. 7 (Dorothy L. Sayers).

Devil Kinsmere (1934).
_____ *Times Literary Supplement*, 18 October 1934, p. 717.
_____ *New York Times Book Review*, 10 February 1935, p. 7.
_____ *Saturday Review*, 23 February 1935, p. 508.
_____ *Boston Transcript*, 27 February 1935, p. 2.
_____ *New York Herald Tribune Books*, 31 March 1935, p. 13 (Paul Allen).

Death-Watch (1935).
_____ *Sunday Times* (London), 31 March 1935, p. 9 (Dorothy L. Sayers).
_____ *Times Literary Supplement*, 11 April 1935, p. 246.
_____ *Boston Transcript*, 17 April 1935, p. 2.
_____ *Saturday Review*, 20 April 1935, p. 644.
_____ *New York Times Book Review*, 21 April 1935, p. 14 (Isaac Anderson).
_____ *New York Herald Tribune Books*, 28 April 1935, p. 11 (Will Cuppy).

The Red Widow Murders (1935).
_____ *Saturday Review*, 11 May 1935, p. 22.
_____ *New York Herald Tribune Books*, 12 May 1935, p. 14 (Will Cuppy).
_____ *New York Times Book Review*, 12 May 1935, p. 16 (Isaac Anderson).
_____ *Boston Transcript*, 5 June 1935, p. 2.
_____ *Times Literary Supplement*, 16 November 1935, p. 750.
_____ *Manchester Guardian*, 18 December 1935, p. 7 (E. R. Punshon).

The Three Coffins (1935).
_____ *New York Herald Tribune Books*, 15 September 1935, p. 10 (Will Cuppy).
_____ *Saturday Review*, 21 September 1935, p. 18.
_____ *New York Times Book Review*, 6 October 1935, p. 22 (Kay Irvin).
_____ *Boston Transcript*, 16 October 1935, p. 2.
_____ *Booklist* 32 (February 1936): 171.
_____ *New York Times Book Review*, 11 August 1974, p. 12.

The Unicorn Murders (1935).
_____ *New York Herald Tribune Books*, 17 November 1935, p. 31 (Will Cuppy).
_____ *New York Times Book Review*, 17 November 1935, p. 18 (Isaac Anderson).
_____ *Saturday Review*, 5 December 1936, p. 44.
_____ *Spectator*, 28 February, 1936, p. 364 (Nicholas Blake).
_____ *Times Literary Supplement*, 14 March 1936, p. 223.
_____ *New Statesman and Nation*, 4 April 1936, p. 534 (Ralph Partridge).

The Arabian Nights Nurder (1936).
_____ *Spectator*, 28 February 1936, p. 364 (Nicholas Blake).
_____ *Times Literary Supplement*, 29 February 1936, p. 183.
_____ *Manchester Guardian*, 6 March 1936, p. 7 (E. R. Punshon).
_____ *Boston Transcript*, 7 March 1936, p. 4 (C. W. Morton, Jr.).
_____ *Saturday Review*, 7 March 1936, p. 20.
_____ *New York Times Book Review*, 8 March 1936, p. 16 (Isaac Anderson).
_____ *New York Herald Tribune Books*, 15 March 1936, p. 20 (Will Cuppy).

_____ *New Statesman and Nation*, 4 April 1936, p. 534 (Ralph Partridge).

The Murder of Sir Edmund Godfrey (1936).
_____ *Chicago Daily Tribune*, 19 September 1936, p. 14 (Frank Swinnerton).
_____ *Times Literary Supplement*, 10 October 1936, p. 803.
_____ *Manchester Guardian*, 23 October 1936, p. 7.
_____ *New York Herald Tribune Books*, 22 November 1936, p. 8 (Alfred Kazin).
_____ *New York Times Book Review*, 22 November 1936, p. 12.
_____ *Saturday Review*, 5 December 1936, p. 44.
_____ *Springfield Republican*, 10 January 1937, p. 7e.
_____ *Wilson Library Bulletin* 50 (November 1975): 208.

The Punch and Judy Murders (1936).
_____ *New York Herald Tribune Books*, 7 February 1937, p. 13 (Will Cuppy).
_____ *New York Times Book Review*, 7 February 1937, p. 22 (Isaac Anderson).
_____ *Boston Transcript*, 13 February 1937, p. 4.
_____ *Saturday Review*, 20 February 1937, p. 18.
_____ *Chicago Daily Tribune*, 6 March 1937, p. 16.

The Burning Court (1937).
_____ *Manchester Guardian*, 9 April 1937, p. 6 (E. R. Punshon).
_____ *New York Herald Tribune Books*, 18 April 1937, p. 20 (Will Cuppy).
_____ *New York Times Book Review*, 18 April 1937, p. 24 (Isaac Anderson).
_____ *Boston Transcript*, 1 May 1937, p. 4.
_____ *Saturday Review*, 8 May 1937, p. 18.
_____ *New Statesman and Nation*, 15 May 1937, p. 818 (Ralph Partridge).
_____ *Times Literary Supplement*, 29 May 1937, p. 412.

The Peacock Feather Murders (1937).
_____ *Saturday Review*, 31 July 1937, p. 20.
_____ *New York Herald Tribune Books*, 1 August 1937, p. 8 (Will Cuppy).
_____ *New York Times Book Review*, 1 August 1937, p. 15 (Isaac Anderson).
_____ *Boston Transcript*, 21 August 1937, p. 4.
_____ *Times Literary Supplement*, 30 October 1937, p. 803.
_____ *New Statesman and Nation*, 6 November 1937, p. 742 (Ralph Partridge).
_____ *Manchester Guardian*, 23 November 1937, p. 7 (E. R. Punshon).

The Four False Weapons (1937).
_____ *New York Herald Tribune Books*, 10 October 1937, p. 25 (Will Cuppy).
_____ *New York Times Book Review*, 10 October 1937, p. 22 (Kay Irvin).
_____ *Saturday Review*, 23 October 1937, p. 24.
_____ *Books and Bookmen* 18 (May 1973): 122.

To Wake the Dead (1937).
_____ *Manchester Guardian*, 10 December 1937, p. 6 (E. R. Punshon).
_____ *Times Literary Supplement*, 11 December 1937, p. 946.
_____ *Spectator*, 17 December 1937, p. 1116 (Nicholas Blake).
_____ *New Statesman and Nation*, 18 December 1937, p. 1067 (Ralph Partridge).
_____ *New York Herald Tribune Books*, 6 March 1938, p. 17 (Will Cuppy).
_____ *New York Times Book Review*, 6 March 1938, p. 20 (Kay Irvin).

_____ *Saturday Review*, 12 March 1938, p. 21.

_____ *Wilson Library Bulletin* 34 (May 1938): 112.

_____ *Spectator*, 11 August 1973, p. 187.

_____ *Books and Bookmen* 19 (October 1973): 138.

The Judas Window (1938).

_____ *Saturday Review*, 8 January 1938, p. 18.

_____ *New York Herald Tribune Books*, 9 January 1938, p. 12 (Will Cuppy).

_____ *New York Times Book Review*, 9 January 1938, p. 12 (Isaac Anderson).

_____ *Time*, 31 January 1938, p. 63.

_____ *Times Literary Supplement*, 5 February 1938, p. 92.

_____ *Manchester Guardian*, 18 February 1938, p. 7 (E. R. Punshon).

_____ *New Statesman and Nation*, 26 February 1938, p. 344 (Ralph Partridge).

_____ *Spectator*, 25 March 1938, pp. 544-45 (Rupert Hart-Davis).

_____ *Pratt Institute Quarterly*, Spring 1938, p. 32.

_____ *Armchair Detective* 7, No. 3 (May 1974): 209 (James Sandoe).

Death in Five Boxes (1938).

_____ *Times Literary Supplement*, 24 September 1938, p. 616.

_____ *Time*, 26 September 1938, p. 68.

_____ *Manchester Guardian*, 30 September 1938, p. 7 (E. R. Punshon).

_____ *Spectator*, 30 September 1938, p. 534 (Nicholas Blake).

_____ *New Yorker*, 1 October 1938, p. 80.

_____ *New York Herald Tribune Books*, 2 October 1938, p. 16 (Will Cuppy).

_____ *New York Times Book Review*, 2 October 1938, p. 22 (Isaac Anderson).

_____ *Saturday Review*, 15 October 1938, p. 40.

_____ *New Statesman and Nation*, 12 November 1938, p. 784 (Ralph Partridge).

The Crooked Hinge (1938).

_____ *Boston Transcript*, 8 October 1938, p. 3 (Marian Wiggin).

_____ *New York Herald Tribune Books*, 9 October 1938, p. 15 (Will Cuppy).

_____ *New Yorker*, 15 (October 1938, p. 96.

_____ *New York Times Book Review*, 16 October 1938, p. 16 (Kay Irvin).

_____ *Times Literary Supplement*, 22 October 1938, p. 59.

_____ *Spectator*, 28 October 1938, p. 740 (Nicholas Blake).

_____ *Time*, 31 October 1938, p. 59.

_____ *Manchester Guardian*, 1 November 1938, p. 7 (E. R. Punshon).

_____ *Wilson Library Bulletin* 52 (October 1977): 140.

_____ *Book World*, 19 August 1984, p. 13.

Fatal Descent (1939).

_____ *New York Herald Tribune Books*, 8 January 1939, p. 10 (Will Cuppy).

_____ *Boston Transcript*, 14 January 1939, p. 2 (Marian Wiggin).

_____ *New Yorker*, 14 January 1939, p. 76.

_____ *Saturday Review*, 14 January 1939, p. 19.

_____ *Times Literary Supplement*, 14 January 1939, p. 28.

_____ *New Yorks Times Book Review*, 15 January 1939, p. 14 (Isaac Anderson).

_____ *Time*, 6 February 1939, p. 27.

_____ *Manchester Guardian*, 7 February 1939, p. 7 (E. R. Punshon).

_____ *Spectator*, 24 February 1939, p. 318 (Nicholas Blake).

_____ *New Statesman and Nation*, 11 March 1939, p. 374 (Ralph Partridge).

_____ *Springfield Republican*, 21 May 1939, p. 7e.

The Problem of the Green Capsule (1939).
_____ *Boston Transcript*, 20 May 1930, p. 3 (Marian Wiggin).
_____ *New Yorker*, 20 May 1939, p. 96.
_____ *Saturday Review*, 20 May 1939, p. 20.
_____ *New York Herald Tribune Books*, 21 May 1939, p. 9 (Will Cuppy).
_____ *New York Times Book Review*, 21 May 1939, p. 17 (Isaac Anderson).
_____ *Wilson Library Bulletin* 35 (June 1939): 113.
_____ *Time*, 5 June 1939, p. 88.
_____ *Times Literary Supplement*, 23 September 1939, p. 553.
_____ *Manchester Guardian*, 20 October 1939, p. 3 (E. R. Punshon).
_____ *Spectator*, 20 October 1939, p. 556 (Rupert Hart-Davis).
_____ *New Statesman and Nation*, 21 October 1939, p. 568 (Ralph Partridge).
_____ *Saturday Review*, 23 December 1939, p. 20.

The Reader Is Warned (1939).
_____ *Times Literary Supplement*, 29 July 1939, p. 455.
_____ *Manchester Guardian* 5 August 1939, p. 5 (E. R. Punshon).
_____ *New York Herald Tribune Books*, 27 August 1939, p. 13 (Will Cuppy).
_____ *Boston Transcript*, 2 September 1939, p. 2 (Marian Wiggin).
_____ *New Yorker*, 2 September 1939, p. 64.
_____ *Saturday Review*, 2 September 1939, p. 18.
_____ *Time*, 4 September 1939, p. 56.
_____ *New Statesman and Nation*, 9 September 1939, p. 380 (Ralph Partridge).
_____ *New York Times Book Review*, 10 September 1939, p. 22 (Kay Irvin).

The Problem of the Wire Cage (1939).
_____ *New Yorker*, 4 November 1939, p. 88.
_____ *Saturday Review*, 4 November 1939, p. 19.
_____ *New York Herald Tribune Books*, 5 November 1939, p. 18 (Will Cuppy).
_____ *New York Times Book Review*, 5 November 1939, p. 28 (Isaac Anderson).

And So to Murder (1940).
_____ *Boston Transcript*, 11 May 1940, p. 2 (Marian Wiggin).
_____ *New Yorker*, 11 May 1940, p. 100.
_____ *Saturday Review*, 11 May 1940, p. 18.
_____ *New York Herald Tribune Books*, 12 May 1940, p. 15 (Will Cuppy).
_____ *New York Times Book Review*, 12 May 1940, p. 22 (Isaac Anderson).

The Man Who Could Not Shudder (1940).
_____ *Boston Transcript*, 25 May 1940, p. 2 (Marian Wiggin).
_____ *New Yorker*, 25 May 1940, p. 96.
_____ *Saturday Review*, 25 May 1940, p. 26.
_____ *New York Herald Tribune Books*, 26 May 1940, p. 12 (Will Cuppy).
_____ *New York Times Book Review*, 26 May 1940, p. 17 (Isaac Anderson).
_____ *Bookmark*, 2 (January 1941): 15.
_____ *Spectator*, 10 January 1941, p. 44 (Nicholas Blake).

Nine—and Death Makes Ten (1940).
_____ *New York Herald Tribune Books*, 13 October 1940, p. 19 (Will Cuppy).

_____ *New York Times Book Review* 13 October 1940, p. 24 (Kay Irvin).
_____ *Saturday Review*, 19 October 1940, p. 28.
_____ *Time*, 4 November 1940, p. 84.

The Department of Queer Complaints (1940).
_____ *New Statesman and Nation*, 19 October 1940, p. 392 (Ralph Partridge).
_____ *Spectator*, 25 October 1940, p. 424 (Nicholas Blake).
_____ *Times Literary Supplement*, 26 October 1940, p. 545.
_____ *Manchester Guardian*, 10 December 1940, p. 7 (E. R. Punshon).
_____ *New Yorker*, 21 December 1940, p. 88.
_____ *New York Herald Tribune Books*, 22 December 1940, p. 10 (Will Cuppy).
_____ *New York Times Book Review*, 22 December 1940, p. 7 (Isaac Anderson).
_____ *Saturday Review*, 28 December 1940, p. 20.
_____ *Time*, 6 January 1941, p. 60.
_____ *Reprint Bulletin Book Reviews* 27, No. 2 (1982): 18.

The Case of the Constant Suicides (1941).
_____ *New Yorker*, 28 June 1941, p. 64.
_____ *Saturday Review*, 28 June 1941, p. 17.
_____ *New York Herald Tribune Books*, 29 June 1941, p. 11 (Will Cuppy).
_____ *New York Times Book Review*, 29 June 1941, p. 17 (Kay Irvin).
_____ *Time*, 7 July 1941, p. 72.
_____ *Springfield Republican*, 13 July 1941, p. 7e.
_____ *Times Literary Supplement*, 9 August 1941, p. 385.
_____ *Spectator*, 3 October 1941, pp. 338, 340 (John Fairfield).
_____ *New Statesman and Nation*, 28 November 1941, p. 3 (E. R. Punshon).

Seeing Is Believing (1941).
_____ *New Yorker*, 23 August 1941, p. 68.
_____ *New York Herald Tribune Books*, 24 August 1941, p. 17 (Will Cuppy).
_____ *New York Times Book Review*, 24 August 1941, p. 17 (Isaac Anderson).
_____ *Saturday Review*, 30 August 1941, p. 16.
_____ *Time*, 1 September 1941, p. 92.
_____ *Springfield Republican*, 14 September 1941, p. 7e.
_____ *Bookmark* 2 (November 1941): 18.

Death Turns the Tables (1941).
_____ *Springfield Republican*, 4 January 1942, p. 7e.
_____ *Saturday Review*, 10 January 1942, p. 17.
_____ *New York Herald Tribune Books*, 11 January 1942, p. 14 (Will Cuppy).
_____ *New York Times Book Review*, 11 January 1942, p. 16 (Isaac Anderson).
_____ *New Republic*, 26 January 1942, p. 125 (Mort Post).
_____ *Books and Bookmen* 13 (January 1968): 28.

The Gilded Man (1942).
_____ *Bookmark* 3 (May 1942): 18.
_____ *New Yorker*, 13 June 1942, p. 72.
_____ *Saturday Review*, 13 June 1942, p. 19.
_____ *New York Herald Tribune Books*, 14 June 1942, p. 18 (Will Cuppy).
_____ *New York Times Book Review*, 14 June 1942, p. 18 (Isaac Anderson).

_____ *Time*, 6 July 1942, p. 88.
_____ *Times Literary Supplement*, 31 October 1942, p. 537.

The Emperor's Snuff-Box (1942).
_____ *New Yorker*, 31 October 1942, p. 26.
_____ *New York Herald Tribune Books*, 1 November 1942, p. 26 (Will Cuppy).
_____ *New York Times Book Review*, 1 November 1942, p. 26 (Isaac Anderson).
_____ *Time*, 2 November 1942, p. 104.
_____ *Saturday Review*, 14 November 1942, p. 18.
_____ *Books and Bookmen* 18 (May 1973): 122.

She Died a Lady (1943).
_____ *New Yorker* 30 January 1943, pp. 63-64.
_____ *New York Herald Tribune Weekly Book Review*, 31 January 1943, p. 15 (Will Cuppy).
_____ *New York Times Book Review*, 31 January 1943, p. 18 (Isaac Anderson).
_____ *Time*, 1 February 1943, p. 88.
_____ *Saturday Review*, 20 February 1943, p. 20.
_____ *Bookmark* 4 (March 1943): 20.
_____ *Times Literary Supplement*, 11 September 1943, p. 443.

He Wouldn't Kill Patience (1944).
_____ *Kirkus Reviews*, 1 January 1944, p. 8.
_____ *New Yorker*, 12 February 1944, p. 88.
_____ *Saturday Review*, 12 February 1944, p. 30.
_____ *New York Herald Tribune Weekly Book Review*, 13 February 1944, p. 12 (Will Cuppy).
_____ *New York Times Book Review*, 13 February 1944, p. 12 (Isaac Anderson).
_____ *Book Week*, 20 February 1944, p. 9 (Elizabeth Bullock).
_____ *Time*, 6 March 1944, p. 104.
_____ *Times Literary Supplement*, 1 July 1944, p. 320.

Till Death Do Us Part (1944).
_____ *Kirkus Reviews*, 1 July 1944, p. 288.
_____ *New York Herald Tribune Weekly Book Review*, 27 August 1944, p. 19 (Will Cuppy).
_____ *New York Times Book Review*, 27 August 1944, p. 18 (Isaac Anderson).
_____ *New Yorker*, 2 September 1944, p. 68.
_____ *Saturday Review*, 2 September 1944, p. 23.
_____ *New Republic*, 4 September 1944, p. 286.
_____ *Book Week*, 24 September 1944, p. 11 (Elizabeth Bullock).
_____ *Spectator*, 6 October 1944, p. 322 (John Hampson).
_____ *Times Literary Supplement*, 7 October 1944, p. 489.
_____ *Wilson Library Bulletin* 40 (November 1944): 147.
_____ *Spectator*, 25 June 1977, p. 25 (Patrick Cosgrave).

The Curse of the Bronze Lamp (1945).
_____ *Kirkus Reviews*, 15 April 1945, p. 168.
_____ *New Yorker*, 23 June 1945, p. 72.

180   John Dickson Carr: A Critical Study

_____ *New York Herald Tribune Weekly Book Review*, 24 June 1945, p. 14 (Will Cuppy).
_____ *Saturday Review*, 30 June 1945, p. 34.
_____ *New York Times Book Review*, 1 July 1945, p. 22 (Isaac Anderson).
_____ *New Republic*, 16 July 1945, p. 86.
_____ *Book Week*, 29 July 1945, p. 11 (Elizabeth Bullock).
_____ *Book World*, 21 October 1984, p. 12.

He Who Whispers (1946).
_____ *Kirkus Reviews*, 15 January 1946, p. 25.
_____ *New Yorker*, 30 March 1946, p. 96.
_____ *Saturday Review*, 30 March 1946, p. 54.
_____ *New York Times Book Review*, 31 March 1946, p. 32 (Isaac Anderson).
_____ *New York Herald Tribune Weekly Book Review*, 7 April 1946, p. 22 (Will Cuppy).
_____ *New Republic*, 8 April 1946, p. 48.

My Late Wives (1946).
_____ *Kirkus Reviews*, 1 September 1946, p. 437.
_____ *New Yorker*, 2 November 1946, p. 128.
_____ *New York Herald Tribune Weekly Book Review*, 3 November 1946, p. 24 (Will Cuppy).
_____ *New York Times Book Review* 3 November 1946, p. 24 (Isaac Anderson).
_____ *Saturday Review*, 9 November 1946, p. 23.
_____ *San Francisco Chronicle*, 10 November 1946, p. 23 (Anthony Boucher).
_____ *New Republic*, 11 November 1946, p. 638.
_____ *Book Week*, 17 November 1946, p. 12 (James Sandoe).
_____ *New Statesman and Nation*, 8 November 1947, p. 347 (Ralph Partridge).

The Sleeping Spinx (1947).
_____ *Kirkus Reviews*, 15 December 1946, p. 627.
_____ *New Yorker*, 22 February 1947, pp. 99-100.
_____ *Chicago Sun Book Week*, 23 February 1947, p. 8 (James Sandoe).
_____ *New York Times Book Review*, 23 February 1947, p. 34 (Isaac Anderson).
_____ *Saturday Review*, 1 March 1947, p. 26.
_____ *New York Herald Tribune Weekly Book Review*, 2 March 1947, p. 24 (Will Cuppy).
_____ *San Francisco Chronicle*, 9 March 1947, p. 17.
_____ *New Statesman and Nation*, 8 November 1947, p. 374 (Ralph Partridge).

The Skeleton in the Clock (1948).
_____ *Kirkus Reviews*, 1 August 1948, p. 380.
_____ *New Yorker*, 16 October 1948, p. 136.
_____ *Saturday Review*, 23 October 1948, p. 38.
_____ *Chicago Sun*, 29 October 1948 (James Sandoe).
_____ *New York Herald Tribune Weekly Book Review*, 31 October 1948, p. 22 (Will Cuppy).
_____ *New York Times Book Review*, 31 October 1948, p. 31 (Isaac Anderson).
_____ *San Francisco Chronicle*, 7 November 1948, p. 15 (E. D. Doyle).
_____ *Springfield Republican*, 5 December 1948, p. 12c.

The Life of Sir Arthur Conan Doyle (1949).
_____ *Kirkus Reviews* 15 December 1948, p. 653.
_____ *Library Journal*, 1 January 1949, p. 55 (E. F. Walbridge).
_____ *San Francisco Chronicle*, 30 January 1949, p. 20 (J. H. Jackson).
_____ *Manchester Guardian*, 4 February 1949, p. 3 (R. G. J.).
_____ *Nation*, 5 February 1949, p. 165.
_____ *New York Herald Tribune Weekly Book Review*, 6 February 1949, p. 3 (E. W. Smith).
_____ *New York Times Book Review*, 6 February 1949, p. 5 (Howard Haycraft).
_____ *Sunday Times* (London), 6 February 1949, p. 49 (Dorothy L. Sayers).
_____ *Time*, 7 February 1949, p. 88.
_____ *Times Literary Supplement*, 12 February 1949, p. 102.
_____ *New Republic*, 14 February 1949, pp. 23-24 (Anne L. Goodman).
_____ *Chicago Sun*, 18 February 1949, (James Sandoe).
_____ *Spectator*, 18 February 1949, p. 230 (Cyril Ray).
_____ *Springfield Republican*, 27 February 1949, p. 22a.
_____ *Twentieth Century* 145 (March 1949): 192 (M. G.).
_____ *Wilson Library Bulletin* 45 (March 1949): 46.
_____ *Booklist*, 1 March 1949, p. 224.
_____ *Commonweal*, 4 March 1949, pp. 525-26 (Elizabeth Johnson).
_____ *Saturday Review*, 5 March 1949, p. 19 (Elmer Davis).
_____ *New Statesman and Nation*, 19 March 1949, pp. 279-80 (Arthur Marshall).
_____ *Atlantic Monthly* 183 (April 1949): 82-83 (Charles J. Rolo).
_____ *Christian Science Monitor*, 19 May 1949, p. 14 (Henry Sowerby).
_____ *Catholic World* 169 (June 1949): 236-37 (Robert Wilberforce).
_____ *Publishers' Weekly*, 14 July 1975, p. 61.
_____ *Book World*, 14 September 1975, p. 3.
_____ *Wilson Library Bulletin* 50 (November 1975): 208.
_____ *Esquire* 84 (December 1975): 59.

Below Suspicion (1949).
_____ *Chicago Sun*, 12 August 1949 (James Sandoe).
_____ *New York Herald Tribune Weekly Book Review*, 14 August 1949, p. 12 (Will Cuppy).
_____ *New York Times Book Review*, 14 August 1949, p. 21 (Anthony Boucher).
_____ *San Francisco Chronicle*, 21 August 1949, p. 21 (E.D. Doyle).
_____ *New Yorker*, 3 September 1949, pp. 67-68.
_____ *Saturday Review*, 17 September 1949, p. 37.
_____ *Bookmark* 9 (October 1949): 5.

A Graveyard to Let (1949).
_____ *Kirkus Reviews*, 1 September 1949, p. 489.
_____ *Chicago Sun*, 11 November 1949 (James Sandoe).
_____ *New York Herald Tribune Weekly Book Review*, 13 November 1949, p. 34.
_____ *New York Times Book Review*, 13 November 1949, p. 51 (Anthony Boucher).
_____ *New Yorker*, 19 November 1949, p. 171.
_____ *Springfield Republican*, 11 December 1949, p. 7d.

The Bride of Newgate (1950).

_____ *Kirkus Reviews*, 1 February 1960, p. 78.

_____ *New York Times Book Review*, 9 April 1950, p. 23 (Richard Match).

_____ *Booklist*, 15 April 1950, p. 161.

_____ *Chicago Sunday Tribune*, 15 April 1950, p. 5 (A. F. Otis).

_____ *Chicago Sun*, 21 April 1950, p. 5 (James Sandoe).

_____ *Wilson Library Bulletin*, 46 (May 1950): 22.

_____ *Saturday Review*, 3 June 1950, p. 32 (J. M. G.).

_____ *New York Herald Tribune Weekly Book Review*, 23 July 1950, p. 14.

_____ *New Statesman and Nation*, 25 November 1950, p. 522 (Ralph Partridge).

Night at the Mocking Widow (1950).

_____ *Kirkus Reviews*, 1 April 1950, p. 220.

_____ *San Francisco Chronicle*, 28 May 1950, p. 22 (E. D. Doyle).

_____ *Wilson Library Bulletin* 46 (June 1950): 29.

_____ *Saturday Review*, 17 June 1950, p. 42.

_____ *New Yorker*, 24 June 1950, pp. 99-100.

_____ *New York Times Book Review*, 2 July 1950, p. 11 (H. M.).

_____ *Springfield Republican*, 30 July 1950, p. 8b (D. F. M.).

_____ *New York Herald Tribune Weekly Book Review*, 20 August 1950, p. 11.

The Devil in Velvet (1951).

_____ *New York Times Book Review*, 22 April 1951, p. 4 (Richard Match).

_____ *Booklist*, 1 May 1951, p. 310.

_____ *Springfield Republican*, 6 May 1951, p. 26a.

_____ *Chicago Sunday Tribune*, 13 May 1951, p. 3 (Kelsey Guilfoil).

_____ *San Francisco Chronicle*, 20 May 1951, p. 21 (L. G. Offord).

_____ *Bookmark* 10 (June 1951): 207.

_____ *Wilson Library Bulletin* 47 (June 1951): 165.

_____ *Saturday Review*, 7 July 1951, p. 31 (R. E. Roberts).

_____ *Catholic World* 173 (August 1951): 393 (Riley Hughes).

_____ *New York Herald Tribune Weekly Book Review*,　29 August 1951, p. 6 (E. L. Acken).

_____ *Times Literary Supplement*, 16 November 1951, p. 725.

Behind the Crimson Blind (1952).

_____ *Kirkus Reviews*, 1 November 1951, p. 649.

_____ *New York Herald Tribune Weekly Book Review*, 13 January 1952, p. 12 (James Sandoe).

_____ *New York Times Book Review*, 13 January 1952, p. 20 (Anthony Boucher).

_____ *San Francisco Chronicle*, 20 January 1952, p. 10 (L. G. Offord).

_____ *Springfield Republican*, 20 January 1952, p. 16a.

_____ *Saturday Review*, 26 January 1952, p. 31 (Sergeant Cuff).

_____ *Bookmark* 11 (February 1952): 109.

_____ *New Yorker*, 2 February 1952, p. 80.

_____ *Spectator*, 21 November 1952, p. 712 (Esther Howard).

The Nine Wrong Answers (1952).

_____ *New Yorker*, 1 November 1952, pp. 135-36.

_____ *New York Herald Tribune Weekly Book Review*, 2 November 1952, p. 16 (James Sandoe).

_____ *New York Times Book Review*, 16 November 1952, p. 32 (Anthony Boucher).

_____ *San Francisco Chronicle* 23 November 1952, p. 27 (L. G. Offord).

_____ *Springfield Republican*, 23 November 1952, p. 7c.

_____ *Booklist*, 1 December 1952, p. 126.

_____ *Saturday Review*, 6 December 1952, p. 37 (Sergeant Cuff).

The Cavalier's Cup (1953).

_____ *Kirkus Reviews*, 15 February 1953, p. 133.

_____ *Springfield Republican*, 10 May 1953, p. 6c.

_____ *New York Times Book Review*, 17 May 1953, p. 29 (Anthony Boucher).

_____ *New Yorker*, 23 May 1953, pp. 139-40.

_____ *New York Herald Tribune Weekly Book Review*, 24 May 1953, p. 20 (James Sandoe).

_____ *Bookmark* 12 (June 1953): 209.

_____ *Saturday Review*, 13 June 1953, p. 44 (Sergeant Cuff).

The Exploits of Sherlock Holmes (1954).

_____ *Kirkus Reviews*, 1 February 1954, p. 85.

_____ *San Francisco Chronicle*, 17 March 1954, p. 19 (J. H. Jackson).

_____ *Chicago Sunday Tribune*, 4 April 1954, p. 6 (Vincent Starrett).

_____ *Time*, 5 April 1954, p. 110.

_____ *New York Times Book Review*, 11 April 1954, p. 27 (Anthony Boucher).

_____ *Saturday Review*, 15 May 1954, p. 32 (Sergeant Cuff).

_____ *New Statesman and Nation*, 26 June 1954, p. 840 (Ralph Partridge).

_____ *Cleveland Open Shelf*, December 1954, p. 33.

The Third Bullet and Other Stories (1954).

_____ *Kirkus Reviews*, 15 March 1954, p. 215.

_____ *New York Herald Tribune Weekly Book Review*, 30 May 1954, p. 9 (James Sandoe).

_____ *New York Times Book Review*, 30 May 1954, p. 18 (Anthony Boucher).

_____ *Springfield Republican*, 6 June 1954, p. 7c.

_____ *Booklist*, 15 July 1954, p. 453.

_____ *Saturday Review*, 17 July 1954, p. 32 (Sergeant Cuff).

_____ *San Francisco Chronicle*, 18 July 1954, p. 19 (L. G. Offord).

_____ *New Statesman and Nation*, 25 September 1954, p. 368 (Ralph Partridge).

Captain Cut-Throat (1955).

_____ *Kirkus Reviews*, 1 February 1955, p. 96.

_____ *Booklist*, 15 March 1955, p. 290.

_____ *Booklist*, 1 April 1955, p. 315.

_____ *New York Times Book Review*, 3 April 1955, p. 28 (Alden Whitman).

_____ *Springfield Republican*, 3 April 1955, p. 8c (H. B. H.).

_____ *Chicago Sunday Tribune*, 10 April 1955, p. 3 (Richard Blakesley).

_____ *Bookmark* 14 (June 1955): 214.

_____ *Times Literary Supplement*, 9 September 1955, p. 521.

Fear Is the Same (1956).

_____ *Kirkus Reviews*, 15 December 1955, p. 897.

_____ *New York Times Book Review*, 4 March 1956, p. 36 (Anthony Boucher).

_____ *Saturday Review*, 17 March 1956, p. 42 (Sergeant Cuff).
_____ *New York Herald Tribune Weekly Book Review*, 25 March 1956, p. 14 (James Sandoe).
_____ *Booklist*, 1 May 1956, p. 362.

Patrick Butler for the Defence (1956).
_____ *Kirkus Reviews*, 15 May 1956, p. 345.
_____ *New York Times Book Review*, 1 July 1956, p. 15 (Anthony Boucher).
_____ *Saturday Review*, 7 July 1956, p. 23 (Sergeant Cuff).
_____ *New York Herald Tribune Weekly Book Review*, 15 July 1956, p. 9 (James Sandoe).
_____ *San Francisco Chronicle*, 29 July 1956, p. 19 (L. G. Offord).
_____ *Spectator*, 24 August 1956, p. 268 (Christopher Pym).
_____ *New Statesman and Nation*, 8 September 1956, p. 287 (Ralph Partridge).
_____ *Springfield Republican*, 28 October 1956, p. 8c.

Fire, Burn! (1957).
_____ *Kirkus Reviews*, 15 March 1957, p. 236.
_____ *New York Herald Tribune Weekly Book Review*, 2 June 1957, p. 9 (James Sandoe).
_____ *New York Times Book Review*, 16 June 1957, p. 20 (Anthony Boucher).
_____ *Manchester Guardian*, 5 July 1957, p. 6 (Francis Iles).
_____ *Spectator*, 12 July 1957, p. 66 (Christopher Pym).
_____ *New Statesman*, 3 August 1957, pp. 153-54 (Ralph Partridge).
_____ *Saturday Review*, 24 August 1957, p. 34 (Sergeant Cuff).
_____ *Springfield Republican*, 25 August 1957, p. 16b.

A John Dickson Carr Trio (1957).
_____ *New York Times Book Review*, 10 November 1957, p. 30 (Anthony Boucher).
_____ *New York Herald Tribune Weekly Book Review*, 17 November 1957, p. 11.
_____ *Saturday Review*, 28 December 1957, p. 28 (Sergeant Cuff).
_____ *Springfield Republican*, 29 December 1957, p. 13b.

The Dead Man's Knock (1958).
_____ *Kirkus Reviews*, 15 June 1958, p. 432.
_____ *Manchester Guardian*, 8 August 1958, p. 4 (Francis Iles).
_____ *Times Literary Supplement*, 22 August 1958, p. 469.
_____ *New York Herald Tribune Weekly Book Review*, 24 August 1958, p. 9 (James Sandoe).
_____ *New York Times Book Review*, 24 August 1958, p. 27 (Anthony Boucher).
_____ *New Statesman*, 30 August 1958, p. 254 (Ralph Partridge).
_____ *Chicago Sunday Tribune*, 5 October 1958, p. 4 (Drexel Drake).
_____ *Saturday Review*, 13 December 1958, p. 32 (Sergeant Cuff).

Scandal at High Chimneys (1959).
_____ *Kirkus Reviews*, 15 June 1959, p. 419.
_____ *Spectator*, 24 July 1959, p. 119 (Christopher Pym).
_____ *Times Literary Supplement*, 31 July 1959, p. 445.
_____ *New Statesman*, 22 August 1959, p. 228 (Ralph Partridge).

_____ *New York Herald Tribune Weekly Book Review*, 23 August 1959, p. 11 (James Sandoe).

_____ *Springfield Republican*, 30 August 1959, p. 4d.

_____ *Guardian*, 4 September 1959, p. 6 (Francis Iles).

_____ *New York Times Book Review*, 6 September 1959, p. 13 (Anthony Boucher).

_____ *San Francisco Chronicle*, 13 Spetember 1959, p. 30 (L. G. Offord).

In Spite of Thunder (1960).

_____ *Kirkus Reviews*, 15 April 1960, p. 340.

_____ *New York Times Book Review*, 3 July 1960, p. 12 (Anthony Boucher).

_____ *New York Herald Tribune Weekly Book Review*, 17 July 1960, p. 11 (James Sandoe).

_____ *San Francisco Chronicle* 17 July 1960, p. 21 (L. G. Offord).

_____ *Springfield Republican*, 17 July 1960, p. 4d (L. H. T.).

_____ *Guardian*, 21 October 1960, p. 9 (Francis Iles).

The Witch of the Low-Tide (1961).

_____ *New York Times Book Review* 29 October 1961, pp. 24, 26 (Anthony Boucher).

The Demoniacs (1962).

_____ *New York Times Book Review*, 28 October 1962, p. 55 (Anthony Boucher).

_____ *Saturday Review*, 29 December 1962, p. 39.

The Men Who Explained Miracles (1963).

_____ *New York Times Book Review*, 24 November 1963, p. 65 (Anthony Boucher).

_____ *Best Sellers*, 1 December 1963, p. 326.

_____ *Library Journal*, 1 December 1963, p. 4667 (James Sandoe).

_____ *National Review*, 14 January 1964, p. 30.

_____ *Saturday Review*, 25 January 1964, p. 40 (Sergeant Cuff).

_____ *Book Week*, 8 March 1964, p. 15 (Dorothy B. Hughes).

_____ *New Statesman*, 20 March 1964, p. 460 (John Fuller).

_____ *Observer*, 27 November 1966, p. 22.

Most Secret (1964).

_____ *New York Times Book Review*, 15 November 1964, p. 73 (Anthony Boucher).

The House at Satan's Elbow (1965).

_____ *Kirkus Reviews*, 1 August 1965, p. 790.

_____ *Library Journal*, 1 September 1965, p. 3479 (M. K. Grant).

_____ *Best Sellers*, 1 October 1965, p. 274.

_____ *New Statesman*, 8 October 1965, p. 531 (Brigid Brophy).

_____ *Observer*, 10 October 1965, p. 28.

_____ *New York Times Book Review*, 7 November 1965, p. 84 (Anthony Boucher).

_____ *Spectator*, 19 November 1965, p. 665 (Hester McKeig).

_____ *Book Week*, 21 November 1965, p. 35 (Dorothy B. Hughes).

_____ *Critic* 24 (December 1965-January 1966): 81.

_____ *Saturday Review*, 29 January 1966, p. 37 (Sergeant Cuff).

Panic in Box C (1966).

_____ *Kirkus Reviews* 1 June 1966, p. 556.

_____ *Best Sellers*, 15 August 1966, p. 184.

_____ *New York Times Book Review*, 4 September 1966, p. 20 (Anthony Boucher).

_____ *Critic* 25 (October 1966): 118.

_____ *Punch*, 23 November 1966, p. 793.

_____ *Observer*, 18 January 1970, p. 30.

Dark of the Moon (1967).

_____ *Kirkus Reviews*, 1 October 1967, p. 1232.

_____ *Library Journal*, 1 October 1967, p. 4031.

_____ *Publishers' Weekly*, 2 October 1967, p. 50.

_____ *New York Times*, 17 November 1967, p. 45.

_____ *Best Sellers*, 15 December 1967, p. 370.

_____ *New York Times Book Review*, 31 December 1967, p. 16 (Anthony Boucher).

_____ *Observer*, 21 April 1968, p. 28.

_____ *Punch*, 29 May 1968, p. 795.

_____ *Books and Bookmen* 13 (June 1968): 41.

Papa Là-bas (1968).

_____ *Publishers' Weekly*, 26 August 1968, p. 266.

_____ *Kirkus Reviews*, 1 September 1968, p. 1007.

_____ *Library Journal*, 1 November 1968, p. 4168 (M. K. Grant).

_____ *New York Times Book Review*, 10 November 1968, p. 65 (Allen J. Hubin).

_____ *Best Sellers*, 1 December 1968, p. 380.

_____ *Book World*, 29 December 1968, p. 12 (A. L. Rosenzweig).

_____ *Spectator*, 7 June 1969, p. 758 (Cyril Ray).

_____ *Catholic Library World* 41 (January 1970): 323.

The Ghosts' High Noon (1969).

_____ *Kirkus Reviews*, 15 September 1969, p. 1032.

_____ *Publishers' Weekly*, 15 September 1969, p. 61.

_____ *Library Journal* 1 November 1969, p. 4028 (M. K. Grant).

_____ *New York Times*, 4 November 1969, p. 43.

_____ *Best Sellers*, 15 December 1969, p. 377.

_____ *New York Times Book Review*, 4 January 1970, p. 21 (Allen J. Hubin).

_____ *National Observer*, 5 January 1970, p. 21.

_____ *Saturday Review*, 31 January 1970, p. 38 (Sergeant Cuff).

_____ *Observer*, 7 June 1970, p. 31.

Deadly Hall (1971).

_____ *Kirkus Reviews*, 1 January 1971, p. 26.

_____ *Publishers' Weekly*, 1 February 1971, p. 68.

_____ *Library Journal* 1 March 1971, p. 864 (M. K. Grant).

_____ *New York Times Book Review*, 14 March 1971, p. 22 (Newgate Callendar).

_____ *Saturday Review*, 27 March 1971, p. 51 (Haskel Frankel).

_____ *National Review*, 8 October 1971, p. 1127 (W. Murchinson).

_____ *Books and Bookmen* 17 (December 1971): 68 (John Boland).

The Hungry Goblin (1972).

_____ *Kirkus Reviews*, 1 April 1972, p. 430.

_____ *Publishers' Weekly*, 3 April 1972, p. 71.

____ *Best Sellers*, 15 June 1972, p. 149.

____ *Book World*, 16 July 1972, p. 14.

____ *New York Times Book Review*, 16 July 1972, p. 32 (Newgate Callendar).

____ *Library Journal* 97 (August 1972): 2654.

____ *Saturday Review*, 26 August 1972, p. 62 (O. L. Bailey).

____ *Observer*, 10 September 1972, p. 32.

____ *Wilson Library Bulletin* 47 (January 1973): 456.

The Door to Doom and Other Detections (1980).

____ *Publishers' Weekly*, 27 June 1980, p. 83.

____ *Booklist*, 1 July 1980, p. 1574 (Connie Fletcher).

____ *Kirkus Reviews*, 1 July 1980, p. 873.

____ *Book World*, 21 September 1980, p. 6.

____ *Wilson Library Bulletin* 55 (December 1980): 294.

____ *Voya* 4 (April 1981): 37.

____ *British Book News*, July 1981, p. 391 (Jessica Mann).

The Dead Sleep Lightly (1983).

____ *Publishers' Weekly*, 18 March 1983, p. 54.

____ *Booklist*, 1 June 1983, p. 1262 (Connie Fletcher).

____ *Best Sellers* 43 (August 1983): 171.

Appendix: Unidentified Translations

[Listed below are translations of Carr's work whose originals I have not been able to ascertain.]

French:
A la vie...à la mort, tr. Jean Barré (Paris: La Jeune Parque, 1946; rpt. Paris: Néo-Nouvelles Editions Oswald, 1982).

Un Fantôme peut en cacher un autre, tr. ? (Paris: Champs-Elysées, 1987).

Impossible n'est pas anglais, tr. Maruice-Bernard Endrèbe (Paris: Champs-Elysées, 1986; originally published as *La Fantôme frappe trois coups*).

La Mort en pantalon rouge, tr. Jean-André and Claudine Rey (Paris: Champs-Elysées, 1987).

Quand le Diable y serait, tr. ? (Paris: Champs-Eylsées, 1987).

Qui a peur de Charles Dickens?, tr. Claude Antoine Ciccione (Paris: J'ai Lu, 1970).

German:
Mit einem Messer im Knopfloch, tr. ? (Hamburg: Kelter, 1978).

Morde à la Manila, tr. ? (Hamburg: Kelter, 1979).

Tagebuch eines Mörders, tr. ? (Dusseldorf: F. M. Bourg, n.d.; rpt. Munich: Heyne, 1962; rpt. Hamburg: Kelter, 1978).

Die Treppe des Königs, tr. Heinz Zürchner (Zurich: Albert Müller, 1939).

Greek:
Ho mauros ephialtēs, tr. ? (Athens: Galaxie, 1962).

Portuguese:

A morte misteriosa, tr. Romariz Monteiro (Lisbon: Empresa Nacional de Publicidade, 1950).
Aviso sinistro, tr. M. da Motta Cardoso (Lisbon: Belagrafia, 1950).
Crime no lago, tr. César Dinis (Lisbon: Empresa Nacional de Publicidade, 1951).
Desafio à polícia, tr. Baptista de Carvalho (Lisbon: Livros do Brasil, 1948).
Um ladrão na noite, tr. José de Natividade Gaspar (Lisbon: Editorial-Século, 1945).
O mistério do parque, tr. Ester dos Santos (Lisbon: Editorial-Século, 1944).

Serbo-Croatian:
Hudobni gostje, tr. Maila Golob (Ljubljana: Radiotelevizija, 1970).
Nori klobucar, tr. ? (Ljubljana: Delo, 1971).

Spanish:
El cuarto cerrado, tr. ? (Buenos Aires: Acmé, 1953).
Empezó entre fieras, tr. Francisco Rodríguez Arvas (Madrid: Saturnino Calleja, 1948).
La estatua de la viuda, tr. ? (Buenos Aires: Emecé, 1953).
Jaque mate al asesino, tr. ? (Buenos Aires: Emecé, 1951 [2nd ed.]).

Turkish:
Aranilan kaatil, tr. Vâlâ Nurettin (Istanbul: Ak Kitabevi, 1963.
Düsman dostlari, tr. Vâlâ Nurettin (Istanbul: Ak Kitabevi; 1963).
Gemideki katil, tr. Sedat Elman (Istanbul: Türkiye Yayinevi, l945).
Iğne deliği, tr. Enver Günsel (Istanbul: Akba Yayinevi, 1964).
Kanli eldivenler, tr. Gülten Suveren (Istanbul: Akbaaba Matbassi, 1965).
Kanli oyun, tr. Sedat Elam (Istanbul: Türkiye Yayinevi, 1945).
Karanlik bir yüz, tr. Oğuz Alplâçin (Istanbul: Yalçin Ofset, 1968).
Kiral merdiveni, tr. Sedat Elam (Istanbul: Türkiye Yayinevi, 1944).
Kiralik daire, tr. Orhan Ş. Yüksel (Istanbul: Tifdruk Matbaacilik Sanayii, 1963).
Ölüm anaforu, tr. Tarik Gürcan (Istanbul: Ahmet Halit Yaşaroğlu, 1958).
Onu bu oda öldürdü, tr. Enver Günsel (Istanbul: Akba Yayinevi, 1982).
Viran kule, tr. Vâlâ Nurettin (Istanbul: Ak Kitabevi, 1963).
Yalan içinde yalan, tr. Vâlâ Nurettin (Istanbul: Ak Kitabevi, 1964).
Yaldizli eller, tr. ? (Istanbul: Altin Kitaplar Yayinevi, 1965).

Index

www.ingramcontent.com/pod-product-compliance
Lightning Source LLC
Chambersburg PA
CBHW030411100426
42812CB00028B/2913/J